GENDER

THE BASICS

Gender: The Basics is an engaging introduction which encourages the reader to pay attention to the impact of cultural, historical, biological, psychological and economic forces on the qualities which have come to be defined as masculine or feminine in particular contexts. Highlighting that there is far more to gender than biological sex, it takes a global perspective to examine the interaction between gender and topics including:

- Relationships, intimacy and concepts of sexuality
- The workplace and labor markets
- Gender-related violence and war
- Public health, poverty and development
- The aging process.

Supporting theory with a wide range of examples, suggestions for further reading and a detailed glossary, this text is an essential read for anyone approaching the study of gender for the first time.

Hilary M. Lips is Professor of Psychology, Chair of the Psychology Department and Director of the Center for Gender Studies at Radford University, USA.

The Basics

GENDER

THE BASICS

Hilary M. Lips

Routledge
Taylor & Francis Group

LONDON AND NEW YORK

First published 2014
by Routledge
2 Park Square, Milton Park, Abingdon, Oxon OX14 4RN

and by Routledge
711 Third Avenue, New York, NY 10017

Routledge is an imprint of the Taylor & Francis Group, an informa business

British Library Cataloguing in Publication Data
A catalogue record for this book is available from the British Library

Library of Congress Cataloging in Publication Data
Lips, Hilary M.
Gender : the basics / Hilary M. Lips.
pages cm
Includes bibliographical references and index.
1. Sex role. 2. Sex differences (Psychology) 3. Sex differences. I. Title.
HQ1075.L578 2013
305.3--dc23
2013016672

ISBN: 978-0-415-68950-2 (hbk)
ISBN: 978-0-415-68954-0 (pbk)
ISBN: 978-1-315-88317-5   (ebk)

Typeset in Bembo
by Saxon Graphics Ltd, Derby

Printed and bound in Great Britain by
TJ International Ltd, Padstow, Cornwall

To Marlan, Karen, and Tom:
Siblings who are also friends

CONTENTS

LIST OF FIGURES

ACKNOWLEDGEMENTS

I am grateful to Sophie Thompson, who first suggested I should take on this project and provided initial guidance. As the writing has progressed, I have much appreciated the help and encouragement of Siobhán Poole and Iram Satti at Routledge. Working with them has been a joy; their optimism, understanding and support helped move the project forward even when I was feeling overwhelmed. Thanks are also due to the reviewers of the initial proposal and sample chapters, who provided suggestions and insights to make this a better book.

I owe a special deep debt of gratitude to Wayne Andrew, who designed all the charts and graphs for this book, and whose caring and enthusiastic participation in this and so many other projects over the years has made them better, more meaningful, and more fun.

Finally, thanks go out to my students, who inevitably ask tough questions, remind me when things are not clear, and push me to find out what I do not know.

Hilary Lips
April, 2013

1

GENDER: EVERYBODY HAS/DOES ONE

Years ago, Ursula LeGuin (1969) described a fictional world in which there were no "women" or "men," but only individuals. Gender categories were absent from this society—except for a few days in each individual's monthly cycle when sexual desires became insistent and individuals became "female" or "male" for the time it took to establish a sexual relationship. Even then, no persistent biological or social tendency toward maleness or femaleness was established: one individual could be the father of some children and the mother of others.

My students are intrigued but discomfited by this fantasy. Most say they cannot imagine a world without gender categories. It would be boring, bland, they protest. Everyone would be the same; relationships would be uninteresting. And how would anyone decide who was supposed to do what? Most react with similar perplexity and stubbornness when I ask them to "imagine yourself as still 'you,' but as a different gender." They argue that they would not, could not, be the same person if they were a different gender—and anyway they would be unskilled and awkward at doing what the other gender is supposed to do.

These responses provide some clues to the pervasive importance of gender categories in our lives. They also suggest that we view gender not as a category that someone simply biologically "is" but as something that individuals do or act out. So what exactly is gender?

GENDER AND SEX: IS THERE A DIFFERENCE?

Most of us are used to dividing people up into two categories: female and male. If pressed, we might say the distinction is based on simple biology: male and female individuals look different, have different reproductive organs. Women have breasts. Men can grow beards. A woman can get pregnant and give birth. A man can inseminate a woman—even against her will.

However, we also know that individual women and men vary a great deal in how close they are to society's ideals of femininity and masculinity. Apparently, simply being biologically female does not ensure that a person is "womanly," and being biologically male does not mean an individual is "manly." Some people who are clearly men are described as not very masculine; some women are termed unfeminine. This suggests that there is something more complicated going on than placing people into well-defined biological categories. In fact, with respect to these issues, there seem to be two dimensions on which individuals might be categorized: biological and socio-cultural.

In recognition of these two dimensions, people who study the differences and similarities between women and men have sometimes made a distinction between sex and gender. They may use the term *sex* to refer to biological femaleness and maleness, and the term *gender* to refer to culturally-mediated expectations and roles associated with masculinity and femininity (e.g. Unger 1979). Although this is the general approach that will be followed in this book, it must be acknowledged that the biological and social dimensions that define women and men cannot be cleanly separated. Social expectations for femininity, for example, are shaped in some ways by the biological fact that women can become pregnant. Men's biologically-based propensity to have larger, stronger bodies is enhanced by social norms that encourage men to work at becoming strong and reward them for doing so. Thus sex and gender are intertwined, and it is usually impossible to separate them completely. Furthermore, gender itself is multidimensional. One dimension is *gender identity*: thinking of oneself as male or female. Another is *gender role*: behaving in ways considered appropriate for women or men in the surrounding culture. Still another is *sexual orientation*: attraction to members of one's own and/or other genders.

A BRIEF HISTORY OF IDEAS ABOUT GENDER

History is filled with pronouncements about the nature of, and differences between, women and men. Recently, for example, Nobel-prize-winning author V.S. Naipaul opined to an interviewer that no woman could be his equal as a writer because of women's "sentimentality, the narrow view of the world" (Fallon 2011). Such comments have roots in a long tradition of theories about differences between women and men, some centered on the notion of women as deficient or incompletely developed human beings, and some based on the idea of men and women as complementary—but relatively equal—opposites. Proponents of the "deficiency" view have included Western philosophers, theologians, and scientists, including Aristotle, Thomas Aquinas, and Sigmund Freud. Advocates of the complementary opposites view have included early medical researchers who viewed female and male reproductive organs as being the same except "inside out;" Chinese philosophers who conceived of two complementary energies as "yin" (darkness, coldness, femininity) and "yang" (heat, brightness, masculinity) and taught that they should be properly balanced in each person; and a variety of theorists— from Carl Jung to present-day psychologists—who have explicated the concept of androgyny: the joining of masculine and feminine qualities in a single individual. Of course, the hierarchical and complementary approaches can overlap, as in cases where people argue that women have special qualities (such as unselfishness) that complement those of men but are not competent enough or tough enough to be placed in leadership positions.

Some specific types of theories about gender are at least somewhat familiar to most people. For example, *psychoanalytic theory*, developed by Sigmund Freud (1960/1924), is often linked to his controversial idea that "anatomy is destiny." He postulated that children learn to identify with their gender through complicated childhood processes centering on their response to having or not having a penis. This process, in which three- to five-year-old children of both sexes attach a high value to the possession of a penis, so that boys learn to fear castration and girls develop "penis envy," was said by Freud to result in feminine or masculine identification. Boys, according to his theory, suppress their early attraction to their mothers and identify with their fathers because they fear their fathers will see them as rivals and castrate them. Girls identify with their mothers as a kind of resigned, fall-back strategy: they realize they can't have a penis of their own, so they hope they can instead attract a man and have a male child.

Also controversial are theories about gender that are grounded in *evolutionary psychology*. Such theories posit that every species, including humans, changes over time as a result of genetic changes that are passed along across generations. Qualities that enhance the likelihood of survival are more likely to be passed on because individuals who have them are more likely to grow to maturity, find a mate, and reproduce. This approach argues that some qualities that are relevant to reproductive success are different for males and females, and they locate female–male differences in the different mating strategies that favor women's and men's reproductive success. For instance, this approach suggests that because men have millions of sperm, their best bet for reproducing their genes is to scatter them as far as possible by mating with many different women. Women, on the other hand, have to devote a lot of time and energy to each pregnancy and birth, so they maximize their chances of passing on their genes by being careful and selective in choosing a mate. So men have evolved to be promiscuous and women to be selective.

A third category of theories of gender involve various aspects of *socialization*. These approaches emphasize that children learn from their culture to identify as male or female and how to behave in masculine or feminine ways. Such lessons may be directly taught by parents, teachers, or peers, or simply absorbed through observation. The theories tend to assume that conformity to expectations about being feminine or masculine is motivated by individuals' desire to "fit in" and to be socially competent.

Finally, there are **social-cultural theories** that focus on how women's and men's behavior is shaped by the way power is distributed in the broader culture. These theories posit that, because so many cultures assign higher status and power to men, behavior associated with masculinity tends to be powerful behavior and feminine behavior tends to be powerless behavior. Such approaches focus not on anatomy, biology or learning, but on the direct impact of the social-cultural environment on women's and men's behavior.

IS GENDER "BUILT-IN," OR DO WE CONSTRUCT IT?

As this brief overview of theoretical approaches shows, one key to the arguments surrounding gender is the debate about how strongly it is rooted in biology. Do our bodies predispose us to be, feel, and behave differently as males and females? How much are such differences affected by the way we are raised, by the culture in which we grow up? This nature vs. nurture question is one that has haunted researchers who study every aspect of human behavior; however, it is particularly perplexing and complicated in the realm of gender. And the more we explore the role of nature and nurture, the more we confront the conclusion that virtually nothing in gender development is the result of only one or the other of these forces. Nature and nurture cannot be separated: they are intertwined and work together at every stage of human development. Thus, most people who have studied these issues deeply claim an interactionist position: they do not argue about *how much* nature or nurture influences particular aspects of development, but try instead to figure out *how* the two sets of influences interact to produce certain results.

THE ROLE OF BIOLOGY

The steps in human sexual differentiation

The path to joining the category male or female begins at conception. Through a series of developmental steps, a fertilized egg moves toward developing a body that will be classified as male or female:

- *Step 1: Chromosomes* When sperm meets egg to produce fertilization, each normally contributes a set of 23 chromosomes, which pair up to form the genetic basis for the new individual. The 23rd pair, known as the sex chromosomes, is the pair that initially determines sex. Normally, this pair will be comprised of an X chromosome contributed by the mother's egg and either an X or Y chromosome contributed by the father's sperm. If the pair is XX, the pattern of development is predisposed to be female; if it is XY, the pattern is predisposed to be male. If some unusual combination, such as XO or XXX occurs, development tends to proceed in a female direction— as long as no Y chromosome is present. Only the sperm, not the egg, can contribute a Y chromosome. Thus the genetic basis of sex is determined by the father.

- *Step 2: Gonads* During the first seven weeks after conception, the embryo develops a "neutral" gonad (sex gland) and the beginnings of both female and male sets of internal reproductive structures. Up until this point, the embryo has the potential to go either way, to develop either female or male reproductive equipment. In the eighth week, if a Y chromosome is present, it promotes the organization of the neutral gonad into an embryonic testis. If there is no Y chromosome, the neutral gonad will start to become an ovary.

- *Step 3: Hormones* Once formed, the testes or ovaries begin to secrete sex hormones, and these hormones influence the remaining steps in sexual differentiation. Testes secrete both testosterone, which influences the male reproductive tract to develop, and Mullerian Inhibiting Substance (MIS), which causes the female reproductive tract to atrophy and disappear. Ovaries secrete estrogens and progesterone, which organize the development of the female reproductive system.

- *Step 4: Internal Reproductive Tract* Over the next four weeks, the sex hormones gradually organize the internal reproductive structures in a male or female direction. Under the influence of testosterone, these internal ducts become the vas deferens, epididymis, seminal vesicles, urethra, and prostate. If no significant amount of testosterone is present, the internal structures differentiate in a female direction: as fallopian tubes, uterus, and vagina.

- *Step 5: External Genitalia* Also by the end of the 12th week, the external genitalia, which are indistinguishable by sex at 8 weeks, have been influenced by the sex hormones to differentiate as either male or female. Under the influence of testosterone, the "neutral" genitalia develop into a penis and scrotum; without the influence of testosterone, the genitalia develop as a clitoris and labia.

A careful reader may have noticed an overall pattern in these steps: at each stage, without the effect of a Y chromosome or male sex hormone, development apparently proceeds in a female direction. This is true in other mammals too. Some biologists like to say that the basic pattern of mammalian development appears to be female—unless testosterone interferes.

Although we tend to think of female and male as two distinct, non-overlapping categories, the fact that sex develops through a series of sequential steps shows that there are some possibilities for these categories to be fuzzy. If, for example, a genetic male (XY) reaches step 3, in which testosterone is being secreted, but happens to have an inherited condition (androgen insensitivity syndrome) that makes cells unable to respond to testosterone, step 4 will not proceed in a male developmental direction. At birth, the baby will probably appear female and be classified as such; the male genetic configuration and testes may well not be discovered until young adulthood. There are a variety of ways in which the steps of sexual differentiation may be inconsistent, producing an individual whose indicators of biological sex are mixed. Such intersexed individuals make up between 1 and 4 percent of the population.

There are two other aspects of the journey toward maleness or femaleness that appear even more complex than the development of a body that can be classified as male or female. One concerns the sexual differentiation of the brain. The other concerns the different ways in which individuals are treated and taught, once they have been classified as female or male.

Female brains and male brains?

If different levels of prenatal hormones can affect the development of internal and external genitalia, might they not also affect the developing brain—producing different kinds of brains in females and males? In recent decades, a number of popular books and articles have argued that women and men think and behave differently because their brains are different. In general terms, this notion is not new. Late in the nineteenth century, women were said to be intellectually inferior to men because they had smaller brains. When it was demonstrated that women's brains were proportionately larger than men's by weight, the argument shifted to the size of particular areas of the brain—first the frontal lobes, then, when that proved untenable, the parietal lobes—that were said to be smaller in women. More recently, researchers have examined the size and shape of various brain structures in women and men and have found some evidence for sex differences, for instance in the corpus callosum (the structure that connects the right and left hemispheres of the brain). Since there is a tremendous amount of individual variation in brain size and shape, it can be very difficult to draw definitive conclusions about sex differences in brain morphology. Furthermore, it is not clear what functional significance these differences may have. Finally, it is uncertain whether the differences are "built in" or are the results of different life experiences—since it is acknowledged that brains are very plastic and responsive to experience.

The complexity of the issues are illustrated in the story of one set of researchers (Wood *et al.* 2008) who set out to find a brain difference that would mesh with the often-reported finding that women show more interpersonal awareness than men. After using magnetic resonance imaging (MRI) to examine the brains of 30 women and 30 men matched on age and IQ, they concluded that one particular brain structure, the straight gyrus (SG)—part of a brain region that had already been linked to the ability to interpret nonverbal cues—was proportionately larger in women than men. Furthermore, size of the SG was correlated with scores on a test of interpersonal perception. So far, this may sound like a clear case of sex differences in brain structure causing sex differences in a particular ability. It turns out not to be so simple, however. In this study, both the size of the SG and the interpersonal perception scores were also correlated with a third variable: respondents' scores on a measure of psychological femininity and masculinity. Respondents (both female and male) who described themselves as having more "feminine" qualities tended to have larger SGs *and* higher interpersonal perception scores. Furthermore, a subsequent study that examined the brains of children aged 7 to 17 found a surprising result: the SG was larger in boys than girls, and interpersonal awareness scores were associated with smaller, not larger, SGs (Wood, Murko and Nopoulos 2009). In this younger sample, both higher interpersonal awareness and smaller SGs were associated with higher scores on psychological femininity. This complicated set of findings illustrates how perilous it can be to try to draw sweeping conclusions about sex differences in the brain and their relationship to female–male differences in behavior. It suggests, for example, the possibility that children's experiences as boys or girls may affect brain development. It leaves us wondering whether women's larger SGs come from many years of being socially sensitive, or whether their social sensitivity stems from their larger SGs—or whether both things may be true.

Another current research emphasis is on exploring possible sex differences in the ways various cognitive abilities may be organized within the brain. This is not something that can be discerned from examining brains directly; rather, researchers ask respondents to perform specific tasks, such as reading, listening, and recognizing objects, and they use various methods to determine which part of the brain is being activated and used to accomplish these tasks. Using this approach, some investigators have found results consistent with the idea that women and men may differ in the ways basic abilities, such as language, are distributed across the two hemispheres of the brain or among the different areas within hemispheres. The findings often involve small differences, are complex and often contested, so it is not possible to sum them up in brief generalizations. This complexity has not stopped media commentators from trumpeting misleading headlines such as "Women are significantly more right-brained than men."

If there were differences in the ways female and male brains were organized, how might this occur? For some decades, there have been efforts to understand the extent to which prenatal hormones might be involved and might organize the developing brain in ways that produce average differences between girls and boys in certain interests and social behaviors. This too is a complicated area, but a reasonable amount of evidence suggests that levels of prenatal androgens are associated with later levels of certain kinds of interests (e.g. interest in babies) and behaviors (e.g. rough and tumble play) which are more strongly associated with one gender than the other. For example, one study measured testosterone levels in amniotic fluid (the fluid that surrounds the fetus in the womb), and tested the association between those levels and the levels of masculine-typical play, measured when the children were aged 6 to 10 years (Auyeung *et al.* 2009). For both boys and girls, parents reported more masculine-typical activities and interests for children whose samples of amniotic fluid *in utero* had shown higher levels of testosterone. The association between prenatal hormone levels and later behavior does not prove definitively that one causes the other. However, this and other studies have been used to suggest that prenatal concentrations of sex hormones may contribute to female–male behavioral differences, and that, to the extent that hormones are responsible for these differences, they may also be responsible for the large individual differences in such qualities *among* both girls and boys.

When we learn about scientific findings of differences in the brains of men and women in any particular sample—findings that involve sophisticated techniques such as neuroimaging—it is tempting to conclude that something really definitive has been proven about brain sex differences. However, experts caution that it would be wise to remain skeptical. For one thing, neuroimaging results can be affected by extraneous variables such as breathing rates or caffeine intake—a problem if samples are small. For another, it can be difficult to interpret the functional significance of differences in the size of brain structures or of more or less activation of a certain area of the brain. And if scientists are trying to link brain differences to behavior that is "feminine" or "masculine," they have to define what behaviors fall into these categories—a daunting and controversial task.

The role of biology in producing gender-related behavior is complex and fascinating; we have only scratched the surface of it here, and much more research remains to be done. However, biology always works in interaction with the environment, and that interaction is always a "work in progress" as each individual develops. As one eminent group of reviewers recently noted (Berenbaum, Blakemore and Beltz 2011: 814), biology is not destiny. Genes are activated or suppressed by environmental factors. Hormones and brain functioning are almost certainly influenced by the different environments in which girls and boys are raised, by their different behaviors, and by joint effects of genes and the social environment.

THE ROLE OF CULTURE

Socialization: learning to be gendered

By the age of 6 months, infants can distinguish women's from men's voices; by nine months, most can discriminate between photographs of men and women—and sometime between the ages of 11 months and 14 months, they show the ability to accurately pair women's voices with pictures of women and men's voices with pictures of men (Martin and Ruble 2004). Clearly, children learn very early of the existence of gender categories and quickly become competent at figuring out who fits into which category.

Not only do children figure out these categories very early, they also quickly become adept at associating activities and items with the appropriate gender. By the middle of their second year, infants reliably look at a female face when presented with images of items such as ribbons and dresses, and at a male face when presented with pictures of things such as fire hats and hammers (Eichstedt et al. 2002). And by this age too, children have learned to link more metaphorical, abstract qualities with gender. Infants in this same study associated bears, fir trees, and navy blue with men, and hearts, cats, and bright pink with women. Children are unlikely to have seen all these items with women and men (for example, most infants will not have seen men with bears); however, they may have learned to connect the attributes of these things with gender. For example, a bear may be seen as strong and fierce; a cat may be seen as soft and quiet. Even very young children have absorbed the message that these characteristics are linked to gender.

How do children arrive at these conclusions? On the one hand, according to psychologists, they respond to instructions, rewards and punishments from people such as parents, teachers, and peers, who let them know how to act as girls or boys and try to shape their behavior to fit expectations for the appropriate gender categories. A boy may be praised for acting "like a little man;" a girl may reap approval for behaving "just like Mommy." Peers may tease a boy for "throwing like a girl"; teachers may criticize a girl for being "unladylike." To cultivate approval and avoid criticism, children bring their behavior into line with the gendered expectations communicated to them. But on the other hand, children do not simply react to rewards and punishments; they are not mere putty in the hands of socializing agents. On the contrary, it now seems clear that children are active searchers for cues about how to behave in gender-appropriate ways.

According to cognitive theories of gender development, once children figure out that there are two gender groups and that they belong to one of them, there are some important consequences. For one thing, they begin to evaluate their own group as better than the other group: children as young as 3 years old like their own gender group more, attribute more positive qualities to members of that group, and show a strong preference for same-gender playmates. They also appear to be more interested in information about their own group, and tend to use gender stereotypes to form impressions of others. They do not seem to need much of a push to conform to gendered expectations; rather, they seem to be motivated to learn as much as they can about this important social category—gender—which is so important to their social identity. Thus the instructions, the presence of adult or peer models who can be imitated, rewards, and punishments are all used by children as sources of guidance to doing the best possible job of fitting into the "girl" or "boy" category. In fact, children become quite rigid for a while as they try to work this out. During early childhood, children try to consolidate their knowledge about gender into hard and fast categories; these categories can be very inflexible, particularly between the ages of 5 and 7 years. In this period, children are prone to make quick and strong judgments about people based solely on gender, and they are likely to be "sure" that women and men can't do certain things (Martin and Ruble 2004). After the age of 7 children tend to relax the categories a little and become more flexible.

Socialization does not end with childhood, however. It is a continuing process, affecting the ways individuals understand and enact gender at each life stage. As children approach adolescence, they fall more and more under the influence of peers and less under the influence of parents. Older children and adolescents who are not "typical" for their gender often feel pressure from their peers to conform to gender norms; when this happens, they are vulnerable to low self-esteem and depression. On the other hand, adolescents who view themselves as gender-atypical but feel accepted by their peers are less likely to face such difficulties. Through the media, children, adolescents and adults are presented with a continuous stream of gendered expectations and models to imitate. One study, for example, examined the portrayals of male and female characters in 101 top-grossing US films across the 15-year period from 1990 to 2005 (S.L. Smith *et al.* 2010). They found that male characters outnumbered females 2.57 to 1—a ratio that had not changed over the 15 years. They also found that female characters were more likely than males to be depicted as young, as parents, and as being in a married or committed relationship. Males were more likely than females to be portrayed as strong and funny; females were more likely to be presented as physically attractive. Both male and female characters were likely to be depicted in gender-traditional occupations. Another study (Paek, Nelson and Vilela 2011), which examined gender portrayals in television advertising across seven countries, found that males were reliably shown in more prominent visual and auditory roles than females, and that both women and men were used to advertise gender-typed products. In general, research shows that in television programs and commercials, video games, and popular films, whether created for children, adolescents or adults, male characters are portrayed more often than females and gender stereotypes are very common (Collins 2011). We swim in a cultural sea of gendered images and, at every stage, a desire to "fit in" pushes individuals to conform to those images.

The influence of the gender hierarchy

It may appear that gender socialization involves fitting people into a fairly arbitrary division of activities and qualities labeled masculine and feminine. Indeed, a look at varying gender prescriptions across cultures or historical eras does suggest a strong streak of arbitrariness: in some cultures, men wear long, flowing garments as a matter of course, but in some the idea of a man in a "dress" is viewed with alarm; in some cultures, men who are good friends walk down the street holding hands, but in others that behavior is considered a violation of masculinity norms; there was a time in North America when the now-familiar mantra that "pink is for girls, blue is for boys" was reversed and pink was considered a strong, "masculine" color.

However, not all gender prescriptions are arbitrary. Many, in fact, help maintain a hierarchy in which men hold more power than women. If we consider the behaviors, personal qualities, and appearance that are considered desirable for men, many involve strength, dominance, and leadership; those considered desirable for women encompass delicacy, flexibility, and agreeableness— and a willingness to bend to a situation rather than take charge. A man often demonstrates his masculinity by wielding power; a woman can often indicate her femininity by behaving submissively. Thus, when people violate gender norms, they are sometimes also challenging the gender hierarchy.

For example, traditional gender roles tend to be entwined with the kinds of work women and men do. The expectation that women will be warm and nurturing means that they are considered a good fit for jobs or tasks that emphasize caretaking and supporting others. The expectation that men will be achievement-oriented and assertive implies that they will be viewed as good candidates for positions that involve taking charge and making decisions. Alice Eagly's (1987) *social roles theory* proposed that women are expected to be warm and compassionate and men to be tough and decisive *because* they are so often observed performing roles that require these very qualities. The gendered division of labor is both based on, and gives credibility to, gender stereotypes. Furthermore, Eagly argued, the requirements of the roles reinforce these qualities: women in "feminine" roles have more opportunity to practice compassion and so develop in that direction; men in "masculine" roles have more scope for decisiveness and so become more used to such behavior and better at it. So gender stereotypes reproduce themselves: people are selected for roles congruent with gender stereotypes, and they learn to perform the requirements of these roles, thus enacting the gender stereotypes and helping to maintain both the stereotypes and the gendered division of labor. In maintaining the gendered division of labor, this circular process also maintains the gender hierarchy, since roles requiring masculine-stereotyped qualities such as leadership abilities are almost guaranteed to involve more status and higher pay than those requiring feminine-stereotyped qualities such as warmth and flexibility.

Another approach, *social dominance theory* (Pratto and Walker 2004), suggests that in societies that emphasize hierarchical social arrangements, the values toward which men are socialized and encouraged are hierarchy-enhancing—values that emphasize the promotion of the interests of powerful groups. Women, on the other hand, are encouraged to adopt hierarchy-attenuating values—values that stress equality and minimizing intergroup status and power differences. The expectation that women and men will hold different values promotes their perceived suitability for different kinds of occupational roles: men for roles that involve wielding power and influence, women for roles that involve supporting and empowering others. Indeed, even a cursory examination of labor statistics in Western countries indicates that men are far more likely than women to be in powerful, high-status positions such as corporate, professional, and political leadership, whereas positions such as social worker, counselor, secretary, and nurse, which involve helping and supporting others, tend to be dominated by women.

Gender stereotypes and roles, then, represent more than the expression of biologically-based sex differences and more than an accidental or random division by societies of qualities and behaviors into "feminine" and "masculine". They are expressions of cultural values, social constructions that help to organize behavior and maintain a society's power structures. And since gender is socially constructed, there is room for variation in the ways it is defined.

Multiple genders?

Cultures differ in their accommodation of individuals who are uncomfortable with the gender assigned to them or who do not fit neatly into either the feminine or masculine gender. Among many Native American groups, for example, there is a tradition of categorizing such individuals as "two-spirit" people. Two-spirited people may be individuals with male bodies who identify and live as women, people with female bodies who identify and live as men, individuals of either sex who are sexually attracted to same-sex others, or anyone who lives outside the traditional definitions of gender and combines elements of both female and male genders. Having two spirits has traditionally been considered a special gift in these cultures. Two-spirited persons have been respected and, in some groups, given special roles in religious ceremonies.

The Americas are not the only place where exceptions to a simple two-gender system have been allowed. In some parts of Polynesia, for example, a category called *mahu* incorporates male-bodied individuals who adopt a feminine appearance and perform women's work. In India, the *hjiras* are male-to-female transgendered people who belong to a religious sect devoted to a particular goddess. They are often called upon to provide blessings at ceremonies such as weddings and births. Some researchers define two-spirit people, mahu, hjiras, and other similar groups as separate gender categories, referring to them as a *third gender*. They argue that such a label is appropriate, since these individuals are not completely incorporated into either the female or male gender, but live by a separate set of rules and expectations. It is probably too simplistic to categorize all these groups in the same way, given the many differences among them. However, the notion that gender categories need not be limited to male and female underlines the idea that gender is a social construction, maintained by agreement among members of a culture.

GENDER IDENTITY

Early in the chapter, we considered the difficulty of imagining oneself as a member of a different gender. For most people, this is quite difficult. Gender identity, the powerful conviction that one is female or male, is apparently developed very early in life. What is responsible for this conviction? Do children simply accept the category into which they are told they belong? Do they try to figure out which category is the "best"? Are there biological underpinnings to gender identity? One thing we know with certainty is that there are limits to the extent children will passively accept their assignment to a gender category. In one very famous case, a young boy's penis was destroyed in a circumcision accident when he was only 7 months old (Diamond and Sigmundson 1997). Following what they thought was the best expert advice, this child's parents decided to raise him as a girl. Starting at the age of 17 months, "John" became "Joan." This child had an identical twin brother, and, for the first few years, the doctor supervising his case wrote optimistic descriptions of how the two children were developing: one as a traditional masculine boy and the other (reassigned) as a well-adjusted, feminine girl. The case was offered as proof of the malleability of gender identity in individuals younger than 24 months: at such an early age, it was said, a child would adopt the gender identity s/he was given, regardless of biological factors.

However, this case did not turn out well. As a young teenager, "Joan," who, according to her family, had never been happy as a girl despite their best efforts to support that identity and to socialize her in a feminine direction, discovered the truth about her history and demanded to reclaim a masculine gender identity. He went through genital surgery, adopted a masculine name, and began living life as a young man. Eventually, he married and became the father of an adopted family. He spoke up about his experience, in an attempt to protect other children from what he viewed as tragic manipulation by the medical community. Yet he remained troubled for the rest of his life, and later committed suicide.

Supporting the notion that gender identity is fixed very early and not easy to change are the first-person accounts of many *transgendered people*: individuals whose gender identity does not match their body's configuration. Most of the people who have written about this experience report that they became aware in early childhood that their bodies did not match their inner conviction about their gender—and that they found it impossible to change that inner conviction despite considerable external pressure. One therapist who collected such narratives reported that 85 percent of her clients recognized before they entered grade school that their gender identities and their bodies were discrepant (Brown and Rounsley 1996).

If an awareness of a mismatch between inner identity and bodily form occurs so early and is so intractable, might there be some neurobiological dimension to gender identity? There is some limited research suggesting differences between one small aspect of the brains of transgendered and non-transgendered individuals (e.g. Kruijver *et al.* 2000), but samples are small, and conclusions based only on correlations. As yet, there is no definitive proof that such differences are routinely present or that they *cause* variations in gender identity. It is reasonable to assume, however, that biology and environment interact in complicated processes to produce gender identity—and that the details are simply not yet fully understood.

Adding to the complexity are reports suggesting that, under some circumstances, gender identity has proven to be flexible. In one case, a male child who was the victim of a surgical accident to his penis at the age of two months was reassigned as female at the age of seven months. That individual, who has since been followed up as an adult, apparently successfully adopted a feminine gender identity (Bradley *et al.* 1998). The researchers speculate that her successful transition to a feminine gender identity is due to the early age (seven months) at which she was reassigned, in contrast to the later age (17 months) in the unsuccessful case described above. In another set of cases, children in the Dominican Republic born with male (XY) genetic configurations and ambiguous genitalia were raised as girls, but then were found to change to a masculine gender identity at puberty when male secondary sex characteristics developed (see Imperato-McGinley *et al.* 1979). In these cases, some researchers argue, the children's early gender identity was not "set" as female because their ambiguous genitalia caused them to be recognized in their community as members of a special category: "first woman, then man." Thus, the way was paved for them to slip easily from a feminine to a masculine gender identity.

Clearly, the causes, processes, and timing of the formation of core gender identity are still in need of clarification. Research tells us that it usually solidifies very early and that it is almost impossible, once that happens, to "convince" an individual that it should be changed. Yet there is more to gender than that basic, private experience of belonging to a gender category. The ways in which that category is defined and expressed can vary a great deal across social and cultural environments.

GENDER AND OTHER CATEGORIES

Some years ago, two researchers (Sugihara and Katsurada 1999) asked a group of Japanese college students to complete the Bem Sex Role Inventory (BSRI), a test often used in North America to assess psychological masculinity and femininity. In North American samples, men usually score as more "masculine" and women as more "feminine" on this measure, meaning that men tend to describe themselves as more like the US men and women as more like the US women on whom the test was developed. For Japanese students, however, these differences did not appear. There were no differences between Japanese women and Japanese men on either the Masculinity or Femininity scales of the BSRI, and both genders scored higher on the Femininity scale than on the Masculinity scale. The authors note that traits desirable for women and men in Japan may be different from those thought desirable in American culture, and they comment that "Japanese have described the 'ideal' woman as 'Yamato-nadeshiko' which represents a gentle and quiet female with internal strength," and that the ideal man is someone with "internal strength rather than physical strength" (p. 645).

Clearly, the ideals and norms for femininity and masculinity are not the same across all cultures. Research also shows that even within cultures, racial and ethnic identities intersect with gender norms. For example, one researcher (Tabar 2007) reports on a cultural category of ethnicised masculinity, labeled *habiib*, among second-generation Lebanese-Australian youths. The term *habiib* emphasizes not only a sense of kinship and shared experience among young Australian men of Lebanese ancestry, but also, according to Tabar's informants, "a hypersexualised masculinity with a particular style of dressing, posturing and even speaking."

Gender norms, stereotypes and roles also intersect with factors such as age, social class, sexual orientation, and ability/disability. For example, there is evidence from several sources that women develop more confidence and power as they move into middle age. Research also shows that gender stereotypes are different for women of low and middle social class. We will explore these intersections further in later chapters.

THE EMPHASIS ON DIFFERENCES

Sometimes the entire focus of inquiries into gender and sex seems to be on defining the differences between categories. Perhaps this is not surprising; academic researchers know that one sure way to get findings published is to show a "significant" difference between two groups. Indeed, "no-difference" findings often languish, unpublished and unrecognized, in academic file cabinets.

The issue of difference is a loaded one, however: in many times and places, women have been excluded from occupations and from participation in aspects of public life *because* of presumed differences from men that made them unsuitable for such activities. Thus researchers oriented toward gender equality have often focused on showing that women and men do *not* differ on important abilities and temperamental qualities.

But might an emphasis only on debunking differences cause us to miss some important issues? Whereas a focus only on illustrating differences may solidify gender stereotypes and uphold the status quo, a focus only on showing similarities might result in the glossing over of important issues such as differences among women and men of different cultures, ethnicities, racial identities, sexualities, ages, and social classes; the different resources and sources of power available to women and men; or the different needs of women and men with respect to biologically-connected issues such as health, reproduction, and longevity.

Clearly, a single-minded emphasis on either differences or similarities is likely to miss something important. Canadian researcher Meredith Kimball (1995) has argued that it is important not to choose one emphasis over the other, but instead to practice "double visions," engaging the tension between the two approaches. Maintaining this perspective is difficult, but it is more consistent with the complexities of women's and men's lives and the ways they entwine and connect. In the next chapter, as we excavate the assumptions and ideas underlying gender stereotypes and prejudice, we will repeatedly run up against this tension between seeing similarities and seeing differences.

FOR FURTHER EXPLORATION

Blakemore, Judith E. O., Berenbaum, Sheri A. and Liben, Lynn S. (2009). *Gender Development*. (New York: Psychology Press, Taylor and Francis Group.) This detailed yet reader-friendly book provides a fascinating and balanced look at different aspects of the development of gender. Chapters on the history of the field and on biological, social and cognitive approaches to understanding how gender takes shape will leave the reader well-informed.

Boylan, Jennifer (2003). *She's Not There: a life in two genders*. (New York: Broadway Books.) This lively and personal book is one of several interesting autobiographies of individuals who have transitioned as adults to a different gender.

Colapinto, John (2001). *As Nature Made Him: the boy who was raised as a girl*. (New York: HarperCollins.) A journalist tells the fascinating story of the famous "John/Joan" case.

Fausto-Sterling, Anne (2000). *Sexing the Body: gender politics and the construction of sexuality*. (New York: Basic Books.) A biologist uses her expertise to warn against over-simplified interpretations of research on biological sex differences. Among the controversies she takes up are the idea that there should be only two genders, and the notion that scientific language is neutral.

Fine, Cordelia (2010). *Delusions of Gender: how our minds, society, and neurosexism create difference*. (New York: W.W. Norton.) An accessible critique of research on sex differences in the brain.

Jordan-Young, Rebecca M. (2010). *Brain Storm: the flaws in the science of sex differences*. (Cambridge, MA: Harvard University Press.) The author presents a sophisticated analysis of the methodological problems with research linking prenatal hormones to sex differences in the brain. She challenges researchers to come up with a new, dynamic model that focuses on the processes of development instead of trying to measure "essential" male–female differences presumed to be the outcome of prenatal hormone differences.

Maccoby, Eleanor E. (1998). *The Two Sexes: growing up apart, coming together*. (Cambridge, MA: Harvard University Press.)

A well-respected pioneer in the psychology of gender development summarizes research showing how the sex-segregated "two cultures of childhood" merge gradually into a more gender-integrated adult culture—and some of the problems that result.

Roughgarden, Joan (2004). *Evolution's Rainbow: diversity, gender, and sexuality in nature and people.* (Berkeley: University of California Press.) The author, a biologist and transgendered woman, provides a tour of the sexual diversity present in the natural world. She shakes up traditional ideas about evolution and helps the reader question what is "natural" with respect to sex and gender.

2

POWER, INEQUALITIES, AND PREJUDICE

Beliefs about the differences between women and men have consequences. In a recent demonstration of this principle, two Canadian researchers (Funk and Werhun 2011) brought men into their lab and asked them to squeeze a handgrip as hard as they could. Afterward, some of the men were told they squeezed "like a girl." Would such a judgment make men feel badly? Interfere with later performance? Indeed. On later tests, men who received this feedback showed a threatened sense of masculinity, reduced performance on a cognitive task, and less attentional self-control than men who were not told their grip strength was girl-like. And when given another chance to use the handgrip, these men squeezed more strongly than other men—perhaps trying to prove their masculinity. Believing that they had violated gender-related expectations apparently shook these men's self-confidence, interfered with their ability to think straight, and motivated them to work hard to prove their masculinity.

The finding that gender stereotypes can exert such effects is a clue to how integral they are to societal norms. These stereotypes are such a pervasive part of our social environment that often we don't even see them as stereotypes, but rather as "the way things are."

GENDER STEREOTYPES:
INSTRUMENTALITY VS. EXPRESSIVENESS

Decades ago, two sociologists (Parsons and Bales 1955) characterized the main themes in gender stereotypic expectations for femininity and masculinity. Women were viewed as more expressive, with qualities that emphasized an orientation to emotion and relationships; men were viewed as more instrumental, with qualities that focused on action, leadership, and accomplishment. To a large extent, the core aspects of these stereotypes have been found repeatedly by researchers, even across cultures. For example, 75 percent of adults surveyed in 25 countries associated six adjectives (adventurous, dominant, forceful, independent, masculine, strong) with men and three (sentimental, submissive, superstitious) with women (Williams and Best 1990).

Gender stereotypes do change over time, but fairly slowly—and the feminine stereotype seems to have been more fluid in recent decades. For the 20 years between 1973 and 1993, US college women's attribution of masculine-stereotyped qualities to themselves increased significantly, while men's attribution of feminine-stereotyped qualities to themselves did not change (Twenge 1997) and, when asked to project what women and men would be like in the future, respondents predicted women would take on more masculine-stereotyped qualities and roles (Diekman and Eagly 2000).

Changes in gender stereotypes and the related expectations for women and men are probably linked to cultural, political and economic changes. In the United States, women have increasingly moved into the paid workforce and taken on occupational roles previously occupied by men, whereas men's roles have not changed so much. It is not surprising, then, that only women's self-views and the perceptions of women have changed to incorporate more masculine traits and behaviors. In countries such as Chile and Brazil, social change has pushed both men and women into more urban, industrial environments and greater technological competence, leading to an increased emphasis on the masculine-stereotyped qualities of independence and problem-solving skills. Perhaps not surprisingly, then, perceptions of increases in stereotypically masculine characteristics not only in women, but also in men, were found to increase over time in these countries (Diekman *et al.* 2005).

Descriptions and prescriptions

Gender stereotypes are more than just descriptive—beliefs about what typical men and women are like. Stereotypes of masculinity and femininity certainly contain this descriptive element, which can influence expectations and even what we notice or ignore about individual men and women. However, they also incorporate a very important prescriptive element. Prescriptive stereotypes specify what women and men *should* be like; they are unwritten but powerful rules about what women and men ought to do to conform to society's expectations about femininity and masculinity. The men in the opening example who were told they squeezed "like a girl" were implicitly being told not just that they differed from the typical man, but that they had violated one of the prescriptions for masculinity by being weak. No wonder they had trouble thinking straight!

The prescriptive aspects of gender stereotypes can be broken down into several categories (Prentice and Carranza 2002). First, there are *intensified prescriptions*: positive qualities that are considered especially desirable for either women or men. For example, in North America it is considered very important for women to be warm, kind, and interested in children. Men who have these qualities are also viewed positively, but for women it is more important. Then there are *relaxed prescriptions*: positive qualities that are viewed as desirable for anyone, but for which either women or men are more easily forgiven if they fall short. For example, intelligence is valued in both men and women, but women are judged less harshly than men if they are seen as lacking in this quality. Next, there are *intensified proscriptions*: qualities that are undesirable in general, but viewed as especially undesirable in one gender or the other. For example, promiscuity is viewed as a bad thing—but promiscuous women are the targets of more disapproval than promiscuous men. Finally, there are *relaxed proscriptions*: socially undesirable traits that nonetheless receive more approval when displayed by one gender than the other. For example, it would be hard to argue that it is a good thing to be shy, but a shy woman is more likely than a shy man to be excused for this quality.

There are important implications of the notion that one gender may be more likely than the other to be stigmatized or punished for displaying a particular undesirable quality. For example, it is considered more important for women than for men to be physically attractive—and one key aspect of attractiveness in Western cultures is thinness. Being overweight is considered undesirable—but more so for women than for men. Employers apparently attribute negative characteristics to heavy women such as laziness, emotional instability, incompetence, lack of self-discipline and low supervisory potential (Puhl and Brownell 2001), and women's (but not men's) body mass is associated with lower wages and lower career success (Glass, Haas and Reither 2010). There is some evidence that the impact of heaviness on women's occupational outcomes begins very early: overweight women are less likely than other women to earn college degrees (Glass, Haas and Reither 2010). For men, on the other hand, weight seems to have no relationship with educational attainment. Why would heavy women be less likely to complete college? Perhaps their high school teachers and peers judge them more harshly and are less likely to provide encouragement. Stereotypes may appear ephemeral and unimportant, but they have very tangible consequences.

The prescriptive masculine stereotype appears more rigid than the feminine one; indeed, some researchers have shown that a significant and very upsetting form of harassment for men is the claim by others that an individual is "not man enough" (Waldo, Berdahl and Fitzgerald 1998). Men and boys react strongly to feedback that they are gender-deviant: in one study, men who were told they scored high on a feminine knowledge test declined to publicize their scores and later expressed stronger masculine interests (Rudman and Fairchild 2004). In another study, men who were told falsely that their personality score was similar to that of a typical woman were more likely than other men to harass a female partner by sending her pornographic material (Maass et al. 2003).

Both women and men can be caught in "double binds" in which the prescriptive stereotype for their gender directly conflicts with the prescriptions for an occupational or social role they are performing. A woman in a leadership position must display decisiveness and toughness that are antithetical to the feminine role. If she appears too tough and decisive, she is likely to be criticized as unfeminine. A man who decides to earn his living as a nurse may find that the compassion and willingness to accept direction necessary for the performance of this role are viewed by others as signs that he is not sufficiently masculine.

"Truth" and stereotypes

It is commonly thought that stereotypes contain a "grain of truth." Such a claim is difficult to evaluate with respect to gender stereotypes, particularly since gender stereotypes are somewhat dynamic. However, some researchers have shown that women's and men's self-descriptions tend to differ less than their estimates of male–female differences in general. So apparently people do not see themselves in ways that match the stereotypes—even if they think those stereotypes are accurate for others. Another researcher (Swim 1994) found that respondents' estimates of gender differences fairly mirrored research findings, but that they underestimated the impact of situations on such differences. Indeed, this is likely to be the main problem with evaluating the accuracy of stereotypes. As noted in the previous chapter, many of the attributes we associate with women and men are not essential, built-in, aspects of personality, but rather responses to social conditions that differ for the two genders. If gender is a social construction, as argued in Chapter 1, then gender stereotypes are social constructions too.

The impact of the media on gender stereotypes

In one episode of the well-known sitcom *Friends*, Ross, a recent father divorced from his wife, spends time caring for his infant son. Dismayed to find the boy clinging to a Barbie doll, Ross tries to get him interested in a GI Joe "action figure" instead. The message that boys aren't supposed to play with dolls (and that, if they do, those dolls are actually not "dolls" but "action figures") comes through loud and clear. Whereas it is meant, in part, to poke fun at gender stereotypes, the episode reinforces both the descriptive and prescriptive aspects of stereotypes. It reminds viewers that boys don't play with dolls and, perhaps more importantly, it reminds them that the adults in a boy's social environment get very upset if he *does* seem interested in dolls.

The media contribute strongly to the construction of gender stereotypes. The stereotypic instrumental–expressive distinction between women and men is reinforced by a steady stream of media images. Content analyses of prime-time television programming, commercials, and films have shown for years that male characters are portrayed more often in work-related roles, whereas female characters tend to be shown in interpersonal roles in families, friendships, and romance. Both female and male characters are most likely to be portrayed in gender-traditional roles and occupations. The work roles in which female characters are seen usually involve clerical or service occupations and are unlikely to include the exercise of authority and instrumental behavior. These portrayals do affect viewers: a stream of studies in different countries has shown that the more television young viewers watch, the more they accept stereotypical beliefs about gender. It is difficult to see how gender stereotypes can change if media portrayals do not.

WOMEN ARE WONDERFUL—BUT INCOMPETENT? EVALUATING WOMEN AND MEN

A discussion of gender stereotypes may lead us to wonder whether they are really so bad—especially for women. After all, the qualities stereotypically attributed to women tend to be rather desirable. Women are seen as warm and caring, empathic, supportive. By contrast, masculine qualities (assertiveness, dominance, leadership orientation) may not seem quite so likeable. Such reflections are a reminder that stereotypes imply more than beliefs about the qualities associated with particular groups—they also involve feelings about favorability, approval, liking and admiration for those groups. In other words, they are connected with evaluation. As we move from the notion that women and men have certain qualities to the notion that we like, admire, or disdain women or men because of those qualities, we are moving from stereotyping to prejudice. Evaluative judgments based on individuals' gender represent a type of prejudice labeled *sexism*.

There is plenty of evidence, to be explored throughout this book, that women are frequently the targets of sexist discrimination. Historically, they have often been excluded from roles, places, and behaviors. Currently, they are underrepresented in most powerful positions, underpaid in comparison to men, and, in many parts of the world, have less access than men to education, medical care, and political power. Strangely, all this does not seem to mean that people *like* women less than men. Indeed, researchers have found that both women and men evaluate women as a group more favorably than men—a finding dubbed the "women are wonderful" effect (Eagly, Mladinic and Otto 1991). However, liking does not necessarily translate into respect, and favorable attitudes toward women do not seem to translate into confidence that they will perform well in situations that require competence, decisiveness, or leadership. Similarly, unfavorable stereotypes of men, that they are less empathic and sensitive than women, may support the notion that men are less likable than women —but make better leaders. Masculine qualities such as these may be less "warm and fuzzy," but they are associated with power. One group of researchers argues that a succinct summary of gender stereotypes and prejudice would be "Men are bad, but bold, and women are wonderful but weaker" (Glick *et al.* 2004: 714).

Stereotypes and status

Social psychologists Laurie Rudman and Peter Glick (2008) argue that the strong prescriptive aspect of gender stereotypes is largely rooted in twin factors: a social structure that assigns men more power and status than women, and the intimate interdependence of gender roles. Prescriptive masculine stereotypes help to maintain gender hierarchy by ensuring that boys and men are trained in, and reinforced for, behaviors that keep their status and power high: leadership, decision-making, dominance, achievement-oriented behavior. Prescriptive feminine stereotypes safeguard the hierarchy by keeping pressure on girls and women to assume traditional supportive, nurturing roles. Because these two sets of status-differentiated roles are interdependent, promoting a great deal of everyday role–guided social contact between women and men (e.g. female secretaries interacting with male executives, female dental assistants interacting with male dentists, female aides interacting with male political leaders), there are plenty of opportunities to reinforce the prescriptive stereotypes.

An example of the impact of associating power and status with masculinity can be seen in the differing reactions to female and male political leaders. Participants in one study reacted negatively to female politicians portrayed as interested in seeking power, but men's power-seeking intentions did not affect participants' reactions to them (Okimoto and Brescoll 2010). Not only did respondents express less desire to vote for a "power-seeking" woman politician than for a woman not perceived as seeking power, but they were also more likely to express feelings of moral outrage toward her: emotions of contempt, anger, and disgust. The researchers concluded that this moral outrage was based on the woman's violation of the prescription that she should be

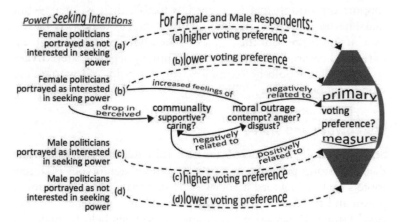

Figure 2.1: Power seeking and the backlash against female politicians. When respondents in this study read a description of a hypothetical female politician, they responded differently, depending on whether or not she appeared interested in seeking power. If she was interested in seeking power, they viewed her as less communal and caring, expressed more reluctance to vote for her, and reacted with more negative emotions than they did if she appeared uninterested in power. Male politicians, on the other hand, were not penalized for being interested in power.

Source: Based on Okimoto and Brescoll (2010), Study 2.

communal in her focus. Such reactions to women perceived as ambitious or power-oriented serve to keep women out of powerful positions and maintain a status difference between women and men.

In support of the idea that prescriptive gender stereotypes serve to maintain status differences between women and men, Rudman and Glick note that the most intensified proscriptions for women, the traits or behaviors that generate the most negative reactions, are those that involve women in claiming or asserting power: rebelliousness, stubbornness, dominance. For men, on the other hand, the most intensified proscriptions involve traits or behaviors that undermine masculine power: emotionality, approval-seeking, readiness to yield to others. These proscriptions are captured in the derogatory labels flung at individuals who fail to conform: women who act "uppity" are characterized as bitches; men who are too easy-going and do not enact masculine prerogatives for power are labeled wimps.

Since men are likely to gain the most from a gender hierarchy that puts them on top, it makes sense that they would hold stronger prescriptive gender stereotypes than women. Research supports this prediction. Men score higher than women on endorsement of traditional gender roles, and react more negatively than women to people who violate gender prescriptions (Glick *et al.* 1997; Glick *et al.* 2004).

An important thing to remember about stereotypes, though, is that they often operate below levels of awareness. We have been discussing the explicit endorsement of gender stereotypes, but researchers have demonstrated that stereotypes can also operate implicitly. Implicit stereotypes guide our reactions and judgments of others even when they are contrary to our explicit beliefs. Thus, for example, women may explicitly reject the idea that women should be subservient, yet be just as likely as men to show automatic negative reactions to women who act authoritative, ambitious, or competitive (Rudman and Glick 1999). Thus, both women and men may, knowingly or unknowingly, enforce gender prescriptions by their negative reactions to individuals who violate them.

SEXISM IS COMPLICATED

Types of prejudice abound. We can think, for example, of racism, ageism, classism: each one an evaluative reaction to individuals based on their group membership. Every type of prejudice is complicated, but sexism is perhaps more complicated than most. This is because, unlike most forms of prejudice in which the prejudiced individual is motivated to, and often can, avoid contact with the target group, people who harbor sexist beliefs are usually in close, even intimate contact with members of the target group. Men and women who hold very sexist attitudes form intimate partnerships with members of the other gender. Women and men work together, parent children together, make decisions together, and often enjoy each other's company a great deal, sometimes while holding firmly to sexist beliefs. Thus theorists and researchers have struggled to analyze sexism and its different manifestations.

Old-fashioned vs. modern sexism

How frequently do we hear openly sexist statements such as "women have no head for politics," or "men are just overgrown babies"? Such overtly derogatory comments reflect the blatant sexism that used to be routinely expressed in many contexts. In recent decades, such comments have become less acceptable, less "politically correct." Does that mean sexism is on the wane? Perhaps, but equally likely is the possibility that it has gone underground. Openly sexist comments that endorse stereotypic judgments about women and men and differential treatment of them would now be characterized as old-fashioned sexism, and are often greeted with disapproval. However, researchers have identified a more subtle form of prejudice, labeled *modern sexism* (Swim *et al.* 1995) or *neosexism* (Tougas *et al.* 1995). Modern sexism entails a lack of support for policies designed to promote equality-oriented changes in gender relations, antagonism toward women's demands for access and inclusion, and denial that gender discrimination still exists. An expression of modern sexism might be, for example, "I'm all for women's rights, but these women complaining about discrimination in employment are going too far: they're too pushy and unreasonable."

Hostile and benevolent sexism

A breakthrough in understanding the maintenance of sexist attitudes even in the context of intimate relationships came when researchers zeroed in on the ambivalence that often characterizes gender-related attitudes. Remember the evidence that people like women more than men, but still don't necessarily respect their abilities or leadership potential? Those mixed feelings are a sign of *ambivalent sexism*: a constellation of attitudes made up of both hostile and benevolent feelings toward the other gender.

Whereas most theories of prejudice have focused only on the hostility directed at the targets, Peter Glick and Susan Fiske (1996) developed an analysis of sexism that explored how individuals maintain the balance between male dominance and intimate interdependence between women and men. Their research identified two intertwined sets of attitudes that support gender ideologies: *hostile sexism* and *benevolent sexism*. Whereas hostile sexism comprises derogatory beliefs about the other gender, benevolent sexism entails warmer but condescending attitudes. Hostile sexism toward women includes attitudes that men should be in charge of, and look after, women, that women are incompetent and untrustworthy, and that heterosexual relationships with women are dangerous and confining for men. Benevolent sexism directed at women includes the attitudes that men should be protective and chivalrous toward women, put women on a pedestal, and that a man needs an intimate relationship with a woman to be complete.

Hostile sexism directed at men includes resentment of their presumed control and dominance, the belief that men are incompetent in certain domains, and the idea that male–female relationships tend to be adversarial. Benevolent sexism toward men includes the attitude that men need to be taken care of, the belief that men are naturally better at some things (especially dangerous or difficult things), and the notion that women need romantic partnerships with men in order to feel fulfilled.

Why would hostile and benevolent attitudes co-exist? Perhaps because, despite the resentments that can accompany the hierarchical relationship between men and women, each gender gets something out of that relationship and so has some stake in maintaining it and feeling good about it (Rudman and Glick 2008). The traditional masculine and feminine gender roles are interdependent: despite resenting men for their dominating behavior, women may depend on men and feel grateful to them for protection; despite viewing women as incompetent and so feeling contemptuous of them, men may depend on, and feel grateful for, women's warmth, care and nurturing.

Women are consistently less likely than men to endorse hostile sexist attitudes toward women. However, women do not always see benevolent sexist attitudes as a problem, often endorsing these attitudes as strongly, or even more strongly, than men do. It is tempting to think that benevolent sexism cannot be so bad if it entails positive feelings toward the target. However, as Rudman and Glick (2008) argue, benevolent sexism produces patronizing, even if affectionate, behavior such as "treating her like a pet or mascot, just as one might love a particularly clumsy and not-too-bright pet dog or cat whose incompetence is endearing." Patronizing behavior undermines the target's self-confidence and promotes an image of strength and superiority for the patronizer and weakness for the target—effectively reinforcing the dominance of one over the other. The benevolent attitudes also tend to be directed mainly toward women who conform to traditional femininity; women who "break the rules" are not necessarily viewed as meriting chivalry or protection. Furthermore, benevolent sexism, by seeming positive and "nice," can undermine women's resistance to gender inequality.

What about hostile and benevolent sexist attitudes toward men? These too tend to support traditional male dominance. High hostility toward men is associated with the idea that male dominance is inevitable, even if unpleasant—a necessary evil that women have to cope with. Interestingly, the women who score highest on hostility to men tend to be, not feminists, but rather those with the most traditional gender-role attitudes and the lowest support for feminism. For women, an adversarial view of men may imply a manipulative approach to heterosexual relationships, such as the idea that men have to be "tricked" into marriage. Such an approach is congruent with benevolent sexism toward men, which implies that a woman needs a man to provide for her and protect her—even though she has to take care of him.

Hostile and benevolent sexist attitudes toward both women and men are found to be strongest in societies where gender equality is lowest (Glick *et al.* 2004). In such cultures, women are encouraged to accept male dominance in return for male protection; men are encouraged to provide materially for women in exchange for emotional support, nurture, and submissiveness.

Sexism in the evaluation of work

What kind of person comes to mind when we think of a nurse? An airline pilot? The CEO of a multinational corporation? Most people automatically generate images that conform to gender expectations: a female nurse, a male pilot, a male corporate leader. This tendency would not be so problematic if it did not also entail a tendency to be a little suspicious of gender-nontraditional occupants of such roles and expect them to perform more poorly. It turns out, though, that people's judgments about work performance are often affected by the gender of the person doing the work and the perceived fit between gender roles and certain kinds of work.

If gender stereotypes say generally that men are more competent than women, we might expect men's work to be evaluated more positively than women's. Just such a pattern was shown clearly in an early study by Philip Goldberg (1968), who asked female respondents to judge the quality of a written article that was attributed to either a female or male author. The same article was judged better on several dimensions when it was thought to be written by a man than when the author was listed as a woman. These results were all the more unsettling because the people making these biased judgments were women. Many years later, Goldberg's study was extended to include both male and female respondents and articles designed to reflect a traditionally masculine (politics), traditionally feminine (psychology of women), or neutral (education) area of expertise (Paludi and Strayer 1985). In that study, both women and men evaluated the articles—even those in the feminine and gender-neutral fields— more favorably when they were attributed to male authors. Researchers have since demonstrated that such a pro-male bias is not always found (Top 1991), but that it is most likely to occur in certain kinds of situations: when the domain in question is stereotypically masculine, when raters do not have much specific information about the expertise of the person whose work is being judged, and when people are evaluating a résumé rather than other kinds of written work (Swim *et al*. 1989).

Many of us would protest that we do not allow gender stereotypes to bias our judgments of others' work, competence, or potential. Yet, as noted earlier in this chapter, stereotypic judgments need not necessarily be explicit; they can and do occur without our awareness. Researchers uncover such implicit gender stereotypes through a method that presents respondents with a series of traits adjectives and asks them to pair those traits with either women or men as quickly as possible. The speed with which someone responds is taken as a measure of how easily the association fits into her/his network or associations for that gender. Thus respondents with strong implicit gender stereotypes might, for example, respond more quickly to the pairing of *kind—woman* than to the pairing of *kind—man*. Using this approach, researchers have found, for example, that respondents associate women more readily with egalitarian words and men with hierarchical words (Schmid Mast 2004) and that they associate women with subordinate roles and men with authority roles (Rudman and Kilianski 2000).

Implicit gender stereotypes affect perceptions of workers and work. For example, researchers have found that people implicitly associate women with traits considered characteristic of elementary school teachers and men with traits stereotypic of accountants and engineers (White and White 2006). An interesting example of the operation of such implicit stereotyping in the realm of work is seen in a study of attitudes toward female and male managers (Latu *et al*. 2011). The researchers asked college students to respond to questionnaires measuring hostile and benevolent sexism and also to a questionnaire measuring how motivated they were to respond without sexism. Additionally, they measured the implicit associations students held with respect to gender and traits of successful or unsuccessful managers. All participants showed explicitly positive views of women in the workplace, and those who had the strongest internal motivation to avoid responding in a sexist way did not show implicit prejudice against women as managers. However, on the implicit measure, the men associated men with the traits of successful managers and women with traits of unsuccessful managers. Female respondents showed stronger associations of women than men with successful manager traits. These researchers also showed that implicit stereotypes might have some very practical consequences: the more participants implicitly associated men with the traits of successful managers, the higher was their recommended salary for a male employee.

There is also clear evidence that, outside the laboratory, individuals apply prejudiced evaluations without realizing they are doing so. In one recent study, faculty members at large, research-intensive universities in the United States were asked to evaluate an application from a graduate student for a lab manager position (Moss-Racusin *et al.* 2012). Some faculty members received an application ostensibly from a woman; others received the identical application, ostensibly from a man. The gender of the applicant made a significant difference: respondents rated the applicant as more competent and worthy of being hired, proposed

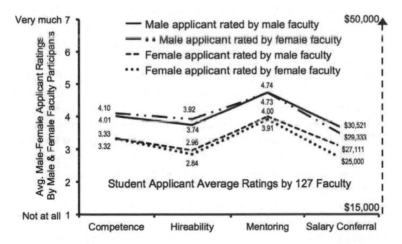

Figure 2.2: Science faculty's subtle gender biases favor male students. When faculty members in science departments of research-intensive universities in the United States evaluated identical male and female applicants for a lab manager position, male applicants received higher ratings and were offered higher salaries.

Source: Based on data from Moss-Racusin *et al.* (2012).

to provide more mentoring, and suggested a higher salary when the name on the application was male than when it was female. In a context of high national concern about attracting more women into science fields, these faculty members had no doubt been encouraged to support and foster female graduate students, yet male applicants were favored.

SEXISM AND THE MEDIA

We have seen that the media reinforce and strengthen gender stereotypes—a process that can, of course, lead indirectly to sexism. However, there is ample evidence that the media promote sexism directly too. Blatant misogyny—hatred of or disdain for women—is all too common in the words of performers and media commentators and in the depictions of women in television, film, music and video games. Rap music, for example, frequently includes derogatory and hostile statements about women, lyrics approving rape and physical violence against women, claims that women are "beneath" men, and references to women as objects to be used and discarded (Adams and Fuller 2006). Rap or hip hop music often fairly drips with hostile sexism and is more likely than other genre to use words such as "bitch" and "hoe" to define women (Frisby 2010). However, themes of benevolent sexism are rampant in pop music, where the lyrics often emphasize that women are valued and appreciated mainly for their bodies and appearance or their "sweetness." Female characters are underrepresented and sexualized in video games (Dill and Thill 2007), and some games glorify the rape or other abuse of women.

Even in the more staid world of media political punditry, prejudice against women is often evident. For example, in one documentary examining the media portrayal of gender, a collection of nasty remarks by radio or television commentators about female political leaders includes reference to "that ugly hag, Madeleine Albright," and a description of US Supreme Court Justice Sonia Sotomayor as having "not the sort of face you'd like to see on a five-dollar bill" (*All Things Considered* 2011). Research is clear that negative portrayals of female political leaders impact people's perceptions—particularly among men who already hold sexist attitudes (Schlehofer *et al.* 2011). When media portrayals are positive, female politicians may be viewed by both women and men as both competent and warm, but men high in hostile sexism exposed to negative media portrayals of women politicians are likely to see those women as both incompetent and cold.

IMPACT OF SEXISM ON ITS TARGETS

Being a target of sexism has consequences: emotional, cognitive, and behavioral. We saw in this chapter's opening example that men told they "squeezed like a girl" had trouble thinking well afterwards. Other studies have shown that men in traditionally feminine occupations may be at special risk of bullying or being "hassled," and have higher rates of absences and turnover in their jobs (Evans and Steptoe 2002).

It is not just being in an occupation that is at odds with gender norms that causes such problems, but the attitudes of an individual's co-workers. One study of German men in non traditional occupations (e.g. nursing, elder care, elementary school teaching, hairdressing) found that the attitudes of their female colleagues were directly related to the men's depressive moods and job dissatisfaction (Sobiraj *et al.* 2011). Men whose female colleagues endorsed statements such as, "It bothers me when a man does something I consider 'feminine,'" were significantly more depressed than their counterparts whose female colleagues did not endorse such attitudes.

Stereotype threat

It can be an uncomfortable feeling to be in a situation where others are skeptical of our qualifications or expect us to perform poorly. That feeling, that uneasy awareness of being judged according to negative stereotypes about our group, has been dubbed *stereotype threat* (Steele 1997). Researchers have found that the awareness that others are applying negative stereotypes to us in our current activities often translates into poor performance. For example, women high in mathematical ability perform more poorly than their male counterparts when told they are taking a math test on which men generally score higher—but not when given the same test with the message that women and men generally have similar scores (Spencer, Steele and Quinn 1999). Researchers theorize that victims of stereotype threat may lose confidence and tend to disengage from tasks associated with the threatened ability, perhaps investing less effort. In the current example, reminding these high-ability women of the stereotype that women are "not good at math" may have made them withdraw effort from the task, resulting in poorer performance.

Another way in which stereotype threat may harm performance is through the necessity to use cognitive energy to counter the stereotype. Researchers have found that when women given math problems to solve are exposed to negative stereotypes about their math performance, they apparently use some of their working memory to counter the stereotype, instead of having all that memory available to solve the problems. When women are "retrained" to associate being female with being *good* at math, they show increased working memory capacity and their math performance improves (Forbes and Schmader 2010). Indeed, some researchers have suggested that stereotype threat is partially responsible for women's historically lower performance in mathematics and the physical sciences (e.g. Good, Aronson and Harder 2008).

One impact of stereotype threat may be a shift in behavior in an attempt to avoid conforming to the stereotype. In a series of studies, researchers exposed women to the stereotype that effective leadership is associated with masculine rather than feminine characteristics. The women were then given the opportunity to respond to hypothetical situations requiring assertive leadership (von Hippel *et al.* 2011). Women exposed to the stereotype tended to alter their communication style in a traditionally masculine direction by speaking more directly, using fewer hedges, hesitations and tag questions. Ironically, these very changes caused a negative reaction. Evaluators rated women who used a more masculine communication style as less warm and likeable and, most importantly, they indicated less willingness to comply with these women's requests. Thus in trying to disconfirm the stereotype that "women can't lead effectively," the women may have undermined their own leadership effectiveness. These women faced a stark example of the double bind produced by prescriptive gender stereotypes: no matter what they did they were violating a norm.

The impact of stereotype threat extends far beyond the social psychology laboratory and beyond simple decrements in performance. Whereas, in life outside the laboratory, individuals are less likely than in previous decades to encounter bald stereotypic statements such as "men do better than women at math" or "women make poor leaders," these and other stereotypes can be communicated and absorbed in many subtle ways. One series of studies of women in various work settings showed that the mere process of comparing themselves with male colleagues seemed to trigger stereotype threat in women (von Hippel *et al.* 2011). Why would this happen? Probably because, in many workplaces, men are paid more, advance more quickly, and are assigned more "important" work than women. A woman in such a workplace, comparing her career progress and success with that of male colleagues, might well begin to wonder if she were being evaluated on the basis of her gender. These researchers showed that women who compared themselves with male colleagues were more likely than other women to experience stereotype threat. Further, that stereotype threat contributed to a set of problematic work-related attitudes. In the first place, stereotype threat was related to identity separation: women's differentiation of their identity into a "work self" (perhaps persuasive, analytical, ambitious) and a "female self" (perhaps warm, sensitive, accommodating). Such identity separation signals a sense of "not belonging" and may have mental health consequences for women who feel they must not express their "female self" when at work. In the second place, the threat was associated with women's belief that their career prospects were limited, a lack of confidence that they would achieve their career goals. Finally, both directly and through these two attitudes, stereotype threat led to lowered job satisfaction and increased intention to quit their jobs. It appears that stereotype threat has the potential to affect individuals' workplace experiences in a variety of complex ways, particularly in work settings where there is an imbalance between women and men and/or where roles have been stereotypically gendered, workers' natural and often irresistible tendency to make cross-gender comparisons may trigger the problems associated with stereotype threat. The only way out of this kind of situation is for workplaces to become more gender-balanced and for occupational roles to be more evenly distributed by gender.

Responding to expressions of sexism

Being the target of sexist comments or actions can be upsetting and stressful: the experience of gender prejudice has been linked to depression, anxiety, lowered self-esteem and anger. Women are far from complacent about such incidents. In one study, women who were targets of scripted sexist remarks by male confederates almost always found the remarks objectionable, viewed the speaker as prejudiced, and felt angry (Swim and Hyers 1999). Yet these women were restrained and cautious when it came to responding publicly to the remarks. Whereas 81 percent of the women in a simulated version of this study predicted they would confront the person making a sexist comment, only 45 percent of the women in the actual study did this.

In a more recent study, participants kept daily diaries for two weeks about their experiences of gender prejudice (Brinkman, Garcia and Rickard 2011). In about a third of the reported instances of gender prejudice, the women said that they had not actually responded in the way they would have preferred. Usually, this discrepancy between desired and actual responses took the form of wanting to confront the perpetrator, but not doing so. The women attributed their reluctance to confront to a variety of reasons, such as not being cost effective (e.g. "it would have escalated the situation"), concern about social norms (e.g. "it would have made someone feel worse"), and being constrained by the situation (e.g. "class was starting"). The most frequent inhibitor of confrontation was concern about social norms—a finding that underlines the power of prescriptive gender stereotypes. Apparently these women were well aware that, if they confronted the perpetrator, they would be negatively evaluated as prickly, oversensitive, and complaining, and that, as women, they were expected to smooth over the situation rather than make it worse. Thus, even though they were the targets of boorish behavior, these women often felt constrained to avoid rocking the boat and violating the expectation that they would be sociable, agreeable, and "nice." Clearly, the social pressure exerted by social norms makes it very difficult for individual women to push back against sexism, even when they feel justified in doing so.

FEMINISM AS A COLLECTIVE RESPONSE TO SEXISM

Outside a New York city rock radio station one day in 2002, a group of angry young women, organized by Riot Grrrl NYC, gathered to protest "cock rock," and the station's male-dominated playlist. Carrying signs such as "Do women have to be naked to get on the radio?" and "We love girl music," and chanting slogans such as "You're teaching girls that women suck ... we won't give in and we won't give up," these women scoffed at the notion that they should be "reasonable" or that the station was blameless and merely responding to audience demand. As one participant later wrote, she was not interested in "a bigger slice of male-dominated pie—I want a different pie, I want a bigger piece of it, and I don't want to cook it" (Ragonese 2002: 27).

In New Delhi, on July 31, 2011, hundreds of women marched in India's first "SlutWalk' to protest the growing sexual violence against women. The title of the march is meant to underline the idea that women should not have to fear sexual assault, no matter what they wear (RFI 2011). The event, one of many similar ones around the world, was designed to challenge the idea that sexual assault is the fault of the victim, caused by her choice of clothing or behavior. The women felt compelled to march because the problem is so pervasive: a recent survey showed that 85 percent of New Delhi's women fear sexual harassment when they leave home.

These protest actions represent collective responses to sexism—something that may be far easier and more effective than the individual responses discussed in the previous section. Research has clearly demonstrated that it is harder to challenge social norms as an individual than with others (Cialdini and Griskevicius 2010), and the history of social movements indicates that such movements can succeed over time in changing rules and expectations. With respect to challenging traditional inequities between women and men, the driving ideologies behind such movements have been various versions of *feminism*. The many shades of feminism have in common a desire to challenge gender inequalities and a belief that women's lives and experiences are important and should be taken seriously. Yet despite the apparent reasonableness of such ideals, the term "feminist" has acquired a dubious reputation in some circles, and some young women reject the label even while endorsing the goal of gender equality.

Feminist movements around the world have, over time, had life-changing impacts: from the early suffrage movements that won women the right to vote, to reproductive rights movements that have strengthened women's right to make decisions about childbearing, to anti-violence movements that have agitated for protection against sexual assault and domestic violence, to a variety of organizations that have pushed for an end to workplace discrimination. Such organizations are driven by the energy and convictions of individual participants—but how and why does an individual identify with, align and coalesce with a feminist movement?

Psychologists have long favored theories of identity development that involve progression through various stages of understanding and commitment. Following in this tradition, Downing and Roush (1985) postulated a model of feminist identity development in which women were said to progress through five sequential stages: passive acceptance (the woman is unaware of discrimination against her based on her sex); revelation (with the realization that discrimination exists, the woman becomes angry and hostile toward men); embeddedness-emanation (she attempts to withdraw from patriarchal culture into a women-only culture); synthesis (she begins to reintegrate with the dominant culture, make more independent decisions, and relate to men as individuals rather than as members of a category of oppressors); and active commitment (she espouses a commitment to social change through feminist collective action). In this model, the development of feminist identity is said to be initially triggered by an experience of discrimination, which jolts the woman out of the initial passive acceptance stage.

This model of feminist identity development has been very popular, but researchers now feel that it may not provide an adequate or accurate description of the experience of today's young women. There is little evidence that women move linearly through the five stages. Furthermore, whereas this model may have captured the experiences of women arriving at a feminist identity in the 1980s, women growing up in the 1990s and later may have a very different "take" on discrimination, gender equality, and feminism. One study found that, in contrast with a model that predicted they would start with "passive acceptance," women developing a feminist identity in the 1990s said there was never a time when they had accepted male superiority and traditional gender expectations; rather, they had always assumed they would be able to "have it all," and only later realized that they were still saddled with traditional expectations associated with marriage and motherhood (Horne, Matthews and Detrie 2001). A study comparing older and younger self-identified feminists and non-feminists found suggestive evidence that as women age they progress from experiencing anger to activism, as the model predicts. However, the study also revealed differences between the experiences of older and younger women (Erchull *et al.* 2009). For the younger women, the starting point seemed more likely to be synthesis—and they moved toward stronger feminist identification and activism as they became aware of subtle discrimination. Erchull and her colleagues suggest the necessity for a new model of feminist identity development:

> Such a model would acknowledge that many young women feel empowered and able to accomplish anything but may not understand the complexities of gender discrimination given that they live in a world where sexism is more subtle than it was in the past.

Regardless of the sequence of stages through which individuals travel to reach an identity as feminists and a commitment to social change, the collective response to sexism that such an identity supports has proven an effective way to challenge gender inequalities and stereotypes that link power and achievement more strongly to men and warmth and relationship concerns more strongly with women. As we will see in the next chapter, both the stereotypes and the challenges to those stereotypes have important implications for relationships between men and women.

FOR FURTHER EXPLORATION

Basu, Amrita (ed.) (2010). *Women's Movements in the Global Era.* (Boulder, CO: Westview Press.) This reader contains a collection of articles on the origins, development and challenges confronted by women's movements around the world, including South Africa, Pakistan, China, Russia, Poland, and Latin American countries. The international focus makes it a good place to start to understand the impact of feminist collective responses to sexism.

Ridgeway, Cecilia L. (2011). *Framed by Gender: how gender inequality persists in the modern world.* (New York: Oxford University Press.) A sociologist describes how we tend to use our traditional beliefs about gender as a framework for organizing new information and dealing with uncertainty—thus unintentionally reproducing old gender stereotypes in new situations.

Rudman, Laurie A. and Glick, Peter (2008). *The Social Psychology of Gender. How Power and Intimacy Shape Gender Relations.* (New York: Guilford Press.) Two social psychologists examine the complex ways in which male dominance co-exists with intimate interdependence to produce our current gender stereotypes and roles.

Implicit Association Test Exercise (2011). http://www. understandingprejudice.org/iat/ This site allows the user to try out a measure of implicit stereotyping: the Implicit Association Test. Versions of the test for both gender and race are available. Trying the test is a good way to get an understanding of what researchers are measuring when they try to assess implicit stereotypes.

3

RELATIONSHIPS, INTIMACY, AND SEXUALITIES

In the rarified early twentieth-century world of British aristocracy, portrayed in the popular television series *Downton Abbey*, individuals' choices with respect to intimate relationships are shaped and constrained at least as much by gender as by class. The eldest daughter of the noble house finds herself unable to marry the man she loves because of an impulsive sexual indiscretion she dares not admit lest it bring scandal on her entire family. A housemaid's liaison with a soldier leads not only to an unplanned pregnancy but also to her rejection by the man in question, disgrace, and the destruction of her chances for a normal life. The valet finds he can divorce his wife for adultery, whereas she would need stronger grounds to divorce him.

Such examples of gender-based uneven distribution of penalties and power in intimate relationships may appear quaint and old-fashioned—but are they? Persistent broad acceptance of a double standard in which women are judged more harshly than men for sexual activity that "breaks the rules," and men's, but not women's, sexual desires are acknowledged as urgent and insistent, is well documented by researchers in countries as diverse as New Zealand, the United States, Turkey, and South Korea. Such an ideology dovetails well with stereotypic notions of male authority and female emotionality. It appears that the gender stereotypes considered in the previous two chapters continue to shape and constrain intimate relationships.

GENDER AND EXPECTATIONS OF POWER AND INTIMACY IN INTERPERSONAL RELATIONSHIPS

Gender stereotypes prescribe authority, leadership and decisiveness for masculinity, and accommodation, interpersonal sensitivity, subservience, and warmth for femininity. These prescriptions may be as strongly enforced in the sphere of interpersonal relationships as in the public sphere of business, politics, and education—and the implications for maintaining a system in which men are in charge are similar in both spheres. For example, some years ago, Australian scholar Dale Spender (1989) used a tape-recorder to document the ways her male and female academic colleagues shared speaking time in their conversations. She found that women virtually always did more listening than speaking: women's share of the speaking time in conversation with male colleagues ranged from 8 to 38 percent. Furthermore, when Spender herself tried, as an experiment, to hold three-minute, two-person conversations in which she held the floor for at least half that time, most of her male colleagues walked away before the time was up. The harder she pushed to try to claim her half of the speaking time, the more uncomfortable she became and the more irritation her male colleagues expressed. Apparently both her colleagues and she had been well-trained to think of male conversational dominance as normal, and female attempts at claiming an equivalent share of speaking time as pushy and rude. One fairly basic rule in interpersonal relationships seems to be that men talk and women listen.

The way we talk with each other has implications for both power and intimacy. Controlling the conversation is a type of power in relationships; keeping the conversation flowing may support and encourage the development and maintenance of closeness, or at least comfort, in a relationship. It appears that, whereas men are expected to dominate relationships, women are expected to do more of the work of sustaining relationships by encouraging and maintaining conversational exchanges. For example, women self-disclose more than men do—especially in cross-sex conversations, and especially with respect to feelings. Women also do more of the work of sustaining interactions—by using non-verbal signals such as eye contact and nodding to show that they are paying attention, by making "listening noises" such as "Mm-hmm" and "I know," and by following up on topics raised by a speaker. In one of the first demonstrations of how hard women work to sustain close relationships, Pamela Fishman (1978) analyzed 52 hours of recorded spontaneous conversation between members of three heterosexual couples in intimate relationships. In these conversations, women did much more support work than men did. Conversational topics raised by the women were far less likely than those raised by men to "succeed" (result in a discussion of those topics); men were far more likely than women to use delayed minimal responses (e.g. a long pause, followed by a uninterested "umm") after women's statements than vice versa. Women worked much harder than men to keep the lines of communication open, but generally men were the ones who decided what the communication was to be about. Again, men are acting in line with a masculine stereotype that prescribes authority and dominance; women are enacting a feminine stereotype of accommodation, warmth, and supportiveness.

Researchers differ as to the reasons for gender differences in communication, but the evidence is consistent with social rather than strong biological explanations. This is because the patterns of differences tend to vary according to the interactive context, such as the relationship between the participants, the type of activity, or the familiarity of the situation. For instance, gender differences in some dominance-oriented conversational tactics, such as talkativeness and interruptions, are more often observed in mixed-gender than same-gender interactions, suggesting that they form part of a tendency for men to try to dominate women rather than simply a gender difference in dominance. And gender differences in both affiliative and assertive speech are more likely in interactions between strangers and in research labs than in natural settings, suggesting that people fall back on gender-related norms and scripts to guide their behavior when in unfamiliar contexts.

Stereotypes connecting gender, power and intimacy are institutionalized in the very trappings of intimate relationships. An old and venerable tradition in many societies is the practice of asking a father for permission to marry his daughter. The tradition in some cultures is for single women to come under the authority of their brothers, should the father die before the women are married. When a woman marries, she often takes her husband's last name. And, lest we think that such "old-fashioned" ideas of male power and female accommodation have no currency in the ways young people think about relationships today, it is interesting to look closely at the media representations of love and romance that are enjoyed by adolescents. In the wildly popular *Twilight* series of books and movies, a young woman, Bella, is courted by a vampire, Edward (and also, for a while, by a werewolf, Jacob). The relationships are marked by numerous instances in which the males rescue Bella from harm—but often harm her in the process. Bella is stalked, bruised, overpowered, frightened, and ordered around repeatedly by Edward and Jacob. Clearly, the males are portrayed as holding and exercising more power; Bella is portrayed as willing to make huge sacrifices in the service of love and intimacy—and, later in the series, for motherhood. These portrayals are redolent of benevolent sexism, a term that was introduced in Chapter 2 to describe a set of attitudes emphasizing that women are vulnerable and need protection and guidance from men. Perhaps because they are so often surrounded by approving depictions of benevolent sexism, adolescent girls may internalize this type of patronizing ideology and fail to recognize such treatment as sexism. Even when they know they are being treated badly, as in cases of sexual harassment and other instances of hostile sexism, young women are apparently so used to being treated in demeaning ways that they often expect such treatment as part of normal heterosexual relationships (Witkowska and Gådin 2005). It appears that the general expectation that men will emphasize power and control and women will emphasize connection and closeness permeates the ways we think about relationships.

WOMEN'S AND MEN'S FRIENDSHIPS

Gender stereotypes that prescribe dominance, competitiveness, toughness and leadership for men may make it difficult for them to be open about feelings with friends. By contrast, stereotypes that prescribe warmth and supportiveness as part of femininity may push women toward both disclosing and listening to accounts of feelings and vulnerability. The result may be a tendency toward emotional restraint and distance among men and toward sharing of emotions among women. Researchers have indeed found girls and women higher in affiliative communication and boys and men higher in assertive communication. Some analysts have characterized the difference between male and female friendships as a divide between shared activities and shared feelings, or between "side-by-side" and "face-to-face" relationships. Men and boys tend to have more friends; women and girls tend to have fewer, more intimate friends.

However, the gender differences are small, do not always appear, and are context-sensitive. A narrow focus on gender differences may obscure large within-gender variations in patterns of communication and friendship. That gender differences in friendship are to some extent a function of history and culture, can be seen by comparing men's friendships in middle-class present-day North America and other settings. For example, one researcher who studied friendship in rural Thailand noted that women were thought not to have really close friends on whom they could rely for serious help and support, but rather simply neighbors and people with whom they enjoy spending time. Men, on the other hand, were thought to have serious "friendships to the death" (Foster 1976). Male–male friendships were sometimes formalized in medieval Near-Eastern countries. For example, one formal contract of friendship between two scholars in Cairo in 1564 stated that the two men would be bound in friendship for their own lifetimes and that of their children and their children's children. They promise to pray in the same synagogue, to lend each other any books they possess, and to never conceal any book from each other (Goitein 1971). Examples such as these reveal a perspective on male friendship that is strikingly different from the activity oriented, emotionally restrained model described by North American researchers.

SEXUALITY IN RELATIONSHIPS

Some scholars suggest that the different communication patterns developed by male and female children as they grow into adolescence significantly shape the way they experience romantic sexual relationships in young adulthood. The impact may be not only on communication and satisfaction in such relationships, but also on the power distribution within them. If girls have relational habits oriented toward self-disclosure and supportive listening, and boys have relational habits that emphasize emotional restraint and conversational dominance, heterosexual romantic relationships appear doomed to be rocky. Women may be unsatisfied with men's listener support; men used to male–male friendships may bask in the unaccustomed warmth of a responsive female listener. Men, used to jockeying for conversational control, may unwittingly neglect to pay attention to conversational topics raised by a female partner, solidifying their culturally-supported role as dominant partners in heterosexual relationships. Learned gendered patterns of communication may shape same-gender romantic relationships as well, by orienting them toward the style practiced most consistently by women or men: more mutual support for women, more power-orientation for men. Thus lesbian couples report somewhat more equality in communication, mutual support and decision-making than do women in heterosexual relationships; gay male couples report less equality of communication, support, and decision-making than heterosexual men (Gotta *et al.* 2011).

What does sexuality mean in relationships?

Gender stereotypes and learned patterns of communication may well affect the ways sexuality is expressed in relationships. If women have learned to emphasize closeness and connection, they may be more likely than men to interpret sexuality in terms of emotion and intimacy. If men have learned to emphasize dominance and emotional restraint, it may be easier for them to think of sexuality in terms of conquest and pleasure without commitment. Indeed, a tradition that to some extent occurs across cultures and historical periods, holds that sexuality carries different meanings for women and men. Women's sexual experience and expression has traditionally not been encouraged, but restrained and guarded. Men's sexual desires, on the other hand, have often been considered irresistible, uncontrollable. This set of attitudes provides the basis for a double standard of sexual behavior, which prescribes that women and men are judged differently for engaging in sexual activity. A woman who engages too easily or indiscriminately in sexual activity is branded with a variety of uncomplimentary labels: slut, promiscuous, loose. Clearly, she is violating the gender-based expectation that she should engage in sexual relationships only when they involve love and intimacy. Such negative consequences do not accrue to a man who "sleeps around" with many women or gets a reputation as being very sexually active. That man may receive a certain amount of disapproval (particularly if he is married or in a committed relationship), but he is also likely to be the target of some envy and admiration from other men, and of nothing worse than an exasperated "boys will be boys" reaction from some women.

These different standards for women and men are more exaggerated in some cultural contexts than others. Sex, or even flirting, outside of marriage (or even outside of an "approved" marriage) can be punishable by death for women whose families subscribe to a traditional strict code of honor. "Honor killings" claim the lives of more than 5,000 women each year, and occur in countries where the propriety of women's behavior is traditionally held to reflect on her family's reputation (United Nations Population Fund 2000). Men, on the other hand, generally do not risk severe punishment for heterosexual activity outside of marriage. In some contexts, however, they do risk physical attack and even death for homosexual activity, and in certain countries such activity can lead to criminal charges and imprisonment.

The cultural scaffolding that props up the double standard is grounded in gender stereotypes, but it is more complex than the prescription that women should reserve sexual activity for intimate relationships whereas men can emphasize "the chase." One contributing factor is that women are the ones who become pregnant and give birth. By controlling women's sexual activity, societies can ensure that children are born into stable family situations and men can ensure that the children they support and help to raise are their own biological offspring. Another aspect is the gender hierarchy. Through controlling women's sexuality and reproduction, men establish, assert, and retain their authority over women and reinforce notions about women's emotionality and lack of suitability for leadership.

Culture, sexual self-schemas, and sexual scripts

Popular media are rife with presentations of sexuality—and it is such presentations that often provide the basis for individuals' ideas about their own sexual selves and how they should be expressed. For example, one study of prime-time television programming found that 77 percent of programs contained sexual content; 20 percent of the instances in which sexual intercourse was portrayed involved characters who knew each other but were not in a relationship; and another 15 percent showed characters having sex soon after they met (Kunkel *et al.* 2005). Viewers may assume such depictions accurately reflect sexual norms; for example, college students seem to believe that their peers are more sexually permissive than they actually are (Chia and Gunther 2006).

Media messages about sexuality are gendered. Women receive conflicting directives that admirable behavior involves being "good" (i.e. restrained) and sexually assertive and sophisticated (Phillips 2000). Portrayals of men's sexuality often emphasize action rather than feelings (Kilmartin 2009). Increasingly, both women and men in North America are presented with media representations of casual, uncommitted sex that support a "hook-up" culture: the notion that there is no need for either women or men to tie sexual activity to emotional commitment (Garcia *et al.* 2012).

Swimming in a sea of such messages is bound to impact individuals' *sexual self-schemas*, their views of themselves as sexual beings. A self-schema about any aspect of the self is a set of cognitive generalizations that help the individual to organize and make sense of incoming information. Thus an individual whose sexual self-schema is heavily weighted with notions of desire is likely to interpret an opportunity for a sexual connection very differently to an individual whose self-schema emphasizes relationship. Not surprisingly, in light of media messages, the sexual self-schemas of women and men tend to differ. Both men and women report the dimensions of passion, romanticism, and openness. However, one dimension that researchers have found among men, but not women, involves power and aggression and includes descriptors such as aggressive, powerful, outspoken, experienced, and domineering. A dimension researchers have found among women but not men involves caution and restraint, and includes descriptors such as embarrassed, conservative, cautious, and self-conscious (Andersen and Cyranowski 1994; Andersen, Cyranowski and Espindle 1999). In describing their sexual selves, men sometimes make a distinction between physical intimacy and emotional intimacy. As one respondent commented, "If you need tenderness and human contact? Rather than talk to somebody, you prove that you're all right, and you get the attachment you need by finding a warm body" (Elder, Brooks and Morrow 2012: 171). Such differences fall clearly in line with gender stereotypes.

Sexual scripts also fall in line with gender stereotypes. Scripts are cultural understandings or shared conventions about how interactions will proceed—understandings that help us to organize and interpret behavior. A sexual script helps organize behaviors into a coherent story, so that once the first behaviors occur, the script suggests how the rest of the interaction will likely proceed (Simon and Gagnon 1987). The scripts are based on past experience, on media representations and on observations of other people. Such scripts are gender-normative: in heterosexual interactions women are expected to behave in certain ways, men in others. Traditionally, sexual scripts for heterosexual interactions have been informed by the double standard: men take the initiative, women set limits; men are interested in casual sex, women are interested in relationships. When in a new situation, people often fall back on scripts to guide their behavior.

Despite the pervasiveness of these traditional (hetero)sexual scripts, most young adults surveyed report that they have engaged in casual sex (Garcia *et al.* 2012). It appears that new cultural scripts are taking root that emphasize non-relational sex, hook-ups, or friends-with-benefits. The initial behaviors in the hook-up script might involve attending a certain kind of party, drinking a substantial amount of alcohol, dancing and flirting—with the anticipation that the subsequent steps will involve casual sex with no expectations of a romantic relationship. Such scripts are celebrated in popular songs such as Katie Perry's "Last Friday Night" (TGIF) and films such as *Friends with Benefits*. On the face of it, these scripts interpret casual, non-relational sex as appropriate for both women and men and they prescribe sexual assertiveness for both genders. However, there is some evidence that the experience of "playing by" these scripts is gendered. Women are much more likely than men to report negative feelings and guilt after having sex with someone they had just met; and women, but not men, appear to show increased depression with the number of sexual partners they report over the past year (Garcia *et al.* 2012). When asked about their feelings on the morning after a hook-up, 82 percent of men, but only 57 percent of women said they were generally glad they had done it (Garcia and Reiber 2008), and more women (42.9 percent) than men (29 percent) said that ideally they would have liked the hook-up to lead to a romantic relationship. Furthermore, in most situations, women more than men report a preference for dating over hook-ups, whereas men more than women report they prefer hooking up (Bradshaw, Kahn and Saville 2010).

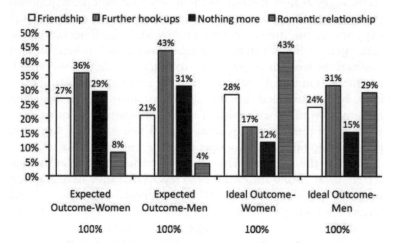

Figure 3.1: Women's and men's expected and ideal outcomes of hooking up. In a sample of more than five hundred undergraduate students in the United States, women and men appeared to differ less in their expectations about the results of hooking up than in their ideals for where they would like such connections to lead. Women were more likely than men to wish that hooking up would lead to a romantic relationship; men were more likely than women to wish for further hookups.

Source: Based on data from Garcia and Reiber (2008).

However, even men are not necessarily completely comfortable with casual sex scripts in heterosexual interactions. Whereas prescriptions for masculinity may include having many sexual relationships while remaining unattached and independent, research suggests that men's feelings about sex are variable and are more complicated than these prescriptions. Men may acknowledge and even subscribe to the notion that they should enjoy non-relational sex, but a significant minority also admit to desiring an emotional connection after having sex with someone several times, even if they did not originally want or plan for a relationship. When men in one sample were interviewed about hooking up, their responses included discomfort with the non-relational nature of such interactions and the articulation of possibilities for real connections and committed relationships (Epstein *et al.* 2009). It appeared that these men often blurred the lines between hooking up and dating, sometimes using the term hook-up to describe a situation where they had wished for a relationship that did not work out. Also, their descriptions of hooking up included a number of instances in which something that started out as casual sex turned into a dating relationship. They also described instances in which they experienced regret and vulnerability after hooking up with people they were not interested in. Thus, although cultural prescriptions may say that men *should* be able to have sex with a stranger without experiencing any emotional consequences, men's reports indicate that such situations are often more complicated.

Sexual scripts for gay men and lesbians seem somewhat reflective of the gender-related expectations spelled out in scripts for heterosexual relationships: scripts for gay men often include casual sex; those for lesbians emphasize that emotional intimacy and sexual attraction are intertwined. However, as has been noted for heterosexual interactions, there are multiple possible scripts, and reality may not fit perfectly with any of them. For example, Rose and Zand (2002) found that the most widely used (though not necessarily most widely preferred) script in relationship formation among lesbians was the "friendship" script. They suggest that many young women have not been exposed to a "romance" or "sexually explicit" script for relationships between women, so they may first treat and label their attraction to another woman as a friendship. The relationship gradually becomes deeper and more committed and is eventually expressed physically. In contrast, the romance script involves flirting and dating and high emotional intensity, leading quickly to an intimate bond and overt sexual contact. The sexually explicit script involves mutual physical attraction and casual sex, and is often initiated in bars or at parties. Even though the latter script is evocative of "masculine" sexuality, 63 percent of respondents in this study said they had engaged in it at least once—though none of the participants endorsed it as the one they preferred.

For young gay men, the cultural script may emphasize being sexually active, being comfortable with casual, non-relational sex and taking sexual risks. Yet, as some researchers have found, though many young gay men in college are well aware of this script and may incorporate it into their self-definition, many do not feel they conform to it (Wilkerson, Brooks and Ross 2010).

DESIRE, AROUSAL, AND SATISFACTION

In her memoir, *Infidel*, Ayann Hirsi Ali (2007) recounts the stark disconnect she experienced as a young woman between her early media-fed sexual fantasies and her first sexual intercourse. Imagination fueled by Harlequin romance novels, she had longed to be swept off her feet by a gorgeous man. She guiltily burned with desire and relished long, passionate kisses with her boyfriend, but followed the rules of her Somali culture to delay sexual intercourse until marriage. As a young girl, she had, according to common practice in her culture, been "circumcised" (had her clitoris cut out and her labia sewn together except for a small hole for urination) to guarantee her purity, and the procedure had left her with a scar in place of a normal vaginal opening. On her wedding night, her new husband "gasped and sweated with the effort of forcing open my scar. It was horribly painful and took so long. I gritted my teeth and endured the pain until I became numb. Afterward, Mahmud fell heavily asleep, and I went and washed again … ."

Ayann had been told by her married girlfriends that sex was unpleasant: that each night was a painful repetition of a scenario in which the husband would push inside the woman, move up and down until he ejaculated, then get up and take a shower—after which the woman would also take a shower and apply disinfectant to her bleeding genitals. Yet she had refused to believe that sex would be that way for her, and, through reading and conversations with friends, had stoked a passionate desire for sexual fulfillment. She dreamed of wildly erotic sexual episodes, but was instead forced into the role of a "good" virgin who lies still and feels nothing. We are not privy to what her husband thought of all this, but we do know that he was the one who was allowed to initiate and direct their sexual activity.

Clearly, sexual desire and arousal are powerful forces—and what they lead to is strongly shaped by societal expectations with respect to gender. The double standard tends to legitimize men's feelings of arousal and desire, but to ignore, downplay, or even condemn such feelings in women. The impact of these gendered expectations can be to encourage men and discourage women in their tendency to recognize, appreciate, and act on their sexual feelings. Indeed, researchers have found that men show a significantly greater degree of agreement between self-reported and genital measures of sexual arousal than women do (Chivers *et al.* 2010). In other words, men's reports that they feel sexually aroused are more likely than women's reports of arousal to match up with the genital changes that signal arousal. Such findings suggest that women and men recognize, label, and interpret the physical signs of arousal differently—probably as a consequence of the very different societal messages about female and male sexuality.

Sexual empowerment for women and girls?

How would relationships change if women were more strongly encouraged to recognize and act on their sexual feelings? Many feminists have advocated for increased sexual empowerment for women, arguing that women should feel free to claim their sexuality: to act on their desires, seek sexual pleasure, dress and behave in sexual ways if they so choose. If women treated their own sexual feelings as legitimate and important, and refused to be embarrassed or hemmed in by a double-standard approach to female sexuality, would the double-standard quickly fade away?

Would the actual balance of power in heterosexual relationships change?

Such questions are particularly vexing in the context of adolescence—the time in most people's lives when sexuality emerges as a force to be reckoned with, when sexual attitudes and scripts take shape, and when individuals may be particularly emotionally vulnerable. On the one hand, it seems obvious that it would be beneficial to adolescent girls to cultivate a sense of efficacy in their sexuality—a sense that they should be aware of and, if they choose, act on their desires, and acknowledge and seek sexual pleasure. Such self-efficacy might well promote self-esteem, responsible decision-making, and equality in heterosexual relationships. On the other hand, it seems equally obvious that girls may not be able to achieve real sexual empowerment in the context of the heavily sexualized and sexist media environment that surrounds them. Can a girl feel subjectively empowered while making choices and behaving in ways that place her under the power of others? Can free sexual expression by one girl help to undermine sexual empowerment for other girls by contributing to the media sexualization of girls in general? Do girls who manage to resist pressures to deny their sexuality and are instead confidently sexually expressive set a standard that is unrealistic for most of their counterparts? Such questions remind us that political and personal power are bound together. Acts of personal empowerment can contribute to cultural change, and political movements can support personal empowerment—but the personal and political approaches work in concert. Clearly, it is too simplistic to urge girls individually to seek sexual empowerment and "take control" of their sexuality.

Sexual satisfaction

In the realm of sexual relationships, one dimension on which empowerment might be assessed is sexual satisfaction. It seems reasonable that part of feeling sexually empowered would be feeling sexually satisfied. Traditionally, there have been differences reported between women and men on variables thought to be related to sexual satisfaction. For example, women more often than men report that they do not reach orgasm during sex with a partner (Michael *et al.* 1994). Men think more about sex than women do and often report a desire for more sex than they are getting (Baumeister, Catanese and Vohs 2001). How are we to interpret such findings with respect to issues of gender, power and justice in relationships?

Sarah McClelland (2010) proposes a theory of *intimate justice* to analyze these issues by focusing on "how social and political inequities impact intimate experiences, affecting how individuals imagine, behave, and evaluate their intimate lives." She argues that in order to evaluate women's and men's reports of sexual satisfaction it is important also to study how entitled they feel to sexual pleasure. In the realm of sexuality, as in many other realms, someone who does not feel entitled to very much may be satisfied with very little. Cultural–political context can affect entitlement, so women and men may feel differently entitled to sexual pleasure. She also notes that it is critical to investigate what respondents mean when they describe their satisfaction as "high" or "low"—and whether there are gender differences in these meanings. For example, in one study, women and men described the low end of a sexual satisfaction scale very differently (McClelland 2009). For women, the low end of the scale was described very negatively, using concepts such as pain, degradation, and depression. For men, the low end of the scale represented less satisfying sex, loneliness, and having an unattractive partner—but men did not mention the severely negative outcomes listed by women.

McClelland's analysis situates the study of personal sexual experiences and relationships clearly within the socio-political context of power relations between groups. Her approach demonstrates why a simple catalog of female–male differences on certain sexual variables is not adequate to an understanding of why and how women and men may experience sexuality differently. The importance of socio-political context is applied in a different way in *sexual economics theory* (Baumeister and Mendoza 2011), which argues that in cultures where women have fewer sources of power than men, women try to enhance their own value and power by restricting sexual activity. These researchers found that, across thirty-seven countries, measures of gender equality were associated with sexual activity: the greater the gender equality in a country, the higher the level of casual sex, the number of sex partners per capita, the tolerance of premarital sex, and the lower the age for first sexual encounter.

Not only sexual behavior, but the entire topic of couple relationships must be placed in the context of power relations between gender groups in order in order to gain a clearer understanding of why and how such relationships function.

Couples: Long-term, intimate connections

Although most people think of long-term intimate relationships as being about love and personal commitment, it is impossible to understand such relationships without recourse to less romantic notions of power, economics, and the way work is divided. Traditionally, norms in most cultures have granted authority in heterosexual couples to men. Such authority is often institutionalized, formally or informally, in the legal and religious frameworks that define marriage. Although, in the modern age, not every bride promises to love, honor and *obey*, there is often an implicit acceptance of male dominance.

Against this backdrop, the roles, rules and habits traditionally associated with male–female couples in many societies have tended to encode the notion that the man is the breadwinner and the woman the homemaker and caregiver. Such a division of roles implies that the man should be the major earner in the family, and that the woman should, in return, perform the bulk of domestic work.

This traditional division of roles does not match the actual situation of most couples in Western countries. For example, in the United States such traditional structures are reflected in fewer than 21 percent of families with children, women make up half of employed workers, and mothers are the primary breadwinners in four out of every ten families (Shriver 2009). In 2009, among married couples where both spouses were employed, almost 28.9 percent of wives earned more than their husbands. The gap between women and men in employment rates has shrunk to less than 10 percent in countries such as Sweden, Denmark and France ("Female power" 2009).

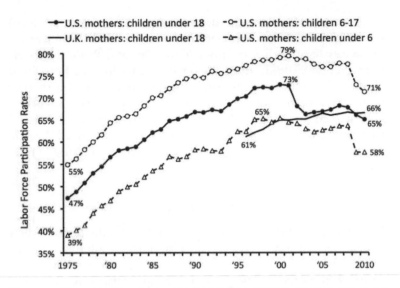

Figure 3.2. U.S. and U.K trends in mothers' labor force participation rates. In both the United States and Britain, labor force participation of mothers of young children increased significantly in the latter part of the twentieth century. Despite some declines in recent years, the majority of mothers, even mothers of very young children, are now in the labor force.

Source: Based on data from U.S Bureau of Labor Statistics (2010b and 2012) and U.K. Office for National Statistics (2011).

If there were no cultural ideology involved, it might be expected that when conditions changed for a couple (e.g. the man lost his job or the woman received a lucrative promotion), women and men would simply and unemotionally adjust their share of domestic work and their decision-making to reflect the change and maintain a fair division of labor. Instead, there is considerable evidence that couples often adhere to traditional patterns of labor division, even in the face of changing situations—and that they may find it uncomfortable to acknowledge discrepancies between their own relationships and the traditional ideal.

For example, women continue to handle well more than their share of housework and childcare responsibilities (US Bureau of Labor Statistics 2011), even though many of them are employed fulltime. And men who earn less than their wives do not necessarily cede decision-making power or the provider role

(Tichenor 2005). Men who hold a strong ideology of traditional masculinity report poorer relationship quality with their wives if the wives have higher incomes (Coughlin and Wade 2012). As noted in one Swedish study, when it comes to dividing household chores and childcare responsibilities, men may insist on sharper boundaries than women do—asserting that they cannot be pressured to do certain kinds of domestic tasks (Magnusson and Marecek 2012). Clearly, then, couples are influenced by the surrounding cultural norms with respect to the gendering of roles within long-term relationships.

Bases and styles of interpersonal power in relationships

The amount and type of influence exerted by individuals in their couple relationships, as well as within friendships, workplace relationships, etc., is shaped in large part by cultural norms and access to resources. As noted above, couple relationships involve roles that have been strongly linked to gender—and these links cannot help but affect power within these relationships.

When one person tries to influence another, the influence attempt must be based upon some resource. If, for instance, a stranger were to stop you on the street and tell you to cross and walk on the other side, there would have to be a *reason* for you to comply with that demand. Perhaps the stranger is pointing a weapon at you, or promising to give you a free box of donuts if you cross the street. Or perhaps she is wearing a police uniform. Or perhaps you are in a culture where it is the norm to accede to such requests when made by strangers. Any of these things would provide the reason for compliance—or, as social psychologists would say, the *bases of power* underlying the influence attempt. Typical bases of power include reward ("I will do this for you if you comply"), coercion ("I will do something bad to you if you do not comply"), expertise ("My expertise tells me this is the best course of action for you"), legitimacy ("I have a right, by virtue of legitimate authority or accepted cultural norms, to demand this of you"), reference ("If you really like, love, or admire me, you will do this for me") and information ("Here are all the good, logical reasons why you should do this") (French and Raven 1959; Raven 1992).

The use of these bases of power depends on having access (or being seen as having access) to particular resources. For example, reward does not work as a basis of power if the influencer does not control any rewards that matter to the potential influencee. Furthermore, access to resources tends to be gendered. For example, in many relationship contexts, men have control over more money than women do, so they are more able to use that as a basis for exerting influence. Perhaps most interestingly from the point of view of long-term couple relationships, cultural expectations with respect to masculinity and femininity can confer strong access to legitimate power. For example, in a cultural context that specifies that the man is the "head" of the household, men have considerable legitimacy-based power with respect to making demands for obedience from their wives and children. And in a cultural context that specifies a man has the main responsibility for providing financial support for the family, a wife has considerable legitimate moral authority when she insists that he do so—whereas a man would have little such authority in insisting that his wife provide major financial support for the family. Legitimacy as a basis of power can also be conferred through the agreements and understandings made between individuals. Thus, for example, if a couple has agreed that they will share the housework equally, each of them has a legitimate right to insist that the other do his/her fair share. If such an agreement violates broader cultural norms, however, it will be harder to enforce on a recalcitrant partner than if it had the additional force of cultural norms.

Both cultural gender role expectations and distribution of the resources on which interpersonal power is based affect the *influence styles* used in couple relationships. For example, interpersonal influence attempts may vary in their degree of directness, from very upfront and direct to very subtle and "sneaky." Gender stereotypes might suggest that a masculine influence style would be direct and "strong," whereas a feminine style would be more subtle and "weak"—and indeed, there is some evidence that that is what people expect. Yet an understanding of the bases of power allows us to look at this situation a little differently. People are likely to be more direct in their influence attempts when they are on firm ground and very sure of themselves—when they control resources of legitimacy, money, physical strength, expertise, and so on to back up their demands or requests. Thus the style of power and influence in any individual couple relationship is likely to depend somewhat on the particular situation: a man who controls all the income may feel comfortable being very direct in demanding it be spent in a certain way; a woman who has reached an agreement with her spouse that they will share equally in the housework may be very direct in demanding that he do his share. Research supports the notion that, among heterosexual, gay male and lesbian couples, individuals who see themselves as having more power than their partners use more direct influence tactics (Aida and Falbo 1991).

Still, the cultural surround that links maleness with higher status seems to have an impact. In one study of long-term same-sex and cross-sex couple relationships, researchers tried to determine what variables were associated with influence strategies. They examined the relative importance of gender, gender-role orientation, control over resources such as money, physical attractiveness, and dependence on the relationship, on the use of "strong" and "weak" influence tactics (Howard, Blumstein and Schwartz 1986). What they found was that the target partner's gender was a key factor in the type of influence used. Both women and men with male partners were more likely to use "weak" influence strategies such as manipulation and supplication. The researchers note that "The power associated with being male ... appears to be expressed in behavior that elicits weak strategies from one's partner."

Finally, the cultural context can have an impact through the adoption of sexist attitudes. Researchers studying heterosexual couples have found that hostile and benevolent sexism affect conflict and resistance to influence (Overall, Sibley and Tan 2011). When men strongly endorsed hostile sexism, couples were less open and more hostile in their conflict interactions, and discussions were less likely to result in the desired change. On the other hand, men who expressed more agreement with benevolent sexist ideals (women are special, need to be protected) tended to behave with less hostility and were able to disarm women's resistance more successfully. Apparently, women were often willing to trade special treatment within the relationship for influence on decisions that went beyond the relationship. On the other hand, when women accepted benevolent sexist ideals but their partners did not, the women were less open and more hostile in their discussions, and seemed to feel that their expectations about how they should be treated were not being realized.

Clearly, cultural norms with respect to gender affect relationships within couples. Gendered expectations may have an even stronger impact when children are part of the family.

Families with children

The birth of a child (or sometimes even pregnancy) can shift the balance of power between a couple. Researchers in North America have sometimes found that a woman's power in a heterosexual couple diminishes with the transition to parenthood (Koivunen, Rothaupt and Wolfgram 2009). Why should this be the case? Again, we must look to the cultural context. Within a social environment that automatically assigns most childcare responsibilities to women, it is women more than men whose lives become changed and circumscribed by childcare responsibilities. It is more likely that a woman rather than a man will be compelled to reduce or give up employment commitments, thus becoming more financially dependent on a partner and less able to leave the relationship. Further, despite its necessity and importance, childrearing is not accorded much status in North America. A full-time mother and homemaker can still feel embarrassed to say she is a "stay-at-home mom." Even mothers who maintain high-powered professional roles find themselves having to minimize and conceal their childcare-related tasks— lest their co-workers or supervisors question their commitment to their jobs (Slaughter 2012).

In some cultural contexts, however, childbearing is regarded as of key importance for married women; the birth of a child (particularly a boy) protects or increases a woman's status and power in the family, and infertility is associated with shame. This is especially true in settings where children are relied upon as a source of economic support (S. Ali *et al.* 2011) and where descent from ancestors is traced only through males (Obermeyer 1992).

Conversely, women's power, both within the family and in the broader social context, affects their children's wellbeing. A woman with more familial and societal power relative to men is better able to ensure that her children receive adequate nutrition, education, and other forms of care. Where women's status is higher, they have more access to prenatal care and to good nutrition themselves—leading to better nutritional outcomes for their children. One large study concluded that if women and men had equal status in South Asian countries, the rate of underweight children under the age of 3 would drop by about 13 percentage points, leading to 13.4 million fewer malnourished children in that age group (L. C. Smith *et al.* 2003). A study of Mexican families showed that greater bargaining power for mothers in their household was associated with fewer hours of child labor for their daughters (Reggio 2010).

Both interpersonal power between a couple and within the extended family, and the surrounding cultural gender stereotypes in which such power relationships are embedded, affect the division of childcare tasks. Mothers, who in almost every culture are expected to do the bulk of childcare, tend to spend far more time on such tasks than fathers (see, for example, Koivunen, Rothaupt and Wolfgram 2009; Lyn and Mullan 2011). Changes in society and in the resources available to women do seem to shift this balance toward more power for women—although never, it seems, to complete equality. Across cultures, women's political and economic power is positively linked to their marital power, and to a more equitable division of domestic work (Rogers 2003). For example, over the course of twenty years in one northern Indian village, an increase in prosperity in the village, along with an increase in women's access to education, was correlated with a rise in the power and status of daughters-in-law with respect to mothers-in-law, and greater assertiveness of mothers in disciplining children (Minturn, Boyd and Kapoor 1978).

However, even in societies that emphasize gender equality, it can be hard for individual couples to overcome completely the overriding expectation that caring for children is "women's work." For example, in the Nordic countries there is a strong cultural and policy emphasis on gender equality, and mothers and fathers have equal rights to paid parental leave. Yet mothers still use most of the available parental leave and continue to do more of the domestic and childcare work than men do—and many parents say this arrangement simply occurred "naturally" (Magnusson and Marecek 2012). Clearly, the impact of cultural stereotypes and expectations with respect to gender runs very deep. Furthermore, the effect of these stereotypic attitudes is to restrict women's choices and their power in heterosexual relationships and to increase their workload. Of course, this set of effects has consequences for women's and men's lives beyond the family as well. In the next chapter, we shall examine ways in which gendered expectations and the gendered division of domestic labor affects men and women in the workplace.

FOR FURTHER EXPLORATION

Tolman, Deborah L. (2002). *Dilemmas of Desire: teenage girls talk about sexuality*. (Cambridge, MA: Harvard University Press.) The author, a psychologist, reports on her interviews with suburban and urban adolescent girls aged between 15 and 18 in two US high schools about their feelings, thoughts and actions concerning sexuality.

Holland, Janet, Ramazanoglu, Caroline, Sharpe, Sue and Thomson, Rachel (1998). *The Male in the Head: young people, heterosexuality, and power*. (London: The Tufnell Press.) The authors analyze power in conventional heterosexual relationships by examining young women's and men's accounts of those relationships. They explore the ways in which sexual empowerment for young men is linked to their ability to access the traditional privileges of masculinity, and explore the ways young women try to achieve sexual empowerment by changing themselves, changing men, and taking control of their sexual encounters.

Feminist forum: adolescent girls' sexual empowerment. *Sex Roles* (2012) **66** (11/12), pp. 703-63. A special section of this journal issue consists of seven articles exploring and debating notions of sexual empowerment for adolescent girls. The first article, by Sharon Lamb and Zoë Peterson, opens the discussion by posing the question of whether girls *are* sexually empowered if they *feel* empowered. Subsequent articles respond to the first, creating a complex and fascinating discussion of gender, sexuality, power, and the media.

Goldberg, Abbie E. (ed.) (2010). *Lesbian and Gay Parents and their Children: research on the family life cycle*. (Washington, DC: American Psychological Association.) This collection of articles provides an overview of research on same-sex parenthood, including chapters on couple relationships, the decision to have children, the experience of raising children, and the perspectives of the children themselves.

Chrisler, Joan C. (ed.) (2012). *Reproductive Justice: a global concern*. (Santa Barbara, CA: Praeger/ABC-CLIO.) This edited book includes chapters on such relationship-relevant issues as partner selection, power in relationships, pregnancy and prenatal care, birthing, and infanticide—all with a cross-cultural emphasis. In each contribution, the authors analyze the role of gender stereotypes and the gendered distribution of power on reproductive issues.

4

THE GENDERED WORKPLACE

In 2011, Christine Lagarde, a lawyer and former French finance minister, became the first woman to become managing director of the International Monetary Fund. Taking on a job that had long been synonymous with masculine-stereotyped expertise and toughness, she has spent her time since then navigating a series of crises in the European Economic Union, negotiating with the heads of European states crafting agreements that run to the trillions of dollars. Now one of the most powerful women in the world, she reports that some men still speak to her as if they assume she is less knowledgeable than they are—and she notes drily that she copes by maintaining "a very good and solid sense of humor" (Sparkes 2012, par. 8).

In 2011, Jeremy Bernard, former chief of staff to the US ambassador to France, was named White House Social Secretary, the first man to hold this position. Now listed by popular media as one of the fifty most powerful people in Washington, Bernard draws on his strong background as White House Liaison to the National Endowment for the Humanities to plan cultural events and high-level state dinners. To do his job well, he relies not only on high energy, creativity and careful planning, but on social skills that have traditionally been stereotyped as "feminine": anticipating the needs of guests, being welcoming, and being nice (Roberts and Argetsinger 2012).

The fact that it is still possible to find stories about the "first woman" and "first man" to hold particular jobs is a reminder of the way work has been gendered. Around the world, women and men work in different jobs. This chapter begins with an examination of these patterns of occupational segregation and the theories about the underlying reasons for them. The discussion includes consideration of both male-dominated and female-dominated workplaces, and the impact of being a gender token in either situation. Included in consideration are a variety of issues, such as discrimination, gendered family roles, and beliefs that women and men differ in certain abilities. There follows a consideration of the gender pay gap, which appears to be caused in part by occupational segregation. Employment discrimination in its many forms is then discussed, along with attempts to ameliorate it through affirmative action strategies. Finally, since family roles seem to be strongly implicated in workplace gender inequalities, the chapter focuses on the evolution of the "family-friendly" workplace and the impact of such changes on both women and men.

OCCUPATIONAL SEGREGATION: WOMEN AND MEN IN DIFFERENT JOBS

Around the world, there has been a trend toward increased access for women to education and participation in the labor force. Since 1970, women's share of the labor force has steadily increased in virtually all regions of the world, and now approaches the 50 percent mark in places such as the Scandinavian countries, the United States, Canada, the UK, and France.

Despite these trends toward equalization of access to employment for women and men, there is persistent gender segregation in the workplace—and, as we have seen, the division of labor in the home also remains strongly gendered. Most clerical and service workers are women; most construction and skilled manual workers are men (Charles and Grusky 2004). Most professional football, soccer, hockey, basketball, and cricket players are men; most childcare workers and nurses are women (US Census Bureau 2012; US Department of Labor 2010). Men are more likely than women to be political leaders, engineers, chief executives of companies, and university presidents (Inter-

Parliamentary Union 2012; Stripling 2012: US Bureau of Labor Statistics 2006). Occupational segregation by gender can be regarded as both vertical (i.e. women tend to be clustered at the low-status, low-paid end of almost every type of work) and horizontal (i.e. women and men at similar status levels are divided into different types of work). There is some evidence that vertical segregation may be slowly diminishing in the most economically developed countries, as more women move into managerial and professional positions. For example, a new report shows that women now make up one-third of physicians and lawyers in the United States—a major shift from a generation ago, when those professions were solidly dominated by men (Mitchell 2012). However, horizontal gender segregation seems to remain stubbornly intact in most situations (Charles 2011).

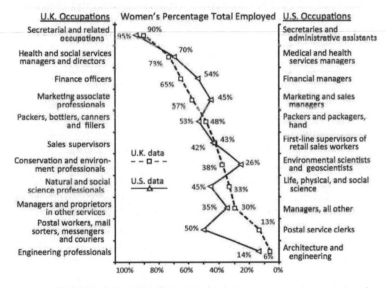

Figure 4.1: Occupational segregation by gender in two Western countries: 2011 data. In both Britain and the United States, as in other countries, occupational segregation by gender is quite dramatic. At the extremes, secretarial and clerical workers are far more likely to be women than men; engineers and architects are far more likely to be men than women.

Sources: Based on data from the U.S. Bureau of Labor Statistics (2011), Table 11, at http://www.bls.gov/cps/aa2011/cpsaat11.pdf, and U.K. Office for National Statistics, Table: Labour Force Survey employment status by occupation, April–June 2011, at http://www.ons.gov.uk/ons/publications/re-reference-tables.html?edition=tcm%3A77-215723.

The reasons for the persistence of occupational gender segregation are probably rooted in a complex interplay between societal and personal gender stereotypes, discrimination by powerholders against outgroups, habit and social inertia—and the repeated lifetime impact of all these on individuals' choices and behaviors. Let us first consider the ways in which expected social roles reproduce themselves.

Why occupational segregation? The impact of social roles

Social psychologist Alice Eagly (1987) proposed a *social roles theory* to explain the persistence of the segregation of women and men into different jobs. Basically, this theory suggests the existence of a positive feedback loop in which certain jobs that require gender-stereotyped qualities tend to be filled by members of the gender group that is presumed to have those qualities—and then the dominance of one gender group in such jobs reinforces the gender stereotyping of both the job and its incumbents. For example, the job of childcare worker is assumed to require warmth, a nurturing orientation, a love of children—all qualities that are stereotyped as feminine. Not surprisingly, then, women will be thought more likely to have these qualities and better suited to this job than men. Someone hiring for this job will likely expect to hire a woman. Women will be more likely than men to apply for this job because both genders have learned the societal expectation that women are appropriate for such work. So, over and over again, women will be more likely than men to be hired as childcare workers. Once in the job, childcare workers use and further develop the nurturing skills necessary to do the job successfully. Observers see childcare workers behaving in warm, nurturing ways, and most of the childcare workers they see behaving in these ways are women. This observation reinforces the idea that women are warm and nurturing and that they (not men) are the appropriate people to fill such jobs. The whole process reinforces gender stereotypes and produces a cycle that is difficult to break: women are selected (and self-select) as childcare workers because they are stereotyped as having the warm, nurturing qualities needed for that job; the job develops and rewards those qualities; and observers, seeing mostly women childcare workers behaving in warm, nurturing ways, are reinforced in their opinion that women tend to be warm and nurturing.

The cycle described here is likely to encourage the persistence of both explicit and implicit gender stereotypes associated with occupational roles. As noted in Chapter 1, the repeated association of women with certain qualities, settings, and behaviors, and men with others, helps us create implicit stereotypes that are virtually automatic in their activation. When we think childcare worker, we think woman; when we think engineer, we think man. This happens even though we know perfectly well that men can be terrific childcare workers and women can be excellent engineers. Individuals whose implicit gender stereotypes are weaker may be more ready to pursue occupational paths that are counter-stereotypic, or to accept gender non-traditional incumbents in gender-stereotyped jobs. For example, a study of French university students revealed that the implicit association of mathematical and reasoning abilities with masculinity was weaker among female engineering students than among female humanities students, or male engineering or humanities students (Smeding 2012).

A social roles approach illustrates how deep and pervasive societal gender stereotypes can bias individuals' evaluations of themselves and others, and can maintain barriers and rules about femininity and masculinity to which people feel they must conform. The thing that makes it so very difficult to break out of this pattern of occupational segregation is the thoroughly ingrained nature of beliefs related to gender. In many situations, everyone knows they are not supposed to make occupational decisions on the basis of gender—but they go ahead and do it anyway, often without realizing it. For example, many people have learned to associate high-prestige positions as orchestra musicians with men. But when auditions for orchestral positions were carried out behind a screen, so that the musical performance could be heard but the musician could not be seen (and his/her gender could not be known), female musicians were more likely to be called back than when auditions were carried out in the normal way (Goldin and Rouse 2000).

Even when making decisions about their own abilities and performance, individuals may, without being aware of it, apply gender-related cultural standards and norms. For example, in one study, when students were told (falsely) that men typically perform better on a test of "contrast sensitivity," male students rated their performance more highly and were more likely than female students to say that they aspired to work in a job requiring that ability (Correll 2004). Simply being given this one-time gender-biased feedback about an ability they had probably never considered before was apparently enough to affect these student's occupational aspirations. Imagine the effect of being told over and over that, for example, men are better than women at math and science. Furthermore, individuals' stereotype-consistent educational or occupational choices, when stated publicly, can be seen as solidifying their conformity to approved behavior. Thus, for instance, if an interest in poetry or dance is considered feminine, a young man can emphasize his masculinity—to himself and to his peers—by declaring his dislike of those fields.

Given the strong cultural messages about what jobs are appropriate and comfortable for each gender, it is not at all surprising if women and men tend to develop different preferences and make different decisions with respect to their occupational paths. One researcher has suggested that these culturally-shaped preferences play a major role in maintaining horizontal occupational segregation—particularly in societies that emphasize the value of individual choice and that have the economic resources to accommodate such choices (Charles 2011). She notes that, in societies where young people are admonished to pursue their own choices and follow their passions, some forms of occupational gender segregation may be especially resistant to change. This is not necessarily because women and men "naturally" want and enjoy different kinds of work, but because the emphasis on personal choice and self-expression provides so much scope for translating internalized gender norms into occupational decisions. In such contexts, she says, "self-expression often results in 'expression of gendered selves'." Young people exhorted to choose a subject they love as a college major are unlikely to zero in on a field they have learned to think of as gender-inappropriate, especially if they are not economically constrained to do so.

These processes of implicit and explicit stereotyping and self-stereotyping conspire to maintain the association of certain occupational roles with men and others with women, producing the persistent cycle described by social role theory.

Different abilities?

The notion that women and men differ in the abilities they bring to their work has a significant history. Up until the nineteenth century, scientists posited that women's brains were smaller than men's, and when that notion was disproven, that the most important parts of the brain were larger in men than women. Even as late as the early twentieth century, women were thought to have far less ability than men for higher learning. The mental effort associated with university-level education was believed by some experts to be damaging and debilitating to women (Rosenberg 1982); this belief was used as a justification for keeping women out of higher education.

Now, however, women are a strong, even majority presence in higher education. Women in the United States earn more undergraduate and master's degrees than men (Associated Press 2011). Globally, the ratio of women to men enrolled in post-secondary education is just over 1.02 to 1.0, and in countries as diverse as Cuba, Kazakhstan, the United Kingdom, Argentina, and Lebanon, women outnumber men in such enrollments (UNESCO 2010). Even in countries where women have historically been underrepresented in higher education, women's enrollments have been steadily increasing. The argument that women "can't handle" higher education no longer has any credibility.

However, there is still a significant difference between women and men in the fields they study in college. The percentage of education majors worldwide who are women is 72.1, but women make up only 36.3 percent of science majors and 23.1 percent of engineering majors (UNESCO 2010). Debate about the reasons for these differences has been fierce. On the one hand, some researchers have focused on the possibility that on average women and men differ in some of the fundamental abilities linked to performance in math, science, and language. Indeed, some small but reliable gender differences in performance *have* been found, with women tending to score a little better on tests of certain specific verbal skills and men tending to score a little better on tests of certain mathematical and spatial skills (Halpern 2012). How much do such performance differences represent different levels of ability? And how much do they reflect the different social–environmental conditions under which women and men are trying to perform?

Beyond the conditions under which individuals are trying to perform, what about the barriers they may face in terms of encouragement or discrimination before they even get into a situation in which they are trying to demonstrate their abilities? Some researchers have focused on the social forces that may push girls and boys, and later women and men, in different career directions, and these forces do not appear to be insignificant. For instance, a study that analyzed natural interactions between mothers and their preschool-aged children revealed that mothers talk significantly more about numbers to boys than to girls— perhaps promoting more early familiarity and liking for mathematical concepts among boys (Chang, Sandhofer and Brown 2011). Parents and teachers often appear to hold and communicate different expectations for girls' and boys' competence in mathematics. As early as second grade, US children demonstrate the stereotype that math is a masculine domain, and boys in this age group identify more strongly with math than girls do (Cvencek, Meltzoff and Greenwald 2011). Italian children show a similar pattern (Muzzatti and Agnoli 2007). In France, fifth-grade children report an awareness of the math–male association, but appear to apply it more to adults than to children; however, they apply the reading–female stereotype to both adults and children (Martinot, Bagès and Désert 2012). As we noted in Chapter 2, when individuals are aware that their group is stereotyped in terms of their abilities in a particular domain, this awareness can impact their performance—a phenomenon known as stereotype threat.

Differential treatment does not end in adulthood. In a recent field study, researchers found that male and female applicants for a lab manager position were evaluated and treated differently by the science faculty from research-intensive universities in the United States—even though their application materials were identical (Moss-Racusin *et al.* 2012). Both male and female faculty respondents rated female applicants as less competent and hireable, and offered significantly lower starting salaries and less mentoring to them than to identical male applicants. It appears that, even among accomplished scientists in research-oriented universities, there is an expectation that women will perform more poorly than men in science careers. Compared to the impact of such differential expectations, it is unlikely that the relatively small gender differences in abilities that have been demonstrated make a large contribution to occupational gender segregation.

THE GENDER PAY GAP

There is a persistent and pervasive gap between women's and men's earnings worldwide. A report from the American Association of University Women (Corbett and Hill 2012) notes that, even controlling for college major, occupation, number of hours worked per week, and economic sector, American women earn less than men just one year after college graduation. The US Census Bureau (Ryan 2012), examining earnings by field of degree, showed men out-earning women in all degree fields among the population aged 25 and older. Even among never-married childless workers, aged 22 to 30 and with the same education, US men earn more than women in every job category (Cohen 2012). Around the world, a similar pattern exists: according to the 2012 *Global Gender Gap* report from the World Economic Forum (Hausmann, Tyson and Zahidi 2012), no country in the world has a ratio higher than 0.82 for female-to-male earnings for similar work. Globally over the past decade, no significant progress has been made in closing the gender pay gap (Tijdens and Klaveren 2012).

As noted above, the gap cannot be completely explained by gender differences in education or specialty. Even in the Nordic countries, where women now make up the majority of the high-skilled workforce, women earn less than men (Hausmann, Tyson and Zahidi 2012). The gap also cannot be completely explained by differences in the number of hours per week or weeks per year that men and women work, or by women's greater likelihood than men to leave work temporarily to care for children (Lips 2013; Roth 2006).

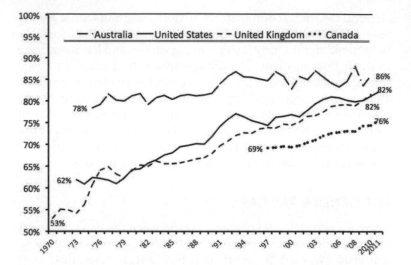

Figure 4.2: Women's percentage of men's gross usual weekly earnings. The gap between women's and men's earnings has narrowed quite slowly since the 1990s, and in no country have women's earnings reached parity with men's. The use of weekly earnings as an indicator, rather than annual earnings, produces a smaller estimate of the size of the pay gap. Many countries do not publish data on annual earnings separately for women and men.

Source: Based on data from Table LMF1.5 *Time Series for Women's Wage Gap by Country: 1970 to 2010,* available at http://www.oecd.org/statistics/ and U.S. Bureau of Labor Statistics *Highlights of Women's Earnings in 2011,* Table 13, available at http://www.bls.gov/cps/cpswom2011.pdf.

The gap may be partially explained by the types of jobs that women and men hold: men are more likely than women to hold jobs that are well-paid and/or that are governed by formal regulations about minimum wage, overtime pay or union-scale wages. One example of this pattern is domestic work: work that is performed in or for private households, such as housecleaning, cooking, childcare, and in-home care for the sick or elderly. According to the International Labour Organization (2012a), women account for fully 83 percent of domestic workers. The women doing this work in developed nations may often be immigrants from poorer countries; their work arrangements are often informally and privately determined; and the work they do, while essential, has historically been assigned low social and economic value. Because these jobs usually fall outside the scope of labor laws, the work arrangements are often unregulated and wages are typically low. At the other end of the income spectrum, in well-paid top management, computing and engineering occupations, men tend to predominate (US Bureau of Labor Statistics 2009a).

Yet occupational segregation is not, all by itself, a satisfactory explanation for the gender pay gap. Indeed, there is some evidence that, at least in developed countries, greater horizontal segregation (i.e. greater division of women and men into different kinds—not levels—of jobs) may be associated both with less disadvantage for women in terms of empowerment and with a smaller gender pay gap. For example, Sweden, a country that has a reputation for gender equality and in which women do rather well on measures of empowerment such as seats in parliament and earned income share, the workforce is highly gender segregated. The researchers suggest that women are less disadvantaged in countries with greater occupational gender segregation, because when women and men are highly segregated into different occupations, there is less opportunity for gender discrimination *within* occupations. In other words, if an occupation is filled mainly by women, women have a greater chance of reaching the highest levels of that occupation because there are more women than men available for promotion. As we will see below in the discussion of tokens, however, men are disproportionately successful in reaching leadership positions in female-dominated occupations—so an occupation would have to be completely filled by women in order to ensure that women would occupy all the senior positions! Still, these findings show that occupational segregation and the pay gap have a complex relationship.

CHANGING PATTERNS AND SCOPE OF EMPLOYMENT DISCRIMINATION

Employment discrimination: a brief history

Employment discrimination on the basis of sex was once an entrenched and accepted practice. Although women have always worked, the notion that they should work for pay was considered scandalous in some circles. A 1918 article in the *Australian Medical*

Gazette, after listing all the harms done when young women spend their days earning money in factories, shops and offices in a "butterfly and parasitic existence," instead of preparing themselves for childbearing and domesticity, concludes by recommending the enactment of legislation "which will prohibit the employment of girls and women in any walk of life which is not unquestionably women's work, until they shall have passed through an apprenticeship in household work" (quoted in D'Aprano 2001: xxii). In certain jobs, there was a long and strict prohibition against women; both verifiable stories and fanciful legends abound of women who, through the centuries, pretended to be men in order to take on roles as soldiers, priests and monks, even pope. In North America, Australia, and elsewhere, until well into the twentieth century, newspaper "help wanted" ads were divided into categories for women and men as a matter of course. It was considered reasonable (and legal) to reject a job applicant by saying "I don't want a woman (or a man) for this position." The capacity to carry out sex discrimination in hiring with impunity was undercut in the UK with the Sex Discrimination Act of 1975, and in the US with a 1961 presidential executive order prohibiting workplace discrimination based on personal characteristics, the establishment of the Committee on Equal Employment Opportunity, and Title VII of the Civil Rights Act of 1964. In Canada, the Canadian Human Rights Act of 1977 also outlawed sex discrimination in employment, and similar legislation now exists in many other countries. Such laws did not wipe out the problem of sex discrimination in hiring, but they made blatant discrimination more difficult.

When women *were* hired, they were routinely paid less than men, with the justification that they could not do the work as well as men, that men, but not women, had families to support, and that paying women the same wages as men would be ruinous for the economy. However, the need to support a family was not extended to women as a justification for employment or fair pay. Rather, when female employees were known to have families, the situation often served as an excuse to bar them from certain jobs—or from being employed at all. For example, beginning in the late 1880s, Australian law provided that married women would not be eligible for employment in the Public Service, and women workers who did marry would be forced to leave their employment. Until the 1970s in the United States, pregnant schoolteachers were often forced to take unpaid maternity leave, on the grounds that not only would continuing to teach be dangerous to the woman and her unborn child but also that the pregnancy would be distracting to the students. Women were also barred from certain manufacturing jobs because of their *potential* to become pregnant, with the justification that exposure to certain chemicals or working conditions might be dangerous to a fetus (Legal Information Institute 2012). Discrimination on the basis of pregnancy was recognized as a form of sex discrimination through a number of court cases, leading to the passage of the Pregnancy Discrimination Act of 1978. This act prohibits discrimination on the basis of pregnancy, childbirth, or related medical conditions. Rulings consistent with the idea that pregnancy discrimination is a type of sex discrimination and is illegal have been made by courts in the European Union, Canada, the UK, and a number of other countries. The problem persists, however: pregnancy discrimination complaints continue to be filed at high rates (e.g. Elmer 2012).

The justification of unequal pay began to erode as legislation mandating equal employment and/or equal pay was introduced and passed in various countries. For example, Canada's first federal pay equity legislation was passed in 1977, as part of the Canadian Human Rights Act. In Britain, the Equal Pay Act was passed in 1970, but its implementation was slowed for 5 years, giving employers time to adjust. In Australia, the National Security (Female Minimum Rates) Regulation of 1943 officially raised the basic female wage from 54 percent to 75 percent of men's wages; not until 1969 did the first Federal equal pay case establish the principle of equal pay for equal work, and the Equal Pay Act was subsequently passed in 1972. In the United States, the Equal Pay Act of 1963 made it illegal to pay a woman less than a man for performing the same or substantially similar job. In New Zealand, the Government Service Equal Pay Act of 1960 eliminated separate pay scales for women and men in public service jobs, but not until 1972 did the Equal Pay Act extend pay equity legislation into the wider workforce. Section 5 of the 1979 Norwegian Gender Equality Act stipulated that women and men in the same enterprise would earn equal pay for the same work or work of equal value. Such legislation has moved women and men toward equal pay, but, as we have already seen, the gender pay gap remains a stubbornly persistent problem worldwide.

Beyond hiring and pay, employment discrimination on the basis of gender has also affected promotion and advancement. In a landmark case in the United States, Ann Hopkins, a broker for the financial firm Price Waterhouse, was denied partnership in the firm even though she had generated more money for the firm than others who were made partners. The reasons given included that she needed to dress and act in more feminine ways and that she would benefit from a "charm school" course. Reasoning that these points were evidence of thinly disguised gender discrimination, Hopkins sued the company and ultimately won her case in 1989. After considering expert testimony from psychologists about gender stereotyping, the judge agreed that Hopkins was being unfairly held to a standard (to be feminine and charming) that men were not expected to meet. The case made it clear that the situation is ripe for discrimination, particularly when evaluation criteria are ambiguous and members of a previously excluded group are moving into new employment roles, (Fiske *et al.* 1991). Furthermore, this case made it clear that such discrimination often goes unrecognized, even by its perpetrators. As noted in Chapter 1, our reactions to others are often affected by implicit stereotypes; we do not even know we are reacting in a biased way.

Sexual harassment

One form of gender-based discrimination at work is sexual harassment: unwelcome sexual advances that intimidate or bother an individual and/or the creation of a hostile work environment through sexual innuendos, teasing, touching, etc., that unreasonably interferes with an individual's workplace experience and performance. Such behavior was at one time considered the stuff of workplace humor rather than a serious problem. Television comedies featured secretaries being chased around their desks by lecherous male bosses—all in supposed good fun! The problem was not even publicly named as sexual harassment until the 1970s

(Brownmiller 1999). However, researchers have now shown that, far from being a joke, sexual harassment can impact victims in serious ways, causing feelings such as helplessness, lower self-esteem, shame, anxiety, and depression (Yoon, Funk and Kropf 2010) and symptoms such as sleeplessness, nausea, suppressed immunity, and increased inflammation (Chan *et al.* 2008). Individuals who are being sexually harassed are also likely to be tardy or absent from work, withdraw socially, value their occupation less, and show an overall decline in job performance (Chan *et al.* 2008).

Sexual harassment at work is now acknowledged to be a common problem around the world, but because the behavior often goes unreported, reliable numbers are difficult to come by. For example, one Singapore study of 500 respondents across 92 companies found that more than half had experienced sexual harassment at work; almost four-fifths of these victims were women (AWARE 2008). In an online survey conducted by AOL, about one in six respondents—the majority of them women—reported being sexually harassed at work (Mahabeer 2011). A *Washington Post* poll found that one in four women said they had been sexually harassed (Clement 2011). A survey of British women workers showed that half reported experiencing some form of harassment based on their gender; 40 percent of those reporting harassment said they had been touched in ways that made them feel uncomfortable (Equality Law 2012).

In the United Sates, sexual harassment is classified as sex discrimination and prohibited under Title VII of the Civil Rights Act of 1964. The Equal Employment Opportunities Commission (EEOC) files civil suits against employers based on employee complaints. In 2011, more than 11,000 sexual harassment complaints were filed with the EEOC, which investigates and acts on them. Recently, for example, Carrols Corporation, a large Burger King franchisee, was forced to pay $2.5 million to settle a sexual harassment lawsuit brought by the EEOC. The suit charged that a number of female employees, many of them teenagers, had been targets of harassment—ranging from obscene comments and jokes to unwanted touching, stalking, and even rape—by managers, and that women who complained were subject to retaliation (US Equal Employment Opportunity Commission

2013). In some other countries, such as France, Britain, Israel, Mexico, and Sweden, sexual harassment is a criminal offense and can be punishable by jail time (Neft and Levine 1997). In India, some protection is provided through a Supreme Court action known as the Vishaka Judgement (Manohar and Kirpal 1997), which defines sexual harassment, prevention strategies, and mechanisms of redress.

Glass ceilings and glass escalators: Is the impact of being a token different for women and men?

For a male- or female-dominated occupation to tilt in the direction of becoming more gender-balanced, someone from the under-represented gender has to be first. The woman or man who makes a foray into a job dominated by colleagues of the other gender, thus becoming a *gender token*, faces a number of issues, first noted by Kanter (1977). For one thing, this person will necessarily stand out among her/his co-workers—which can be either a good or bad thing. The negative aspect of standing out is that it can make a person more self-conscious and anxious, and thus more prone to make mistakes. Indeed, this outcome is exactly what researchers found when they examined the performance of female and male tokens in small groups in the laboratory (Lord and Saenz 1985). Not only did the tokens not perform at their best, but also their mistakes were more likely to be noticed and remembered than those of other group members.

But a gender token faces more than simply being perceived as unusual. He or she must also contend with specific gender stereotypes that undermine the perception of his/her suitability for and/or competence at the job. Because of the content of gender stereotypes, their impact may be somewhat different for men and women in token positions. For instance, some studies show that male tokens find it easier than female to connect with (often male) supervisors, and thus may be taken more seriously (see, for example, Floge and Merrill 1986; Yoder and Sinnett 1985). A possible explanation for this phenomenon is the stereotypic expectation of greater male than female competence.

Furthermore, a token may find it more difficult than others to find routine support and friendship from workplace colleagues. Here too, women and men in such positions may differ in their experience. One study of nationally representative US data revealed that, whereas women in male-dominated occupations perceived relatively low levels of support from co-workers, men in female-dominated occupations perceived relatively high levels of support (Taylor 2010). Thus being in a numerical minority was apparently a disadvantage for women but an advantage for men.

Particularly in managerial and professional occupations, women seem to become increasingly rare—and so seem more and more like tokens—at higher levels of advancement. There are quite a few women in middle management, but very few female CEOs of top companies or female members of corporate boards, for example (International Labour Organization 2012b). This situation has been described by some as a *glass ceiling*: it feels as though there is an invisible barrier that women smash against when they try to move up past a certain level. A recent report titled *Breaking the Glass Ceiling* examined the presence (or absence) of women on corporate boards in Europe, North America, and Australasia—to find that even in countries that have made significant efforts to get rid of the glass ceiling, women are still underrepresented in certain top positions (Giunta 2011). In Norway, for example, the report showed that despite a strong quota rule about the representation of women on corporate boards, most of those boards are still chaired by men and only 2 percent of public companies listed on the Norwegian Stock Exchange have female CEOs. And in the United Kingdom in 2010, only 12.5 percent of the executive directors of FTSE 100 companies were women and 21 percent of FTSE 100 companies had exclusively male boards.

The "glass ceiling" imagery suggests that women make reasonable and smooth progress in their careers until they approach the upper levels of advancement and then are suddenly and inexplicably stopped by something they cannot see. Some analysts have taken issue with this way of looking at the barriers women face, arguing that the shortage of women at the top is not caused by a sudden collision with a glass ceiling, but by the cumulative effect of a whole series of barriers and obstacles that winnow down the number of women at each step of advancement. As we will see in the next chapter, a different way of looking at the issue may be to think of women pursuing career advancement as traversing a labyrinth, with lots of dead ends and blind alleys, or as an inexorably narrowing pipeline, with many leaks along the way.

In contrast to the extra barriers faced by women who are tokens, men who are tokens in female-dominated professions appear to experience a glass escalator: a constellation of subtle mechanisms and pressures that enhance men's advancement in women's professions (Williams 1992). The escalator effect may be based on stereotypes about men's abilities, skills, and styles of leadership—stereotypes that affect the ways men behave and others' perceptions of their behavior and potential. The effect is often to facilitate men's advancement and privilege them for leadership opportunities, even in professions such as nursing or social work where they form a numerical minority. However, this advantage in upward mobility appears to accrue most easily to white men, and is less likely to be available to men from minorities who work in feminized occupations—perhaps, in part, because minority men are less likely to receive support from majority women (Wingfield 2009).

MOTHERHOOD PENALTIES AND FATHERHOOD PREMIUMS

Another thing that can apparently be an employment-related disadvantage for women but an advantage for men is parenthood. It appears that a *motherhood penalty* is one of the major contributors to the gender wage gap. For example, one study showed that the cumulative earnings of non-mothers in the United States were 64 percent of men's, whereas mothers earned between 52 and 57 percent of men's earnings, depending on how many children they had (Sigle-Rushton and Waldfogel 2007). Having 2 to 4 children can decrease a woman's wages by 4 to 8 percent, according to one researcher (Glauber 2007). Others have found a 7 percent reduction in wages per child (Budig and England 2001). This same decrease in wages does not appear to affect men with children. In fact, for men—particularly those who are white married professionals in "traditional" households, having children results in an increase in wages—a *fatherhood premium* (Glauber 2008; Hodges and Budig 2010).

It seems obvious that, among parents, the gendered division of labor with respect to childcare responsibilities could contribute to a motherhood wage penalty. In the United States, for example, most women work full-time, yet women still engage in more hours of childcare activities than men (US Bureau of Labor Statistics 2010a). This heavy share of domestic responsibility could lead women to work fewer hours outside the home, to choose more flexible, part-time work with lower pay, or have lower productivity rates while at work. That interpretation fits well with a *human capital approach* to understanding the gender pay gap: the idea that women, especially mothers, simply invest relatively less than men do in their employment, and thus harvest fewer rewards.

The human capital approach contains the assumption that women's choices about how much time and energy to invest in employment or family are free, not forced. However, there is plenty of evidence that mothers are constrained in these choices. For example, between 2001 and 2003 just under 40 percent of US women who were pregnant with their first child had to take time off work that was unpaid (Johnson 2008). Although just over half of first-time mothers now have access to at least some paid maternity leave, this flexibility tends to be available mainly to educated women. According to one US study, among first-time mothers with less than a high school education, only 18.5 percent were given paid maternity leave; 50 percent quit their jobs and 10.9 percent lost their jobs (Laughlin 2011). Inadequate leave policies and lack of childcare resources for mothers may cause them to feel as if they must decide between work and family. Working fewer hours, taking time off for children, or completely stepping out of the work-force for young children comes with an economic cost, resulting in lower earnings for mothers—but it is not a cost they freely choose.

But what about the wage premium or bonus that fathers receive? This effect has sometimes been attributed to men's increased effort at work when they know they have a child to support. And indeed, men do tend to increase their effort at work when they become fathers. However, the fatherhood premium is still evident even after researchers adjust for fathers' longer hours, work effort, and other factors (Glauber 2008). It appears that fatherhood, especially among men who fit society's ideas about ideal or normative upper-class masculinity (i.e. heterosexual, white, well-educated, married) is regarded by employers as a positive quality—representative perhaps of responsibility, loyalty, dependability (Hodges and Budig 2010). Thus fathers may benefit from positive stereotypes while mothers suffer from structural discrimination based on traditional assumptions about parental roles.

AFFIRMATIVE ACTION AS A SOLUTION?

In her memoir, US Supreme Court Justice Sonia Sotomayor (2013), the first Latina American to hold this position, recounts the reaction she received from the school nurse at her high school when Sotomayor received word from Princeton University that she was being considered for admission to that prestigious institution. The nurse asked her why she, and not the number one and number two students in the graduating class, was on the list for consideration. Sotomayor had not heard the term "affirmative action" at that time, but says she realized from the tone of the question that the nurse felt there was something unfair going on. Now an unabashed supporter of the principle of affirmative action, Sotomayor calls it something that opened doors for her and changed the course of her life. She argues that it is important to have some structures in place that deliberately counter the tendency for people to unthinkingly prefer to recommend, admit, hire, and promote individuals who are like themselves. Yet the whole idea of affirmative action remains controversial—so controversial that some advocates of the basic principle have sought to avoid the term altogether. When authoring a groundbreaking report about the need to fight employment discrimination in her country, Canadian judge Rosalie Abella (1984) consciously chose to go beyond the framework of individual rights implied in the affirmative action concept. Instead, she wrote about *employment equity* strategies to counter unintentional systemic discrimination that produced barriers to women and minorities.

Affirmative action is a broad concept that encompasses a variety of proactive strategies to increase the proportion of women and minorities who have access to educational and employment opportunities. In the workplace, such strategies may include expanding recruitment efforts to ensure they reach under-represented groups, offering special training opportunities to targeted groups, and educating supervisors about their potential biases. In some countries, affirmative action strategies can include aspirational or mandatory quotas for the proportion of women or minorities in certain positions. For example, the European Union recently set an aspirational target for member countries that by 2020 at least 40 percent of non-executive directors of corporate boards should be women (BBC News 2012).

Affirmative action stirs strong debates. Some people feel that it is not fair to consider the gender or race of an applicant for a job or a spot in an educational program. They argue that affirmative action can result in discriminating against traditional applicants while unfairly giving opportunities to less qualified women or minorities. Others argue that many decades of disadvantage to women and minorities cannot be undone without deliberate action to include them in arenas where they have historically faced barriers—and that critics of affirmative action ignore other instances of preferential treatment such as legacy admissions to colleges, or hiring based on personal networks. Some research suggests that affirmative action may, in some circumstances, undermine the self-confidence of its beneficiaries and promote the stereotype that they could not succeed on their own (e.g. Heilman and Alcott 2001). However, under "real world" conditions, when an individual knows she or he is qualified, such concerns appear to be minimal. Affirmative action tends to be resisted most strongly by those who benefit from the status quo; however, after years of discrimination, it is unlikely that a truly "equal-opportunity" workplace can be created without such strategies (Crosby, Iyer and Sincharoen 2006).

MOVING TOWARD FAMILY-FRIENDLY WORKPLACES

We have noted that parenthood is linked to different workplace outcomes for women and for men. Are there ways to level the playing field for female and male workers who are trying to balance paid employment and family responsibilities? A variety of strategies, such as part-time work, flexible hours, telecommuting, job sharing, and parental leave have been offered by employers as ways to help parents allocate their time and energy efficiently across work and family domains. Yet there are clear costs to employees who choose "family-friendly" flexibility options offered by employers. Many employees are aware that if they take advantage of flexible work arrangements, their commitment to the job may be questioned and they may suffer negative career consequences. Women are particularly trapped by this situation: they may be judged as wavering in their career commitment if they take maternity leave or reduce their hours, and as bad parents if they combine demonstrably serious work commitment with family. Workers deciding whether to avail themselves of these opportunities must consider the possibility that they will be judged according to both gender stereotypes and norms that women always tend to put family first, and an "ideal worker" norm that prescribes prioritizing work over all other responsibilities.

The kinds of family-friendly options that are made available to workers seem to reflect societal assumptions and norms about gender roles and parenting. For example, in countries where there are strong traditional attitudes toward motherhood, extended maternity leave and part-time work options are likely to be offered to employed mothers—and these women may feel strongly pressured to accept such benefits, despite potential harm to their careers (Den Dulk 2005). If societal norms promoting the assignment of caregiving tasks primarily to women are not challenged and undermined, "family-friendly" workplace reforms can help solidify the gendered division of household labor by making it possible for women to continue to carry the major share of household work and putting little pressure on men to do more (Daly 2011).

Research suggests that professionals, both women and men, who deliberately reduce their load at work to accommodate family responsibilities can, under some circumstances, achieve both career success and satisfaction with family roles—though they may receive fewer promotions than their colleagues (Hall *et al.* 2012). A great deal more research is needed to understand the long-term consequences of various ways of combining work and family, and to find the most sustainable ways of doing so. It is clear, however, that stereotypes and norms about gender and parenting play an important role in determining what kinds of arrangements are tried and how well they work.

FOR FURTHER EXPLORATION

Babcock, Linda and Laschever, Sara (2003). *Women Don't Ask: negotiation and the gender divide.* (Princeton, NJ: Princeton University Press.) Using a wide variety of research findings, the authors provide an excellent overview of the many ways in which socialized gender role expectations affect women and men's sense of entitlement and their readiness to negotiate for what they want in the workplace and other settings. Using real-world examples, they also provide a convincing summary of the many impacts of gender differences in negotiation—along with some practical advice.

Kessler-Harris, Alice (2001). *In Pursuit of Equity: women, men, and the quest for economic citizenship in 20th-century America.* (New York: Oxford University Press.) A pre-eminent labor historian provides an overview of the history of the development of women's participation in paid work in the United States, including careful consideration of the role of marriage, discrimination, and equal pay.

D'Aprano, Zelda (2001). *Kath Williams: the unions and the fight for equal pay.* (Melbourne, Australia: Spiniflex Press.) The author provides a fascinating social history of the struggle for equal pay in Australia, while introducing the reader to some of the main characters in this fight.

Crosby, Faye J. (2004). *Affirmative Action is Dead: long live affirmative action.* (New Haven, CT: Yale University Press.) The author draws from research in psychology, law, political science, education, and sociology to describe affirmative action, analyze the often ambivalent public reactions to it, and delineate the arguments for and against it.

Halpern, Diane F. and Cheung, Fanny M. (2008). *Women at the Top: powerful leaders tell us how to combine work and family.* (Hoboken, NJ: Wiley-Blackwell.) Using an overview of existing research and personal interviews with sixty-two prominent women in the US, China and Hong Kong, the authors explore what strategies may work for managing successful careers and family lives together.

5

GENDER, LEADERSHIP, AND PUBLIC LIFE

In a blistering speech before Parliament in late 2012, Australian Prime Minister Julia Gillard fought back against the opposition leader Tony Abbot's repeated use of blatant sexism to try to undermine her leadership (Little 2012). Noting his previous public comments that it might not be a bad thing that there were fewer women than men in leadership positions, and that women might be less adapted by temperament or physiology for command, his condescending references to the housewives of Australia, and his willingness to be photographed standing next to signs that labeled Gillard personally as a "witch" or a "man's bitch," Gillard asserted that, if the opposition leader wanted to "know what misogyny looks like in modern Australia, he ... needs a mirror."

It is difficult to think of a man in a prominent leadership position who has had to take women to task in any similar way for using sexism to undermine his leadership. This is likely because, as we have seen in earlier chapters, masculinity, and not femininity, is stereotypically linked to public leadership—so people do not derogate a male leader just because he is a man. However, gender stereotypes can also be used to damage men who are leaders. If a man in a position of public leadership displays qualities that are seen to be too feminine, he risks criticism and loss of respect for being too "soft"—unless his masculine credentials as tough, decisive, and hard are firmly in place. Once he is seen as sufficiently masculine, a male leader is permitted to display some compassion and vulnerability at appropriate moments—such as the press conference where US General Norman Schwartzkopf shed some tears when talking about the troops killed during the Gulf War of 1990-91. Male leaders who can deploy compassion and care in rationed doses without losing their commanding edge are admired. Yet one of the most devastating attacks on a male politician still seems to be that he is "soft" on something: on crime, on communism, on terrorism, on corruption.

GENDER AND POLITICAL LEADERSHIP: GLOBAL TRENDS AND SOME EXAMPLES

The World Economic Forum, which compares women and men within countries on their health, educational, economic and political outcomes, reported in 2012 that, whereas gender gaps in health and educational outcomes were on average closing fairly rapidly, only 60 percent of the economic outcomes gap and 20 percent of the political outcomes gap had been closed (Hausmann, Tyson and Zahidi 2012). Clearly, political leadership is a domain where gender equality is lagging. Despite some progress in recent decades, women still make up less than 20 percent of the members of parliaments in the countries of the world (QuotaProject 2013). As of 2012, only one country, Rwanda, had women as more than half of its parliamentary representatives (Inter-Parliamentary Union 2012). Just over 11 percent of the world's self-governing countries have female presidents or prime ministers; just under 7 percent of monarchies have female royals at their head (Institute for Women's Leadership, 2011).

Among the newest women at the helm of a country is Dilma Rousseff, who took over as President of Brazil in 2011—the first woman (and the first economist) to hold this position. Dubbed the "mother of the nation" during her election campaign, she has also been called the Iron Lady (a nickname that has, in the past, been given to many other women political leaders, including Margaret Thatcher of Britain, Golda Meier of Israel, Benazir Bhutto of Pakistan and Yulia Tymoshenko of Ukraine). Rousseff

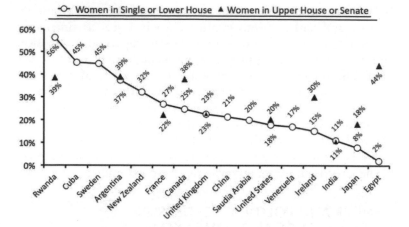

Figure 5.1: Representation of women in national parliaments and upper houses or senates. Women are underrepresented in the legislative bodies that govern nations. Although women form a majority of the world's population, in only one country (Rwanda) are women a majority among elected parliamentary representatives.

Source: Based on data from Inter-Parliamentary Union (2013), at http://www.ipu.org/wmn-e/classif.htm.

came to electoral politics via a circuitous route, moving from an upper-middle-class background to involvement in left wing politics and the underground resistance in her teens. Jailed and tortured in her early twenties, she emerged to go to college and continue her involvement in politics, helping to restructure her country's democracy and eventually becoming a career civil servant. She served as energy minister and as chief of staff to the former president before launching her own run for president in 2010. Rousseff is only one of several women to head Latin American countries in the last decade; these include Christina Fernández de Kirchner, president of Argentina, Michele Bachelet, former president of Chile, and Laura Chinchilla, president of Costa Rica. In fact, Latin America and the Caribbean, often stereotyped as bastions of machismo and male privilege, have an enviable recent record with respect to female political leaders: a number of countries in the region (Cuba, Nicaragua, Costa Rica, Argentina, Mexico) have almost as high or a higher percentage of female members of parliament as the Nordic countries (Inter-Parliamentary Union 2012).

In Africa, two female heads of state, Ellen Johnson-Sirleaf of Liberia and Joyce Banda of Malawi (both of whom have also been dubbed "iron ladies"), have committed themselves to advancing women's rights on that continent. Both have presided over a strengthening of the voices of women in government, increases in the proportion of girls in school, and initiatives on maternal health and safety. Each comes by her dedication to these issues through life experiences that mirror those of many other women: Banda survived an abusive marriage and once worked as a market vendor—a job held by many African women (Opolade 2012). Sirleaf was married at the young age of seventeen (and later divorced), and is mother to four sons and grandmother of eight.

Female political leaders must often struggle to bridge the perception that, because they are powerful, they cannot be "real" women. Some emphasize the conjunction of femininity with power by taking on a maternal persona—as in Dilma Rousseff's "mother of the nation" title (a title which has also been applied to a variety of female political leaders over the years, including Gro Brundtland, former prime minister of Norway, Fatima Jinnah, one-time candidate for the presidency of Pakistan, and Winnie Mandela, well-known activist of South Africa). For many powerful women, however, labels such as "iron lady"—implying not only toughness, but perhaps a cold and unfeeling style—seem unavoidable. German chancellor Angela Merkel has been called the Iron Frau; US Secretary of State Madeline Albright was labeled the Titanium Lady; and critics of Jane Byrne, the first female mayor of Chicago, mocked her by calling her Attila the Hen. Rather than fight such labels, some women leaders—such as Ellen Johnson-Sirleaf and her female cabinet members, known collectively as Liberias' "iron ladies," have adopted them as badges of honor (*Iron Ladies of Liberia* 2008). And some leaders seem to have managed to project an image that spans the gap between "masculine" toughness and "feminine" softness: media coverage of former US House of Representatives Speaker Nancy Pelosi describes her both as having a "spine of steel" and a "heart of gold" (Dabbous and Ladley 2010).

Although the rise of some high-profile female political leaders appears to herald a new set of attitudes about women and leadership, in most countries the rate of progress for women in politics has not been particularly rapid. For example, in the decade between the end of 2002 and the end of 2012, the percentage of women among elected representatives in lower houses of congress or parliaments inched up only from 13.8 to 17.9 in the United States, from 17.9 to 22.3 in the United Kingdom, from 20.6 to 24.7 in Canada, and from 29.2 to 32.2 in New Zealand. In some countries (e.g. Saudi Arabia, Micronesia, Qatar), the number of women in national legislative bodies remained at zero during this time, while in others (e.g. Kenya, Ukraine, Hungary, Malta, Brazil, Ghana, Myanmar, Haiti) the numbers never reached 10 percent. Important and interconnected barriers to women's political progress include being ignored or stereotyped by the media, a lack of access to financing for their campaigns, and a cultural tendency to treat women as second-class citizens (Llanos 2011).

Yet there are a few countries where women have made dramatic gains. During the same decade, women's representation in Cuba's legislative body rose from 27.6 percent to 45.2 percent, and their representation in Rwanda's parliament more than doubled, from 25.7 percent to 56.3 percent (Inter-Parliamentary Union 2012).

What factors underlie the uncommon success of Cuba and Rwanda in increasing the representation of women? The key in both cases seems to be that gender equality has not been left to chance: there has been an explicit effort to overcome traditional anti-woman biases and to support the entry of women into politics. And in both cases, a new system of government has been crafted by men and women who fought together to replace an older one. Analysts argue that in Cuba, women's rights were broadly incorporated into the changes that grew out of the revolution, so that women's access to resources such as health and literacy increased. Furthermore, a commitment to women's rights as a "revolution within a revolution," called for by Fidel Castro, was implemented through policy changes that encouraged and supported the advancement of women. Affirmative action models have been used to build a database of candidates with equal numbers of men and women, and the Cuban government has implemented a platform of goals and strategies to support women's leadership (Oxfam 2012). In Rwanda, the constitution adopted in 2003 prescribes that women and men have equal access to elective offices, and specifies that at least 30 percent of the posts in decision making bodies will be held by women (Constitution of the Republic of Rwanda 2003). In addition, the tragic genocidal conflict in that country left many women as widows or as sole supporters of their families because their husbands were in jail, making it necessary for women to take on leadership positions (Bikorimana 2012). In both Cuba and Rwanda the situation for women is still far from perfect. Indeed, women in Cuba refer to a "gender paradox" in which their country has a strong legal commitment to gender equality but is rooted in a long tradition of patriarchal attitudes and structures (Torregrosa 2012). And in Rwanda, although some people complain of "positive discrimination" toward women, women are still underrepresented in secondary schools and universities because they are tasked with domestic responsibilities that interfere with their access to higher education (Bikorimana 2012).

The comparatively rapid growth toward gender equality in political leadership in Rwanda and Cuba illustrates that it is possible to make dramatic changes in women's representation, but it is far from easy. Furthermore, the paths taken by these countries suggest that gender equality in access to political leadership does not just happen, even in the presence of good will and a general belief that equality is a good thing. Rather, equality requires a comprehensive, proactive, and determined set of strategies— perhaps affirmative action strategies, as in Cuba, or quotas, as in Rwanda.

One reason why it may sometimes require extraordinary measures to speed up women's integration into high-level political leadership roles is the persistence of a perceived disconnect between femininity and political power. Research on reactions to hypothetical politicians has shown that respondents tend to react negatively to female politicians who are seen as interested in seeking power—but not to male politicians (Okimoto and Brescoll 2010). Respondents who viewed a female politician as having power-seeking intentions said they were less likely to vote for her; on the other hand, likelihood of voting for a male politician was unrelated to his perceived power-seeking intentions. Furthermore, when a female politician was described as ambitious and having a strong will to power, respondents viewed her as less competent and deficient in communality (low in supportiveness and caring)—and reported feeling emotions toward her that indicated moral outrage: anger, contempt, disgust. When a male politician was similarly described as ambitious and power-oriented, he benefitted by being viewed as having more desirable agentic qualities (assertiveness, strength, toughness), but was not viewed as lower in communality or competence and did not stir reactions of moral outrage. These findings suggest that women who aspire to high political leadership are still viewed, not just as unusual and as violating expectations, but rather as stepping out of line—breaking the rules. These women are seen as violating prescriptive stereotypes with respect to femininity, whereas men who aspire to political leadership are fulfilling prescriptive stereotypes with respect to masculinity.

GENDER AND ORGANIZATIONAL LEADERSHIP: GLOBAL TRENDS AND SOME EXAMPLES

As is the case with formal political leadership, access to formal organizational or corporate leadership has not been easy for women. As of January 2012, the average representation of women on the corporate boards of Europe's largest listed companies was 13.7 percent, up from 11.8 percent in 2010; more than 96 percent of the presidents of the 600 largest companies were men (European Commission 2012). In the same year, just 20.1 percent of *Fortune 500* companies had 25 percent or more women executive officers, up from 19.9 percent the year before (Catalyst 2012a), and only 3.8 percent of these companies had women as CEOs (Catalyst 2013). In the Asia-Pacific, the numbers for female representation on corporate boards were even lower than those in Europe: 8.5 percent for China, 5.3 percent for India, and 0.9 percent for Japan (Catalyst 2012b). As noted in the previous chapter, European countries have responded to the shortage of women in such positions by setting an aspirational quota for member countries: at least 40 percent of non-executive directors of corporate boards should be women by 2020 (BBC News 2012). Some countries, such as Norway, that have already implemented such quotas have found that the resulting increased representation of women at director level has increased the likelihood of women being

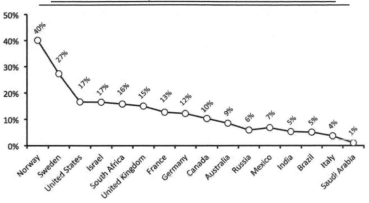

Figure 5.2: Representation of women on corporate boards by selected countries. Women are underrepresented on the boards of major corporations around the world. In Norway, where quotas have been in place for some years, women's presence on boards is significantly higher than in many other countries.

Source. Based on data from Catalyst (2012b).

appointed to top leadership roles such as corporate CEOs or board chairs (Wang and Kelan 2012).

Among the most powerful women in the business world are Ginni Rometty, the first woman CEO of IBM, Christine Lagarde, first female managing director of the International Monetary Fund, and Maria Das Graças Foster, head of giant oil-producer Petrobras. Among the "top 50" women in business listed by *Fortune* magazine in 2012 (50 Most Powerful Women in Business 2012), each of these women worked her way up over many years to head an extremely male-dominated institution. Their success demonstrates the possibility for women of breaking into the very highest corporate levels, but the very presence of the list illustrates the novelty of women at the top.

"Uncounted" leaders: Activist women

Although women are underrepresented in formal positions of organizational leadership, there is no basis for the idea that women and men differ in their motivation to lead. Women and men do not differ on measures of power motivation (Winter 1988).

Researchers have found a small tendency for men to score higher than women on certain dimensions of the motivation to manage in hierarchic organizations (desire to engage in competition with peers; desire to behave in an active, assertive way; desire to impose wishes on subordinates; and desire to stand out from the group) (Eagly, Karau, Miner and Johnson 1994). These dimensions are congruent with the masculine definition of leadership in top-down organizations, where men tend to predominate in administrative positions, and managers have considerably more power than subordinates. Women score higher on two other dimensions of leadership in such organizations: desire to have positive relationships with superiors, and desire to meet day-to-day managerial role requirements. However, women's leadership has historically not been limited to hierarchic organizations. In fact, many of the most accomplished female leaders have *not* worked in traditional male-dominated organizations, but have instead directed their energy to forming and nurturing grass-roots activist groups seeking social change.

Because they have not worked under formal labels such as CEO, board chairperson, senator, or president, the contributions of numerous women leaders are frequently uncounted and overlooked. However, it would be difficult to argue, for instance, that women such as Susan B. Anthony, Elizabeth Cady Stanton, Emmeline and Sylvia Pankhurst—warriors in the fight for women's suffrage—were not effective and critically important leaders who made an enormous difference in their world. Many women have devoted their leadership drive and skills to advancing women's rights. Their names are often forgotten, but their impact may well go beyond that achieved by individuals who hold more traditional leadership positions. We may think, for example, of Meena Keshwar Kamal, founder of the Revolutionary Women of Afghanistan (RAWA), defying restrictions on education of women and girls by developing and supporting a secret network of underground schools. Or of Nawal Saadawi of Egypt, Maryam Rajavi of Iran, Salwa Charfi of Tunisia, or Ghada Jamsheer of Bahrain—all outspoken activists for women's rights in their countries, in often risky defiance of cultural and religious restrictions (Halila 2008). And then there is Tawakkol Karman of Yemen, youngest-ever recipient of the Nobel Peace Prize in 2011, speaking passionately at rallies and organizing demonstrations in support of peace and women's rights. As we consider the barriers to women's leadership, it is important to remember that most of these barriers are linked to the socio-cultural environment, and do not represent essential differences between women and men.

GENDER STEREOTYPES AND THE EVALUATION OF FEMALE AND MALE LEADERS

Decades ago, research documented that the notion of formal leadership was entwined with masculinity. When people thought of managers, they thought of men (Schein 1973; Schein et al. 1996). When respondents were asked to think of powerful people, they envisioned men (Lips 2001). When asked if they would vote for a female political candidate for president, they expressed uneasiness (J. L. Smith, Paul and Paul 2007). Although there are more women in high-profile leadership positions these days, the stereotype of leaders continues to reek of masculinity (Koenig et al. 2011). In fact, researchers have explained the dearth of women in leadership by citing a clear *lack of fit* (Heilman 1983) or *role incongruity* (Eagly and Karau 2002) between the requirements of stereotypical femininity (niceness, care, compassion, consideration) and the qualities expected of leaders (goal-orientation, decisiveness, determination). The attempt to fulfill the contradictory requirements of both roles can make leadership problematic for women by putting them in a double bind.

A double bind for women

Women leaders are caught in a double bind. In 2007, the American research firm Catalyst surveyed more than 1,200 executives in the United States and Europe to determine their views of leadership and of women and men in leadership roles. The report, appropriately titled *Damned if You Do, Doomed if You Don't*, revealed that when women behaved in ways consistent with feminine gender stereotypes, by, for example, showing concern for others' perspectives, they were viewed as less competent. On the other hand, if they behaved in more masculine ways (acting assertively or displaying ambition, for instance), they were judged unfeminine and overly tough (Catalyst 2007). The report showed that women leaders consistently faced higher standards than men, and tended to be viewed as either too soft or too tough—rarely just right. Women leaders seemed to have to settle for either being seen as competent or being well-liked, but rarely found themselves in the position of being both liked *and* admired as competent.

A number of other studies also show that women in professional roles are penalized for the behaviors or attributes that are ignored, tolerated, or even praised when exhibited by men. Women reap more disapproval than men do when they are not "nice" or display poor social skills (Rudman and Glick 1999). Women who express anger over a colleague's mistake are seen as being emotional and out of control; men who express the same sentiments in the same situation gain stature (Brescoll and Uhlmann 2008). Powerful women, but not powerful men, incur disapproval and backlash if they talk more than others (Brescoll, 2011).

Female executives who dress in what others regard as a provocative way suffer a large drop in perceived competence—a drop that is not experienced by women in lower-status jobs (Glick *et al.* 2005). There is no evidence that male executives incur a loss of respect or status if they dress provocatively—but that may be because, for men, power is sexy and so dressing provocatively doesn't even come up. Both attractive women and attractive men sometimes benefit from a "beauty premium" in earnings (Adreoni and Petrie 2008), but attractive men seem to benefit more than attractive women, and only women are sometimes penalized for being *too* attractive (Bennett 2010). Women in low-status and/or "feminine" positions tend to be penalized if they are not seen as attractive, but women in (or applying for) high-status and/or "masculine" positions who appear too beautiful or sexy are sometimes subject to what some have labeled the "beauty is beastly" effect (Heilman and Stopeck 1985). According to this idea, attractiveness may be seen as detrimental for female applicants for leadership positions because attractiveness is associated with femininity—and femininity is seen as incongruent with the requirements for these jobs. In other words, beautiful women are seen as displaying a lack of fit for the position. In one study, participants were shown photos of attractive and unattractive women and men and were asked to sort them according to suitability for particular jobs (Johnson *et al.* 2010). Attractive women were discriminated against for masculine jobs for which physical appearance was unimportant.

Another study examined the impact of attractiveness on evaluations of female and male leaders who exhibited different leadership styles (Braun, Peus and Frey 2012). These researchers found that attractiveness was a disadvantage for women leaders who used a transformational leadership style. The differential impact of attractiveness on reactions to female and male leaders was pronounced for transformational leaders (leaders who used charismatic behavior to inspire and motivate followers), but not for leaders using a more traditional, transactional style (i.e. who focused on task completion, rewards, and punishments). Attractive women using a transformational leadership style elicited less trust and loyalty from followers than did unattractive women using a similar style. For male transformational leaders, attractiveness made no difference. The negative impact of attractiveness on followers' reactions to female transformational leaders—but not to male—was linked to gender stereotypes. In the case of female leaders, attractiveness appeared to strengthen followers' perceptions of a lack of fit between the leaders' femininity and the strong, influential behavior required of a transformational leader.

What makes leadership even more difficult for women is that, even though the qualities thought to be important for leaders may vary across cultures, women's strengths seem to be consistently underestimated. In a study of managers from ten Western European countries and the United States, researchers found that, across cultures, there was a relatively consistent tendency to view women leaders as more supportive and men to be more oriented to problem-solving. The strength of these stereotypes about women's and men's leadership capabilities varied somewhat by culture, but what is especially disheartening for women is that, at least in some countries, they were believed to have less of whatever qualities were deemed important—particularly by men. In Nordic cultures where the ideal leader was expected to be a delegator, for instance, men were seen as better delegators; in Anglo cultures, where the ideal leader was expected to be good at inspiring others, men were seen as more effective than women on these dimensions (Catalyst 2006).

One study recently showed that the women leaders who get the most promotions are those who are good at being chameleons: they can project assertiveness and confidence, but can, depending on the circumstances, "turn those traits on or off" (O'Neill and O'Reilly 2011). In fact, among the managers they studied, women who had masculine traits and were good at tailoring their behavior to the social environment received three times as many promotions as masculine women who tended *not* to adapt their behavior, 1.5 times more promotions than masculine men, and twice as many as feminine men. For the men with feminine traits, being a chameleon apparently conferred no advantage.

One reason why men may be leery of female leaders is that culturally perceived masculinity is fragile—and men's own status can be affected by being in a subordinate position to someone who violates gender stereotypes (Brescoll *et al.* 2012). Researchers found that male subordinates of either a female supervisor in a masculine domain (a female construction-site supervisor) or a male supervisor in a feminine domain (a male human resources supervisor) were paid less and viewed as having lower status than men whose supervisors were in gender-congruent domains. The status loss for these men appeared to be caused by the perception that they lacked masculinity, because the situation could be remedied by providing information that bolstered the men's perceived masculinity (in this case, that they enjoyed watching football, eating steak and ribs, and driving fast cars). Women's status or pay was not affected by working for a gender-atypical supervisor. In this kind of situation, then, gender stereotypes can harm men as well as women.

Leadership, self, and identity

Given the gendered stereotypes about leadership, it would not be surprising if women and men had different perceptions, expectations, aspirations, hopes, and fears with respect to holding leadership positions. One way to think about these perceptions is in terms of *possible selves*: individuals' particular visions and fantasies of what they could be or become in the future (Markus and Nurius 1986). Everyone has a set of many possible selves, created from their social experience and from exposure to models and images portrayed in the media. These different possible selves may include visions both positive (e.g. successful businessperson) and negative (e.g. failed political candidate). They are not necessarily aspirational goals but rather possibilities that a person can imagine for the self.

Gender differences in leadership-related possible selves among young women and men may reveal ways in which they have absorbed cultural messages about gender, power and leadership. Several studies have examined these issues among university students—a population from which many leaders are likely to spring. Lips (2000) asked a sample of US students to imagine themselves as persons with power, to rate how possible and how positive it would be for them to actually occupy that role, and then to describe what they would be like in their imagined powerful role. Next, the students were asked to envision themselves in three specific powerful roles: CEO of a major corporation, political leader, and director of a scientific research center, and respond to the same questions. Women rated the possibility of occupying both their imagined powerful role and the political leader role lower than men did. Furthermore, an analysis of their written responses showed that women were more likely than men to anticipate that powerful roles, particularly the political leader role, could entail relationship problems. The relationship concerns they expressed included difficulties associated with being respected by subordinates, being categorized according to their femininity rather than their position, and figuring out how to have time and energy left over for relationships outside of work.

Ways of trying to integrate power with cultural femininity may differ somewhat across cultures. In a similar study that included students from Puerto Rico as well as the US mainland (Lips 2001), women respondents were significantly more likely than men to anticipate relationship problems in powerful roles, and the political leader role was listed as the least possible role by women in both samples. Female respondents were also more likely than males to mention appearance as a way of trying to manage perceived contradictions between femininity and power, emphasizing that they would look attractive, even though powerful, or that they would convey power by looking elegant and stylish. Women in both samples expected relationship issues to crop up in powerful roles. However, only the women in the US mainland sample connected this expectation to lower ratings of possibility and positivity of occupying powerful roles. This may reflect a greater emphasis by mainstream US culture than by Puerto Rican culture on the notion that femininity involves being generally accommodating and nonabrasive, even with strangers. Cultural differences in perceptions of acceptable ways to mix femininity and power are also suggested in another study (Killeen, Lopez-Zafra and Eagly 2006), in which researchers asked undergraduate students in the US and Spain to envision themselves in a leadership role and then indicate how positive and possible the role would be. Here again, men perceived the powerful role as more possible for themselves than women did, but only in the Spanish sample did men rate powerful roles as more positive for themselves than did women. The latter finding may be due to the lower percentage of women occupying managerial positions in Spain, making such positions more stereotypically masculine. In this study, men were more likely than women to report that holding a powerful role would facilitate close relationships with spouse, children and friends and relationships with men in general or women in general—echoing earlier findings that powerful roles present fewer relationship concerns for men than for women. Taken together, these findings suggest that women's ambivalence about holding powerful positions transcends cultural boundaries, although the ambivalence may be linked to somewhat different issues in different cultural contexts. They also suggest that one factor slowing down women's entry into leader roles may be women's weaker sense that these roles are possible for them—particularly in combination with close relationships.

Might an individual's sense of possibility as a leader be changed by strategies designed to encourage the construction of an identity as a leader? This is the notion behind a number of leadership development programs aimed at women in educational and corporate organizations. Building an identity as a leader, like the construction of other identities, involves a series of interactive processes in which a person engages in certain actions and others react and provide feedback that informs the person's self-view. A positive spiral is created when one's exercise of leadership is recognized and affirmed by others, strengthening one's identity as a leader and increasing the motivation to look for new opportunities and take the risks associated with adopting a leadership role. Thus, women are often encouraged to try out leadership behaviors and seek out opportunities for advancement, under the assumption that they can thus build confidence in capacity for leadership. However, this process does not take place in a vacuum, but within a cultural context that often defines leadership as masculine. For a woman in most cultures, developing an identity as a leader and integrating that identity as a core part of her self has to be done in contexts where the notion of feminine authority is met with suspicion (Ely, Insead and Kolb 2011). Attempts to develop women's leadership identities and skills must integrate an awareness of the many subtle biases and barriers that will greet women as they work to advance. One way of thinking of this set of obstacles is to imagine a labyrinth, with many dead ends and blind alleys that must be negotiated in order to reach a goal.

The labyrinth

Social psychologists Alice Eagly and Linda Carli (2007) chose a labyrinth metaphor to describe the situation faced by women in their quest for leadership positions. A labyrinth is full of twists, turns, and impenetrable walls, but there is a viable route to the center to be found. It is an appropriate image, Eagly and Carli argue, because it incorporates the notion of multiple obstacles—from start to finish—rather than a single, impervious barrier (glass ceiling) at the end. According to their analysis, the labyrinth that provides the context faced by women pursuing leadership roles includes prejudice, wage discrimination (often beginning at entry-level jobs), slower promotions to supervisory and administrative positions at all levels, less favorable evaluations, resistance to women's leadership and influence because their style does not match masculine-stereotyped expectations, and demands of family life that fall disproportionately on women, particularly by giving them less time for professional networking. All of these barriers might be labeled chronic; they can appear repeatedly as women advance through the stages of their careers, and their effects are cumulative. They are also often so subtle that they go unrecognized—leaving women to feel frustrated and powerless because they cannot seem to translate their ability and motivation into the leadership roles to which they aspire. If a woman does not recognize the ways in which this context may be holding her back, she is likely to internalize a sense of inadequacy instead of an identity as a leader. Eagly and Carli argue that organizations can adopt a number of strategies that shift the situation in the direction of increasing leadership opportunities for women, including reducing the subjectivity of performance evaluation, changing the norm that employees must put in long hours at work to be seen as productive, and providing mentoring relationships that support networking. They also suggest establishing family-friendly human resources practices and encouraging male employees to participate in those benefits. The latter suggestion is a reminder that making the leadership situation better for women can also improve things for men. As Ely and colleagues (2011) note, some of the subtle biases that hold women back are also likely to interfere with the recognition of talented men who do not fit easily into existing organizational norms and structures. Subtle biases are often built into an organization's routine practices, rather than being the result of intentional actions and decisions; working to eliminate those biases is likely to open doors for a variety of talented individuals.

ARE THERE "FEMALE" AND "MALE" LEADERSHIP STYLES?

Several women world leaders participating in a recent international panel on development were quick to voice opinions about the differences between men and women as leaders. Helen Clark, former prime minister of New Zealand, said that women look at leadership differently than men: that women are more likely to look at leadership as an opportunity for service, perhaps because women are often so directly involved in caring for children or frail relatives (Saine 2012). President Ellen Johnson Sirleaf of Liberia noted that it makes a real difference to have women leadership roles, and President Joyce

Banda of Malawi commented that "Leadership is a love affair …
you must fall in love with the people and the people must fall in
love with you" (Saine 2012, par. 5).

We have seen that women and men in leadership roles are
sometimes evaluated differently, depending on their leadership
style—suggesting that people may believe different styles are
appropriate for women and men. But is there any evidence that
women and men actually lead differently? Researchers attempting
to answer this question have focused on two broad leadership
styles: *transformational* and *transactional*. Transformational leadership
includes four aspects: stimulating followers to think innovatively,
motivating followers to contribute to a shared vision, showing
consideration and support for followers' concerns and
development, and modeling one's own ideals, values and beliefs.
Transactional leadership, by contrast, is a style that focuses more
narrowly on reaching set goals, completing tasks, assigning rewards
and punishments based on performance, and detecting errors
(Bass and Avolio 1994).

Transformational leadership has gained a great deal of attention
and approval in recent years and is often the favored contemporary
approach. At the same time, research indicates that women in
leadership positions show a small but consistent tendency to be
more transformational in their styles than men (Eagly, Johannesen-
Schmidt and van Engen 2003). The difference between women
and men appears greatest for the dimension of transformational
leadership that encompasses supportive, encouraging treatment of
subordinates. Women also differ from men on one dimension of
transactional leadership that is strongly linked to leadership
effectiveness: rewarding subordinates based on performance.
Furthermore, these differences between women and men as
leaders appear to be accurately recognized by observers
(Vinkenburg *et al.* 2011). It would seem reasonable to assume that
these differences might give women a "leadership advantage"—
and indeed, a number of commentators in the popular press have
now speculated that women have the qualities to be better leaders
than men. In light of the relative shortage of women leaders in
politics and business, this assertion is puzzling.

To unravel the puzzle, it is important to remember that
leadership effectiveness is dependent on the context: the type of

task being undertaken and the characteristics and attitudes of those being led (Chemers 1997). We have noted that one source of difficulty for women leaders lies in a perceived lack of fit or role incongruity between the qualities perceived as necessary for leadership and those stereotyped as desirably feminine. This incongruity can be seen as especially stark in jobs that are male-dominated or that are viewed as requiring a large element of masculine toughness—and these are the very leadership roles in which women tend to be most embattled and most scarce. To straddle this perceived divide, women in leadership roles must emphasize both their competence *and* their warmth, their decisiveness *and* their supportiveness, their sensitivity *and* their strength. Given this double set of requirements and the necessity to perform a delicate balancing act between them, it would be surprising if women did not approach leadership somewhat differently than men. Furthermore, because it may help with some elements of this balancing act, the transformational style may provide female leaders with an advantage in certain situations. The transformational style incorporates behaviors that are supportive, considerate, and encouraging—all qualities congruent with expectations for women—so this style may present less incongruity for women than did older notions of leadership. Indeed, research reveals that observers judge individualized consideration as more important for the promotion of women than for the promotion of men, underlining the necessity for women to "demonstrate both sensitivity and strength, whereas male leaders only need to prove they are strong" (Vinkenburg *et al.* 2011).

Even if women manage to carry this double burden, however, cultural change can be slow. Particularly in the most masculine stereotyped leader roles, women may continue to be judged against old-fashioned notions of leadership that emphasized only masculine qualities, even though today's organizations are increasingly likely to be team-based and consensus-oriented. Furthermore, as we have already seen, there is a tendency to view men as possessing more of whatever leadership qualities are culturally valued (Catalyst 2006). Both of these factors may help to put the brakes on any tendency for women to gain a leadership advantage through a transformational style. As Eagly and Carli

(2003) note, however, organizations can now claim credit for innovation and progressive change when they increase the number of women in leadership roles, and this cultural change continues to be a force toward gender equity.

Leaders as role models for women and men

Not surprisingly, people form important aspects of their views of leadership through exposure to leaders. Where most high-profile leaders are men, and where ideals of leadership involve mainly a top-down, directive style, that vision of traditionally masculine, authoritative leadership can be self-perpetuating. The situation may sap women's belief in themselves as possible leaders. It may also undermine the confidence of both women and men in their leadership abilities if they are not comfortable with that leadership style.

It seems logical that presenting people with role models of leaders who do not fit traditional gendered leadership stereotypes would help women and non-traditional men to articulate possible selves as leaders and improve their leadership performance. Paradoxically, however, women often seem to be threatened rather than encouraged when presented with models of successful female leaders. For example, researchers in one study exposed women to successful female leaders, male leaders, or no leaders before they performed a leadership task. The women exposed to the female leaders actually reported lower self-evaluations, more feelings of inferiority, and lower leadership aspirations than did women in the other two groups (Hoyt and Simon 2011). In another study, exposing women to a description of a very successful female CEO seemed to lower their self-ratings of competence (Parks-Stamm, Heilman and Hearns 2008). In a similar vein, women who were presented with examples of women in powerful positions such as business professor, surgeon, or president of a company's financial division responded by associating themselves less with leadership and showing less interest in masculine jobs (Rudman and Phelan 2010). And women who read about a successful woman in a masculine stereotyped professional role rated that role as less attainable than did women who were not exposed to the successful woman (Lawson and Lips in press). The only conditions under which seeing successful female role models seems to bolster women's confidence in their capacity to achieve such positions are when the role models are explicitly presented as being similar to the respondent (e.g. Asgari, Dasgupta and Stout 2012; Lockwood 2006).

Why should it be so difficult to use successful female role models to inspire other women to aspire to leadership positions? One possibility is that women tend to see those role models as very different from themselves—and thus not as appropriate models. Influenced by stereotypes that assert a lack of fit between leadership and femininity, women may view successful female leaders as unfeminine—and thus be repelled rather than attracted by the possibility of becoming like those leaders. Alternatively, women may simply feel that, because they are so exceptional, these successful women are very unusually talented and brave—or very unusually thick-skinned, driven and unlikeable—and may exaggerate the contrast between themselves and the role models. Indeed, when there are few women in senior positions within a company, the women in that company report less likelihood of identifying with senior women or seeking their advice. In the context of an organization in which senior women are scarce, that very scarcity may make these women appear unfit as role models (Ely, Insead and Kolb 2011).

Even if presenting women with role models does not always increase their confidence in their abilities, might it enhance their leadership-related performance in an actual situation? In one study, researchers placed participants in a virtual reality environment and instructed them to give a persuasive public speech (Latu *et al.* 2013). The virtual environment was programmed to depict a room with a responsive twelve-person audience, in which either a picture of a successful powerful woman (Angela Merkel or Hillary Clinton), a picture of a successful powerful man (Bill Clinton), or no picture was displayed. Researchers measured the length and quality of the speeches and the participants' self-evaluations of their performance. They found that, in the presence of either no picture or a picture of Bill Clinton, men spoke longer than women; however, this gender gap disappeared when participants spoke in a virtual room with a picture of Angela

Merkel or Hillary Clinton—because women in those conditions spoke longer. Women's speeches were also rated as higher in quality in the female role model conditions, and the women in these conditions evaluated their own performance more positively. Thus, women seemed to be empowered by their exposure to female role models.

This study helps us to understand why, despite the discouraging results reported at the beginning of this section, female role models may be important in facilitating the movement of more women into leadership positions. In this study, women did not simply compare themselves in some abstract way to Angela Merkel and Hillary Clinton—and thus, perhaps, trigger feelings that they could never measure up to these outstanding women. Rather, they were given the opportunity to perform a challenging, leadership-related task while being presented with these inspiring models. After successfully performing the task, they were able to judge themselves based on having accomplished the task. Rather than contrasting themselves with these exemplary women, perhaps they were able to align themselves psychologically with them, drawing inspiration and empowerment. These findings suggest that the most effective way to use female role models to encourage more women into leadership is to combine the exposure to role models with chances for women to take on leadership tasks.

The study just described, along with a number of others, showed no effect of gender of role model on male participants. This may be because there are so many more visible male than visible female leaders in our social environment—so men have many more available same-gender leader role models and simply take male leadership for granted.

THE IMPACT OF LEADERSHIP POSITIONS ON THE MEN AND WOMEN WHO HOLD THEM

When Hillary Clinton prepared to step down from her post as US Secretary of State, after four years in which she logged some 1700 meetings with world leaders, 956,733 airplane miles and visits to 112 different countries, she said she would like to "catch up on about 20 years of sleep deprivation" and see if she could get "untired"

("Hillary Clinton on life after being Secretary of State" 2013). Veteran US congressman David Obey Clearly, preparing to retire from office in 2010 after 21 terms, commented that "quite frankly, I am bone tired" (Ruffini 2010, par. 2). Clearly, one likely impact of serving in a demanding leadership position is exhaustion. That effect may or may not be linked to gender—but it is safe to assume from our knowledge about the different conditions and expectations that surround male and female leaders, that gender-related expectations can make a difference to the way leadership is experienced.

In a ground breaking study, Erika Apfelbaum (1993) conducted interviews of Norwegian and French women in high leadership positions. She found that the specific contexts provided by Norway and France for these women's leadership apparently made profound differences to their experiences. For the French women, leadership was seen as burdensome, difficult and conflict-laden. By contrast, the Norwegian women enjoyed being leaders and spoke positively about their roles. Apfelbaum attributed these differences, in part, to the differing history of the two countries: Norway had a long history of gender equality and there were already a substantial number of women in high political office, whereas France was not used to women in leadership positions and had relatively few. The Norwegian women felt solidly grounded in their legitimacy as leaders; the French women felt embattled. Most of the Norwegian women were married and said they had few problems balancing marriage with a demanding career; most of the French women were single, and reported difficulties in achieving a satisfactory balance between their personal relationships and their high-powered roles. These findings are a reminder that women are likely to pay a high price for leadership, not in every situation, but in contexts where women leaders are unusual and the culture does not support women as legitimate leaders. Male leaders seem less likely to suffer such difficulties in institutional environments where male leaders are rare—perhaps because male leadership, even when unusual, is almost always seen as legitimate (Cognard-Black 2004). In the absence of societies where female leadership is much more strongly expected than male leadership, it is not possible to examine the impact on men of a situation parallel to the situation that existed for French women in the early 1990s.

FOR FURTHER EXPLORATION

Eagly, Alice H., and Carli, Linda L. (2007). *Through the Labyrinth: the truth about how women become leaders.* (Boston, MA: Harvard Business School Publishing.) Two social psychologists examine the research to determine why it remains so difficult to get women into leadership positions. They argue that the glass ceiling image is less appropriate than a labyrinth metaphor to describe the barriers women face in their careers as they try to negotiate the paths to power.

Ducat, Stephen J. (2004). *The Wimp Factor: gender gaps, holy wars, and the politics of anxious masculinity.* (Boston, MA: Beacon Press.) The author analyzes the history of Western culture from the point of view of gender attitudes. With a particular focus on American politics and foreign policy, he argues that much of the nation's foreign and domestic policy is driven by the desire to demonstrate "masculine" self-reliance and dominance and to reject "feminine" approaches of care and nurturing.

Chin, Jean Lau, Lott, Bernice, Rice, Joy K. and Sanchez-Hucles, Janis (eds) (2007). *Women and Leadership: transforming visions and diverse voices.* (Malden: Blackwell Publishing.) This collection takes a feminist perspective and contains chapters on topics that include communication styles, women as academic and corporate leaders, the impact of diverse cultural contexts, collaborative leadership, and developing transformational leaders, along with chapters dedicated to leadership among Latinas, Black, Asian American, and American Indian women, women with disabilities, and lesbian women.

6

GLOBAL PATTERNS OF GENDER-RELATED VIOLENCE

In January 2013, the US Defense Department announced that it would lift the ban that had prevented American women from serving in combat positions. Although women make up more than 14 percent of that nation's active duty military, and many female soldiers have been injured or killed during the wars in Iraq and Afghanistan, women had been automatically excluded from the 230,000 positions that officially involve direct combat. In certain other countries (e.g. Canada, Australia, New Zealand), women have already been serving in combat roles (Barnes and Nissenbaum 2013).

Resistance to women in combat roles has a long history. Women, it has been argued, cannot meet the high physical standards needed for combat roles. Women are not tough enough to be exposed to the dangers of combat or the rigors, discomfort and dirt of the battlefield. Women who are taken by the enemy in war risk being raped. The presence of women will endanger male military personnel because, in battle, the men will take special risks to protect the women—and the women will not be able to protect the men. Common themes in these arguments are a visceral discomfort with the notion of women engaging in active, potentially lethal, physical aggression, and a feeling that women need protection. These ideas are rooted in the descriptive and prescriptive stereotypes of femininity outlined in earlier chapters: women are supposed to be gentle, nurturing, compassionate, caring, accommodating—not tough, aggressive, decisive, or willing to take physical risks.

These stereotypes feed the notion that women need special protection—an idea that is linked to benevolent sexism—and that society is providing that protection by keeping them out of combat roles. However, military women are often subject to violence, even if they are not officially in combat. This point became starkly clear to the public early in the Iraq war, when Pfc. Lori Piestewa, a member of an army maintenance unit who was driving a transport truck, was killed when her unit was ambushed (Legon 2003). Furthermore, it is not necessary for military women even to be deployed in order to face violence. In the same week as the combat rule change was announced, congressional hearings were being held to investigate a pervasive pattern of sexual assault and rape of recruits and trainees at an Air Force base in Texas. The "enemy" who perpetrated the assaults in this case were the women's instructors during basic training (Bernard 2013). Sexual assault appears to be a continuing and pervasive problem in all branches of the military (Frank et al. 2012), underlining the irony of the claim that women are somehow being protected by being kept out of combat roles.

Considerations of women, men, and violence produce strong emotional reactions, in part because they activate powerful prescriptive stereotypes of femininity and masculinity. The way we have learned to think about aggression and violence is clearly linked to gender.

INTERPERSONAL VIOLENCE IS GENDERED

Violence is associated with men and with masculinity: men are most often both the perpetrators and victims of the types of interpersonal violence, such as assaults and homicides, that end up in the public record (Federal Bureau of Investigation 2011). Researchers who study aggression in laboratory situations or through self- or peer-report find a greater likelihood of male than female direct and physical aggression among children (Lansford et al. 2012), adolescents (Card et al. 2008) and adults (Archer 2004).

Males have also been found to be higher in verbal aggression, though by a smaller margin (Archer 2004). Gender differences in aggression are consistent but fairly modest, and are most likely to appear under conditions where the provocation for aggression is low and where the norms of the situation favor male more than female aggression (Eagly and Steffen 1986; Giancola *et al.* 2002; Hyde 1984). Gender differences in relational aggression (aggression that harms another by damaging her/his social status and/or relationships) are not so consistent (Lansford *et al.* 2012). Relational aggression fits more neatly with femininity stereotypes and is more socially acceptable for women than physical aggression. Thus it is tempting to suppose that this type of aggression may be more characteristic of women than men. However, both women and men, girls and boys, engage in relational aggression, depending on the circumstances (Crick, Ostrov and Kawabata 2007).

In general, it may well be the case that women and men do not differ in how aggressive they are, but rather in the kinds of aggression they display. Men are no more likely than women to get angry, but they appear to choose forms of aggression that are more risky or costly, such as physical aggression, use of weapons, or direct confrontation (Archer 2004). There is abundant evidence that women can and do behave aggressively, and that they have as much potential as men to be aggressive (Richardson 2005; White and Kowalski 1994). However, both women's and men's display of aggression is likely shaped by social norms, the power distribution in a given situation, and the potential costs of various behavioral options.

Men, in particular, often find themselves in situations where they are expected to behave aggressively. As part of the masculine role in many cultures, men are supposed to be the protectors and defenders of their families, their communities, their nations. They are more likely than women to be placed in roles, such as police and military occupations, that require the use of aggression. Yet even when men conform to the requirements of these roles by doing what they must, they can pay a significant cost. For example, Timothy Kudo (2013), US Marine Corps veteran of the war in Afghanistan, writes that he carries with him "every day" the unshakeable memories of the incidents in which he ordered people killed. Noting that the Department of Veterans Affairs has begun labeling this problem as a *moral injury*, Kudo comments that "This isn't the kind of injury you recover from with rest, physical therapy and pain medication."

On the other hand, for men the cost of *not* behaving aggressively in some situations may be humiliation and a devastating loss of status or self-esteem. Perhaps for this reason, one significant trigger for overt aggressive behavior by men appears to be challenges to their masculinity—men may sometimes behave in physically aggressive ways to restore masculine status that has been threatened (Bosson *et al.* 2009). One Canadian study shows, for instance, that when men are in situations where they have lower economic or educational status than their female partners, they are more likely to be emotionally abusive (Kaukinen 2004).

One problem with understanding violence from a gender perspective, then, is that violence is interpreted to mean different things when perpetrated by women and by men. A man behaving violently may be seen as acting out his masculinity, but a woman behaving violently is defying or undermining perceptions of her femininity. Furthermore, because women are viewed as weaker than men, their aggression—particularly against men—may not be taken seriously. Such considerations must inform the analysis of gendered patterns of violence.

Masculinity in a number of situations involves claiming status in a hierarchy and power over others. In particular, masculinity often implies superiority to, and power over, women. Perhaps, then, it is not surprising that acts of interpersonal violence by men are often directed at the women with whom they are in intimate relationships—and that acts of interpersonal violence by women are often directed, frequently in self-defense, at male partners.

INTIMATE PARTNER VIOLENCE

Like other forms of violence, violence in the home and family is not gender-neutral. Although both women and men can be perpetrators or victims of domestic violence, women are far more likely than men to suffer serious injury, to live in terror of a spouse, or to have to flee their homes for their own or their children's safety (Catalano 2012; Crown Prosecution Service

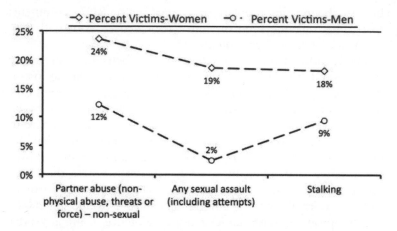

Figure 6.1: Prevalence of intimate partner violence in England and Wales among adults. Both women and men may suffer at the hands of an intimate partner, but crime statistics show women are more likely than men to be targets of all types of abuse from partners.

Source: Based on data from Table 3.01, *Crime in England and Wales*, available at https://www.gov.uk/government/publications/crime-in-england-and-wales-2010-to-2011

[UK] 2011). This pattern holds true all over the world (World Health Organization 2005). However, as we shall see, this does not mean that women are not also perpetrators of intimate partner violence.

The violence that occurs in intimate partnerships can be physical (such as hitting, kicking, choking), sexual (rape, coercion of specific sexual acts), or psychological (such as insults, screaming, isolating the individual from friends or family). All these kinds of violence can have devastating consequences, and they often occur in concert (Black *et al.* 2011). In this section, however, the main focus is on physical violence.

INTIMATE PARTNER VIOLENCE AGAINST WOMEN

Male partner violence against women

The statistics on abuse of women by male intimate partners are staggering. A multi-country study conducted by the World Health Organization (2005) found that, across 10 countries (Bangladesh,

Brazil, Ethiopia, Japan, Peru, Namibia, Samoa, Serbia and Montenegro, Thailand and the United Republic of Tanzania), the proportion of women who reported that in their lifetime they had ever experienced physical or sexual violence from a partner ranged from a low of 15 percent to a high of 71 percent. When asked only about their experience of the previous year, the proportion of women reporting partner violence still ranged from 4 to 54 percent. The proportion of women who in their lifetime had experienced severe physical violence at the hands of a partner (being hit with a fist, kicked, dragged, threatened or harmed with a weapon) ranged from 4 to 49 percent. In the United States, almost one in every four women has experienced severe physical violence by an intimate partner during her lifetime (Black *et al.* 2011).

Since the violence takes place in the context of an ongoing relationship, and in a household, acts of domestic violence tend not to be one-time events but rather become long-term patterns.

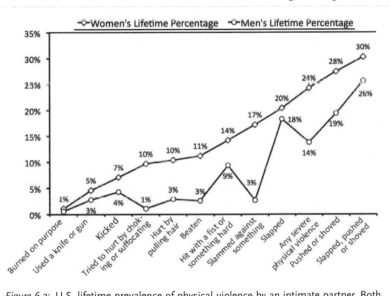

Figure 6.2: U.S. lifetime prevalence of physical violence by an intimate partner. Both women and men may be victims of severe physical violence, such as being beaten, kicked, or choked by an intimate partner. Over a lifetime, the percent of women reporting such violence is higher than men for almost every form of physical violence.

Source: Based on data from Black *et al.* (2011).

The WHO study found that most women who experienced intimate partner violence once experienced it repeatedly—a finding that is consistent with other investigations of domestic violence (Frieze 2005). There may be many different patterns of violence within couples (Frieze 2005, 2008; Williams and Frieze 2005); two that have been identified have been labeled "intimate terrorism," involving one-sided abusive violence, and "common couple violence," involving fairly low-level mutual violence that rarely results in injury (Johnson and Ferraro 2000). Women in the first group, who are being terrorized by a partner, may find it impossible to leave the situation, often because they simply have no safe place to go, are economically dependent on their partner, or have been so demoralized by the violence and the accompanying verbal abuse that their self-confidence in their ability to live independently is shattered (Arias and Pape 1999). However, even if they stay in the situation, and even if they fear for their lives, many abused women develop strategies for survival and coping with the abuse—often including fighting back verbally and/or physically (Ferraro 2003). When a woman does leave, the danger of the situation often escalates as an irate and/or desperate husband or partner tracks her down and vents his anger in a violent, or even lethal, attack (Pagelow 1993).

We have already seen that men do not seem to be more angry or essentially more aggressive than women. What, then, is the explanation for so much male violence directed at female partners? It seems likely that one important part of the explanation lies in cultural gender arrangements. As noted above, men can use violence to act out masculinity—particularly as masculinity implies power over women. Furthermore, in many situations, societal arrangements and norms actually give men formal or informal authority over their wives and daughters, thus providing perceived legitimacy to the use of force against them—and providing women little recourse when they are targets of violence by a spouse. For example, a recent large survey of women in Iraq found that 63 percent agreed that a husband is justified in beating his wife (Linos, Khawaja and Kaplan 2012). Research in India shows that women's risk of intimate violence is linked to tolerance of violence against women in their communities (Boyle et al. 2009). A Canadian study reveals that men who are more accepting of a patriarchal ideology are more likely to be violent toward their wives (Lenton 1995). Thus culturally-supported gender ideology provides some plausible explanations for the pervasiveness of male violence against female intimate partners. However, if enacting masculinity and exerting male authority were the only causes of intimate partner violence, instances of intimate partner violence against women by female partners would be extremely rare. This does not seem to be the case.

Female partner violence against women

Data from a recent national survey in the United States shows that nearly one in three respondents who self-identified as lesbian had experienced at least one incident in her lifetime of severe physical violence by an intimate partner. More than two-thirds of these respondents reported that the perpetrator of the violence was female (Walters, Chen and Breiding 2013). The overall findings of this survey indicate that violence is as common in lesbian and gay intimate partnerships as in heterosexual couples. However, many women who have experienced violence within lesbian relationships report that they feel silenced and isolated because there is little acknowledgement of female on female intimate partner violence, and few sources of support for survivors (Walters 2011). The very invisibility of intimate partner violence in lesbian couples may be linked to gender stereotypes that posit that women are not physically aggressive or violent

Like violence in intimate heterosexual relationships, violence in lesbian couples may be associated with factors specific to the relationship, such as power imbalances or dependency. However, the phenomenon is also responsive to a cultural context of stereotyping and discrimination based on sexual orientation. For women in lesbian relationships, the stresses associated with being in a sexual minority appear to be associated with both lower relationship quality and intimate partner violence. Women in lesbian couples who have most strongly internalized the surrounding culture's negative attitudes about lesbians are most likely to experience poor relationship quality and, in turn, to perpetrate or be victimized by violence in that relationship (Balsam and Szymanski 2005).

INTIMATE PARTNER VIOLENCE AGAINST MEN

Violence against men by female partners

About one in every seven men in the United States reports experiencing in his lifetime severe physical violence (slammed against something, hit with a fist or something hard, or beaten) by an intimate partner; about 2 percent report experiencing this type of violence in the previous year (Black *et al.* 2011). Among heterosexual men, more than 99 percent of those who say they have experienced intimate partner violence report that the perpetrator of that violence was female (Walters, Chen and Breiding 2013). Global statistics on the abuse of men by female intimate partners are less available than comparable statistics for female targets of abuse by men.

On surveys of violence in intimate heterosexual relationships in Western countries, women are as likely or more likely than men to report being violent, and slightly more men than women say they have been targets of one-sided severe violence (Archer 2000; Williams and Frieze 2005). These findings run counter to most people's expectations, and indicate that intimate partner violence is a more complex phenomenon than men battering women. One possible explanation for women's higher reports of perpetrating violence is that women may be more likely than men to fight back against partner violence—because some male victims may feel it is illegitimate to be physically aggressive against a woman. Another possible explanation is the presence of a reporting bias: because male violence against women is not socially acceptable, men may be more reluctant than women to report committing violent acts against an intimate partner of the other gender.

Male victims of severe intimate partner violence may have little recourse if they want or need help and support. There are fewer services available to male victims, and men are less likely than women to report their victimization or call on law enforcement for assistance (Nowinski and Bowen 2012). In the context of gender stereotypes that portray men as tougher than women, it can be very difficult for a man to admit that he is being abused by a female partner, and it can be difficult for others to believe that he is unable to stop the abuse.

Violence against men by male partners

Among gay men in the United States, the reported lifetime prevalence of severe physical violence by an intimate partner is 16.4 percent (Walters, Chen and Breiding 2013). More than 90 percent of these men reported only male perpetrators. It appears that intimate partner violence among gay men is a significant issue, demanding further research (Nowinski and Bowen 2012). The violence may be precipitated by stress in the relationship and, as in other types of couples, gender stereotypes and ideology may play a role. For example, in one study of gay male couples in Cuba, economic hardships appeared to lead to feelings of threatened masculinity, which led in turn to violence as a reassertion of masculinity (Santaya and Walters 2011).

Overall, it appears that, at least in the United States and the few other countries where both male- and female-initiated violence in different kinds of intimate couples have been studied, intimate partner violence occurs in all types of couples with approximately similar frequency, and that the violence may take one of a number of different patterns. In addition, women as well as men perpetrate violence, even severe violence, on intimate partners. However, this does not imply that gender is irrelevant to understanding intimate partner violence. For one thing, it is not at all clear that the same violent behaviors have the same meaning or impact for women and men in intimate relationships, or that all the most appropriate questions are being asked of women and men in surveys of intimate partner violence. For example, it may mean something different to a man than it does to a woman to push or be pushed by a partner. And if a woman's clothes are destroyed by her partner, she may perhaps experience that as more violent than a slap—but destruction of clothing may not even be included in the list of violent acts included in the measures of violence (McHugh, Livingston and Ford 2005). A difference in the underlying meaning may help to explain the robust and consistent finding that being the victim of violence in an intimate relationship is linked consistently with more negative psychosocial outcomes, such as distress and marital dissatisfaction, for women than for men (Williams and Frieze 2005).

STALKING

Stalking is a pattern of threatening or harassing tactics, often involving unwanted contacts or obvious surveillance, that makes the target feel fearful. Examples of stalking might include repeated harassing phone calls or emails, following or spying on the target person, or leaving items for the target to find. A recent report shows that about one of every six women and one of every nineteen men in the United States has been stalked during their lifetime (Black *et al.* 2011). Most stalking is carried out by people who know the target person. For more than two-thirds of female victims and just over 41 percent of male victims, the perpetrator is a current or former intimate partner. Women are much more likely to be stalked by men than by women; men are likely to be targeted about equally by male and female stalkers. Stalking is often considered a "gendered" crime, because of the consistent pattern of female victims outnumbering male victims—particularly when the definition of stalking is limited to behaviors that instill fear and/or that involve credible threats (Lyndon *et al.* 2012). A substantial number of female and male college students report being stalked; on the other hand, many students do not self-identify as stalking victims, even when targeted by behaviors that meet criteria for stalking (McNamara and Marsil 2012). Cyberstalking, which involves the use of computer-mediated communication to harass the victim, was reported by more than 40 percent of students surveyed on one US college campus; this form of stalking was experienced disproportionately by women and by racial and sexual minority students (Reyns, Henson and Fisher 2012). Women experience more severe psychological, physical, and social consequences from stalking than men do, in large part because women's fear responses to stalking tend to be higher than men's (Sheridan and Lyndon 2012). Yet, as with other forms of intimate partner violence, stalking is sometimes not treated seriously by law enforcement, or elicits responses based on gender stereotypes.

RAPE AND SEXUAL ASSAULT

In December 2012, the brutal gang rape of a 23-year old woman on a bus in Delhi triggered mass protests in India and shock around the world. The young woman, who later died of her injuries, was a physiotherapy student who had been to see a film at a local shopping mall. Returning home, she and a male friend were attacked by a group of men on a bus, where both were beaten with an iron bar and she was raped repeatedly while the bus travelled the streets. It was reported that the six men who abused her said they would teach this woman a lesson for going out at night with a man. Protestors demanded action from the government to punish these and other rapists, and argued that crimes of sexual assault against women were too often ignored or trivialized. Commentators suggested that many women were afraid to report sexual assaults because police officers were unsympathetic, and some claimed that the preference for sons in India had nourished a sense of male privilege and entitlement that undermines respect for women (Nelson 2012).

Whereas many rapes do not involve this much physical violence or a gang of strangers, this tragic incident and its aftermath brings into focus many of the key gender-related issues about sexual assault. First, it is far more likely to happen to women than to men, and to be perpetrated by men rather than women. Second, it is a crime that, in many contexts, is not taken seriously by lawmakers, law enforcement officers, and communities—and for this reason is often both under-punished and underreported. Third, reasons for the trivialization of sexual assault include a number of rape-supportive attitudes, such as the belief that female victims deserve or even want to be raped, as indicated by their behavior. And finally, all of the previous issues are rooted in patriarchal notions that men are entitled to judge and dictate behavior to women, to mete out punishment when women do not conform to such dictates, and to have access to sex with women when and how they deem appropriate (Gavey 2005; Jewkes 2012).

Researchers have reported that 28 to 37 percent of adult men in South Africa, 24 percent of men in India, and between 10 and 15 percent of men in Bangladesh have committed rape (Jewkes 2012). The World Health Organization (2005) found that rates of sexual violence against women ranged from 6 to 59 percent within intimate partnerships and from about 1 to 12 percent by non-partner perpetrators across ten countries studied.

In two-thirds of the settings where data were collected for this study, over 5 percent of the women said that their first experience of sexual intercourse had been forced. According to a national survey, 18.3 percent of women and 1.4 percent of men in the United States have been raped at some time during their lives (Black *et al.* 2011). More than half of the women said they were raped by an intimate partner, and more than 40 percent reported being raped by an acquaintance. Of the men who were raped, more than half said that the perpetrator was an acquaintance, and just over 15 percent said the perpetrator was a stranger. For more than 30 percent of female rape victims the first rape occurred before the age of 18; for just over 12 percent it occurred before the age of 10. More than 27 percent of male victims were first raped before the age of 10.

A review of 75 studies of sexual assault against individuals who identify as gay, lesbian or bisexual in the United States found that the prevalence of lifetime sexual assault among lesbian or bisexual women ranged from 15.6 percent to 85 percent; the prevalence of lifetime sexual assault among gay or bisexual men ranged from 11.8 percent to 54 percent (Rothman, Exner and Baughman 2011).

As can be seen from the above statistics, perpetrators of sexual violence are often intimate partners, family members, or acquaintances of the victims; an implication of this pattern is that a victim's sense of security and trust in interpersonal relationships is likely to be profoundly shaken by rape. It is also evident that, although many men have been victims of rape, this type of violence is far more likely to be experienced by women than men in their lifetime. There are a number of reasons why this is so, but one reason is likely the way societies think of and talk about heterosexual activity (Gavey 2005). For instance, as noted in the chapter on sexuality, there is a pervasive tendency to apply a double standard to male and female sexuality, with men designated as aggressors and initiators and women designated as gate-keepers and limiters. In other words, men are supposed to press for sex and women are supposed to resist—and all of this is simply part of a ritual that usually ends in sex. In such a framework, the line between seduction and rape becomes blurred. Rape is, by definition, forcing sex on another person. Yet some men who report they have forced or coerced a woman into having sex also say they have not committed rape (Koss 1988; Lisak and Miller 2002); and some women who report they have been forced or coerced into having sex also say they have not been raped (Kahn *et al.* 2003). Furthermore, a significant number of respondents apparently feel that a man is justified in forcing a woman to have sexual intercourse if she has had sex with him before (Shotland and Goodstein 1992) or behaved in certain ways, such as allowing him to pay for a meal or entertainment, teasing, or "leading him on" and then changing her mind (Bostwick and DeLucia 1992; Emmers-Sommer and Allen, 1999). In a context in which men are thought to need and desire sexual activity more than women do, and in which women do not feel entitled to resist sexual activity unless they have been clear and forceful about that resistance from the start, the stage is set for a high frequency of rapes of women by men.

The situation is even more conducive to rape in cultural contexts where women are explicitly designated as men's property or subject to their husband's authority. Rape in the context of marriage was long considered an oxymoron in many societies, since a husband was thought to be entitled to have sex with his wife, whether or not she was willing. The United Nations *Declaration on the Elimination of Violence Against Women*, published in 1993, established marital rape as a violation of human rights (United Nations 1993), and rape within marriage has now been designated as a crime in many countries (United Nations 2006). Despite this official recognition of spousal rape as illegal, however, women and men in many developing countries continue to believe that a husband is justified in using force to have sex with his wife if she refuses him; women who are married at a young age and who have few resources in terms of education, experience, or finances, are at particular risk (Population Council 2004).

Rape as a weapon of war

A long and painful tradition exists of using rape as a way to demoralize and humiliate opponents in war. There is, of course, a gender aspect to this practice: historically, most soldiers have been male, and women have often been left behind while men went out to fight. By ravaging women "belonging" to the enemy, troops may endeavor to systematically demonstrate their dominance and wreak destruction on communities of the opposing group. Indeed, one explicit goal of rape in wartime has been to dilute the ethnic group of the enemy by forcing their women to give birth to the babies of the rapists (Smith-Spark 2004). Another, less obvious, goal is to strengthen the bonds among combatants (Marino 2011). Hundreds of thousands of women have experienced this war-associated trauma, along with the consequent depression, fear, high suicide rates, risk of unwanted pregnancy, and sexually transmitted disease (Donohoe 2005; Nolen 2005). Men too are raped during wartime, although their stories are even less likely to be told and heard than those of female victims (Sivakumaran 2007). One report notes that 76 percent of male political prisoners surveyed in El Salvador in the 1980s reported sexual torture, and more than 80 percent of male concentration camp inmates in Sarajevo reported they had been raped (Storr 2011). A survey of about 1,000 households in the war-ravaged eastern Democratic Republic of Congo found that almost 40 percent of women and just under 24 percent of men had experienced sexual violence (Johnson *et al.* 2010). Another finding of this and another study (Cohen, cited in Marino 2011) is that female combatants are often participants in wartime rape: holding the victim down, using objects such as a bottle to perpetrate the rape. The finding that men as well as women are vulnerable to rape and other forms of sexual assault during armed conflicts, and that female as well as male combatants participate in rape, underlines the notion that sexual violence is more about power and proof of dominance than about sexual passion. Rape is humiliating, frightening, dangerous and debilitating for women; for men, it is also all of these, with the added dimension of being seen and experienced as emasculating

Wartime victims of rape face a number of special traumas: while dealing with the aftermath of rape, they are also dealing with the deaths and injuries of friends and families, displacement, and many other losses; any normal support systems may have been destroyed; and they are often stigmatized and rejected by others because of the rape, and may even be at risk of further violence by relatives who view them as dishonored (Nolen 2005;

Parrot and Cummings 2006). Victims frequently show symptoms of major depressive disorder and posttraumatic stress disorder (Johnson *et al.* 2010). International courts now prosecute wartime rape as a crime against humanity or as a crime of genocide (Henry 2010).

VIOLENCE AS A PUBLIC PERFORMANCE OF GENDER HIERARCHY AND NORMS

Although the types of violence described in this chapter are often hidden, both intimate partner violence and sexual violence also have a public face. Sometimes violence becomes a public performance of gender hierarchy and male status: an overt enactment of men's claim to ownership of, and right to authority over, "their" women. A tragic example is honor killing: the murder of a woman whose behavior is deemed to have brought dishonor to her husband, father, and/or other family members. Women who are murdered in defense of family honor have usually been judged as transgressing cultural boundaries of propriety by, for example, dressing in unapproved ways, going without chaperones to public places, being seen in the company of unrelated men, having intimate relationships outside of marriage, being raped, or even marrying without family approval. Such killings, often carried out by a male relative such as a brother or through a collaborative effort on the part of several family members (Chesler 2010), have been estimated to claim the lives of more than 5,000 women every year worldwide (United Nations Population Fund 2000), although reliable estimates are virtually impossible. They have been documented in countries as diverse as Turkey, Jordan, Egypt, Pakistan, India, Israel, and Brazil, and are often either not prosecuted, or treated leniently by the courts in those countries (Parrot and Cummings 2006).

The practice of honor killing is rooted in cultural norms that not only legitimize higher status for men than women, but also link a man's honor and standing in the community to his authority over his wife and daughters. In certain poor communities where patriarchal norms are strong, a man may feel that his honor is his only possession of value. An indiscreet, independent, or disobedient woman is seen as bringing shame on her family and as destroying that one important possession—a possession that is ranked higher in importance than the woman herself. The cultural assignment of higher value to men's honor and community standing than to women's lives is a sobering indicator of the damage that can result from rigid adherence to a hierarchical gender system.

For a man in a traditional community, one aspect of protecting his honor is protecting the women in his family from rape and other forms of violation. Ironically, that very man may use rape as a tool of public punishment against women for violating rules of sexual propriety, or for intruding into spaces or situations where they "do not belong." Because of its implications for men's honor, rape can also be used by men as a weapon against other men: one man can lash out at another by raping his wife, daughter, sister, or mother. In one case that created international outrage, a young Pakistani woman, Mukhtaran Bibi, was gang-raped by several men on the orders of the rural village tribal council, and then forced to walk home naked in front of villagers who taunted and insulted her. She was being punished because her brother had been seen with a woman from that village (Kristof 2005).

Public enforcement of the "rules" of gender also takes the form of violent hate crimes against sexual minorities. In such incidents, one or more perpetrators attacks a gay, lesbian, bisexual or transgender individual because they view that individual as transgressing norms, expectations, or values associated with heterosexual masculinity and/or femininity. Hate crimes, by definition, are terrorizing to whole categories of people, each of whom may legitimately worry that they could be the next to be attacked. In the United States in 2011, more than 1,500 hate crimes motivated by bias against a particular sexual orientation, were documented (Federal Bureau of Investigation 2012).

THE BUSINESS OF GENDERED VIOLENCE

There is money in gendered and/or sexualized violence: the profits made by individuals and organizations that sell people (most often women and children) into sexual slavery, or that distribute images of people being raped or sexually humiliated, are significant. For example, pornography, the depiction of sexually explicit images (of which a significant proportion, though not all, are violent) for the purpose of entertainment and sexual arousal, is big business with a global reach. According to some estimates, in 2006 the pornography industry in China generated about 27 billion dollars and the same industry in the United States generated about 13 billion dollars (Nowak 2012).

Pornography

There are three reasons for considering pornography under the topic of gendered violence. First, a significant amount of pornography depicts sexual violence, such as the rape and/or humiliation of women or men. Second, there has been an extensive debate about whether and to what extent the use of pornography may contribute to sexually violent attitudes and behaviors. And third, there is the question of whether the persons depicted in pornography the performers are victims of coercion and violence.

On the first question, there is considerable evidence that portrayals of violence and domination are a significant theme in pornography. For example, a content analysis of top-selling and top-renting popular pornographic videos revealed high levels of both physical and verbal aggression, with mostly male perpetrators (70.3 percent) and female victims (94.4 percent) (Bridges *et al.* 2010). More than 88 percent of the scenes analyzed portrayed physical aggression such as spanking, hair-pulling, gagging, slapping and choking; almost half the scenes contained verbal aggression, such as insulting or name-calling. Women were far more likely than men in these videos to be insulted or referred to in derogatory ways. In these videos, most of the targets of aggression were portrayed as responding neutrally or with pleasure to the aggression—leading to the concern, expressed by the researchers, that viewers of pornography are learning that aggression during a sexual encounter enhances pleasure.

The fastest-growing medium for the distribution of pornography is the Internet. One analysis of 31 free Internet sites depicting sexual violence found that images strongly emphasized the depiction of women as victims, usually with no image of the perpetrator. Pain experienced by the victim appeared to be the main emphasis of such sites; there was little or no attempt to portray rape as seduction (Gossett and Byrne 2002).

Producers of pornography are apparently well aware that violence sells. A content analysis of pornographers' own public descriptions of their products reveals a strong awareness that violence increases the marketability of the films and other media they purvey (Tyler 2010).

The question of whether and how exposure to pornography—particularly violent pornography—may contribute to sexual violence has been extensively debated and studied. Do consumers of pornography become more likely to engage in sexually violent behaviors, to adopt more violence-supportive attitudes, to lose empathy for victims of sexual violence? And does the amount of violent content of the pornographic material make a difference? The answers to these questions are still evolving. Some studies show that individuals' use of pornography may be linked to harsher evaluations of other-gender individuals with whom they interact (Jansma *et al.* 1997), weakened commitment to their real-life partners (Lambert *et al.* 2012), and loss of compassion for female rape victims (Zillmann and Weaver 1989; Zillmann and Bryant 1982). There is convergent evidence from a number of studies that, for men, pornography consumption is associated with an increased risk of sexually aggressive attitudes and behaviors. However, the relationship between pornography and violent outcomes is complicated and does not apply equally to all men and all forms of pornography. For men who are already at high risk for committing sexual aggression because they are hostile and distrustful toward women, gain gratification from controlling women, and take a promiscuous, non-committal approach to sexual relations, the heavy use of pornography, particularly violent pornography, is significantly associated with attitudes supporting violence against women (Malamuth, Hald and Koss 2012). These men may be both more likely to seek out violent pornography, and more likely to be influenced by it, than other men. With respect to sexually violent behavior, too, research shows that consuming pornography is most likely to affect men who are more predisposed to sexual aggression and who use pornography frequently (Vega and Malamuth 2007).

Exposure to violent pornography may also have deleterious effects on women. In one study, women who read an eroticized depiction of rape after ingesting a moderate alcohol dose were less likely than sober women to label the incident as rape and were more callous toward the victim (Davis *et al.* 2006). And viewing media portrayals of sexual or non-sexual violence against women can make women feel disempowered (Reid and Finchilescu 1995).

There is some disagreement as to whether the adult performers in pornographic media are always exploited, or whether this line of work is sometimes a free and rational choice by the individuals who engage in it. There is a great deal of evidence that the practices expected of female performers are dangerous to their health (Bridges *et al.* 2010). Accounts by women who have become well-known performers often present stories of conflicted emotions, abuse by producers and photographers, and the relentless coercive breaking down of their stated boundaries (Boyle 2011). Performers speak of being discouraged from using condoms, the physical pain of certain acts such as multiple penetrations, vaginal and rectal tears, and exhaustion. However, they often seem to construct these harmful consequences of their work as normal outcomes of a life they have freely chosen, and do not critique the ways in which they have apparently been bullied or threatened into engaging in acts they would rather avoid. Their narratives sometimes emphasize their own lack of sexual inhibitions and suggest that the worst outcomes happen, not to themselves, but to other, more naïve, young women, who do not understand what they are getting into when they become performers. It is clear, however, that participation in the pornography industry can have a variety of profoundly harmful impacts on the women who perform before the cameras—indeed the industry itself acknowledges, even advertises, the use of deception, coercion and harm of performers (Boyle 2011; Tyler 2010). This admission raises troubling questions about the extent to which performers in pornography, even if they are adults, are being paid and are choosing to show up for work each day, are victims of sexual violence. With respect to performers who are under-age, there is no doubt that they are being victimized and exploited.

Sex trafficking

Trafficking is another form of violence that is gendered and global; its victims are overwhelmingly women and children (Hodge and Lietz 2007). Victims are deceived, often by false promises of good jobs, or taken against their will from their own countries, deprived of legal documents, often kept imprisoned, and forced to work at prostitution, sweatshop labor, or some other form of forced servitude. Trafficking has been cited as possibly the fastest growing organized crime (Hodge and Lietz 2007); although estimates vary and are difficult to substantiate, trafficking may affect as many as 2 million women and girls per year (Watts and Zimmerman 2002). The girls and women most often come from poor countries or those with high unemployment and are sent to more affluent countries; a disproportionate number of victims come from Asian countries (Crawford 2010). According to one European study, 95 percent of victims experience physical or sexual violence while being trafficked (Zimmerman *et al.* 2006). Trafficking is an organized and very profitable form of gendered violence: global profits are estimated to be 31.6 billion US dollars per year (Besler 2005).

ECONOMIC AND HEALTH IMPACTS OF GENDERED VIOLENCE

Those who have been victimized by physical or sexual violence show physical and mental symptoms of ill health. In the WHO multi-country study, women frequently reported injuries from bruises and punctures, to broken bones and damage to their ears or eyes (World Health Organization 2005). Furthermore, women who had been victims of physical or sexual partner violence were significantly more likely than non-victimized women to report they were in poor health, had difficulties with walking, and experienced symptoms such as memory loss, dizziness, emotional distress, fatigue, and thoughts of suicide. Partner violence frequently occurred during pregnancy, and the rate of miscarriages and induced abortions was higher among women who had experienced partner violence than among other women. A national survey in the United States revealed that both female and male victims of rape, stalking, or intimate partner violence were more likely than their counterparts to report frequent headaches, chronic pain, difficulty sleeping, limitations on their activities, and poor physical and mental health (Black *et al.* 2011).

The physical and psychological impact of violence is energy-draining and thus has profound implications for the victims. In cultural contexts where women hold less power and status than men, the potential for violence affects women's opportunities to achieve success, or improve their status relative to men. For example, women who live in situations where violence against women is common learn to be alert, careful and avoidant (Khalid 1997). Caution limits their mobility and interferes with their economic and social opportunities. In this sense, an atmosphere of potential violence, whether in individual women's homes or in their public streets and communities, serves as an effective way of controlling women's behavior, movements, and aspirations.

The effects of such debilitating consequences for victims go beyond the individual women and men who experience the violence. A 2004 World Health Organization report (Waters *et al.* 2004) showed that intimate partner violence costs the economy of the United States 12.6 billion dollars annually—an amount equal to 0.1 percent of the gross domestic product. The same report showed that such violence had costs equal to 1.6 percent of the gross domestic product for Nicaragua, and 2 percent of the gross national product for Chile. One reason for the high economic costs is that victims of intimate partner and sexual violence impact the health care system: they are more likely than other people to need and seek out health care and to have more and longer hospital stays (Black 2011). Health care costs are significantly higher for victims of intimate partner violence than for non-victims, in large part because there are usually multiple violent episodes and because victims require services, such as psychiatric care, that are less frequently required by non-victims (Kruse *et al.* 2011). One US study found that health care costs attributable to intimate partner violence against women were US$1,727 per year per victim (Jones *et al.* 2006). The annual direct medical costs associated with all types of violence against women have been estimated at 1.1 billion dollars in Canada (Health Canada 2002).

Medical costs are not the only expenses incurred by societies as a consequence of interpersonal violence. Costs of legal services, safe accommodation, and policing are also significant. Furthermore, because they are more likely to be injured or ill, victims are also more likely to miss work, so there are costs to individuals and their employers associated with lost earnings, lost time, and lost opportunities for productivity. All such costs are difficult to measure, but, for example, one Australian study put the costs of refuge accommodation (including legal services, policing, estimated lost earnings and opportunity costs) for victims of domestic violence at 14.2 million dollars per year (Australian Institute of Criminology 2001). A study by the United States Department of Justice (1994) estimated that the annual combined costs of direct medical services to victims, lost earnings and lost opportunities associated with rape was 33 million dollars.

Because violence costs societies so much, programs or interventions to stop interpersonal violence often cost less than the money they save. For example, one report estimates that the Violence Against Women Act (VAWA), passed in the United States in 1994 and providing for severe criminal penalties against perpetrators of intimate partner violence and stalking, saved 12.6 billion dollars in averted costs related to victimization over its first five years (Clark, Biddle and Martin 2002, 2003).

In the light of these diverse consequences, gendered violence is now viewed and treated by international policy analysts not as a private, interpersonal matter, but as both a public health problem and a human rights issue.

FOR FURTHER EXPLORATION

Frieze, Irene H. (2005). *Hurting the One You Love: violence in intimate relationships.* (Belmont, CA: Wadworth/Thompson Learning.) The author carefully examines the research on violence in relationships, including violence against and by both women and men.

Gavey, Nicola (2005). *Just Sex? The cultural scaffolding of rape.* (Hove, UK: Routledge.) The author, a New Zealand psychologist, examines the social science literature on rape from a feminist and social constructionist perspective. She argues that we must pay critical attention to the use of dynamics of heterosexual relations as a justification for rape.

Crawford, Mary (2010). *Sex Trafficking in South Asia: telling Maya's story*. (Abingdon, UK: Routledge.) The author, a social psychologist, provides a critical feminist analysis of sex trafficking, focusing on the case of Nepal. She explores how a discourse that characterizes victims as "backward" may lead to strategies for protecting girls and women that may, paradoxically, restrict their human rights.

Kristof, N. and WuDunn, S. (2009). *Half the Sky: turning oppression into opportunity for women worldwide*. (New York: Random House.) The authors explore, through compelling cases and statistics, some of the most serious problems that women face worldwide. The book includes chapters on trafficking and sexual violence, as well as on individuals and organizations working to empower women in the face of these problems.

United Nations. *The UN Secretary-General's Database on violence against women*. (Accessible at http://sgdatabase.unwomen.org/country.action.) This database contains separate pages for every country that has provided data about the measures it has undertaken to address violence against women.

7

GLOBAL PATTERNS OF GENDER AND HEALTH

The World Health Organization (2010a) reports that 57 percent of the world's blind people are female, and that the proportion of women in the blind population rises at older ages. We do not usually think of blindness as a gender-linked problem, but the WHO Department of Gender and Health notes that gender inequalities explain much of the disproportionate impact of this problem on women. Globally, women with cataracts are less likely than their male counterparts to have the routine surgery that would prevent blindness—because they have less access than men to the financial resources that would pay for medical care or transportation to a health care facility, less access to education and health information, and less autonomy to make decisions and act on them with respect to health care.

It might be expected that women and men would be vulnerable to different health problems because of differences in their bodies. After all, women and men differ in their hormones, their reproductive systems, their secondary sex characteristics, their size, and their muscle strength. However, as the opening example illustrates, there are a number of other differences between women and men that could reasonably be expected to lead to gender differences in health: different kinds of work and stress, different behavioral norms and expectations, different life priorities, different access to resources.

GENDERED PATTERNS OF DISEASE

According to the World Health Organization (2012), in 2009 average global life expectancy at birth was 71 years for women and 66 years for men. Although there was a great deal of variation among regions, income groups, and individual countries, there was a consistent pattern for women to live longer than men. Life expectancy at age 60 was also higher for women (21 years) than for men (18 years). Although women live longer than men, this advantage might be said to be undercut by the fact that they suffer more illness, chronic health problems, and disabilities than men (Rieker and Bird 2005).

These broad statistics obscure a host of differences in the pattern of illnesses that afflict, and kill, women and men. For example, men experience more life-threatening diseases, such as coronary heart disease and cancer, at younger ages than women; women, on the other hand, suffer higher rates than men of certain chronic disorders such as autoimmune diseases, and short-term infectious diseases (Rieker and Bird 2005).

It is impossible to make many broad generalizations about the gendered patterns of specific diseases without paying attention to the impact of socioeconomic development. Access to resources affects health and longevity. In poorer countries, people are more vulnerable to illnesses that may be rare in developed countries— simply because preventive care is not available. Thus, for example, women's death from cervical cancer is far more common in low-income regions, where screening and treatment are less available, than in high-income countries, where such tests and treatment are routine. Almost 80 percent of deaths from cervical cancer occur in low-income countries (World Health Organization 2009). And in poorer countries, diseases of older age may be less prevalent than in richer countries—because people are more likely to die of something else before they have a chance to become old. Thus, for example, Alzheimer's disease and other dementias are the third leading cause of death for women in high-income countries, but are not even in the top ten causes of death for women in low- and middle-income countries (World Health Organization 2009).

In developed countries, a small number of major non-communicable diseases—heart disease, cancer, and stroke—are leading causes of death for both women and men (Rieker and Bird 2005); globally, these diseases, along with chronic respiratory diseases and diabetes, are the major non-communicable diseases that cause death (World Health Organization 2013a). Cardiovascular disease is the leading cause of death for both women and men globally, but it occurs at later ages for women than men. This later occurrence is thought to happen because, until menopause, women's estrogen levels serve a protective function against the build-up of the artery blocking plaque that can produce heart attacks. Also women are more likely than men to suffer from two specific types of heart disease: coronary microvascular disease, and broken heart syndrome (National

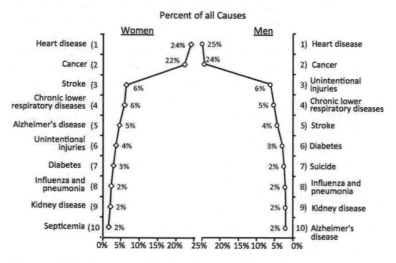

Figure 7.1: Ten leading causes of death in women and men in the United States. There are both strong similarities and notable differences in the leading causes of death for women and men. Whereas heart disease and cancer are by far the top killers of both sexes in the United States, men are more likely than women to die of unintentional injuries or of suicide, and women are more likely than men to die of Alzheimer's disease.

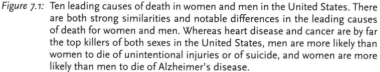

Source: Based on data from the U.S. Centers for Disease Control: Leading Causes of Death in Females, at : http://www.cdc.gov//women/lcod/2008/index.htm and Leading Causes of Death in Males, at http://www.cdc.gov//men/lcod/2009/index.htm

Heart, Lung, and Blood Institute 2011). For women, cardio-vascular disease is the leading cause of death in high income regions, but drops to second place in low income countries, where women are more likely to die of lower respiratory tract infections than of heart disease (World Health Organization 2009).

Cancer is more prevalent in higher income countries, with cancer rates of high income countries more than double those of low income countries. Breast cancer is the most common cancer among women and the leading cause of cancer deaths for them, followed by lung, stomach, colorectal and cervical cancers (World Health Organization 2013a).The incidence of breast cancer varies dramatically across regions of the world, from a rate of about 20 cases per 100,000 women in Eastern and Middle Africa to about 90 cases per 100,000 women in Western Europe (Cancer Research UK 2012). Since women diagnosed with breast cancer are far more likely to survive in developed countries than in less developed countries, there is less variation in mortality rates. For men, the most cancer deaths occur globally from lung, stomach, liver, colorectal, and oesophegial cancers (World Health Organization 2013a). Prostate cancer, which affects only men, accounts for 7 percent of cancer diagnoses and 3 percent of cancer deaths worldwide (Cancer Research UK 2012).

Autoimmune diseases, characterized by problems in the immune system that cause the body to attack its own organs, tissues, and cells, are far more likely to affect women than men. Most common among these diseases are multiple sclerosis, lupus, and rheumatoid arthritis. In the United States, nearly 80 percent of those suffering from autoimmune diseases are women, and these diseases comprise a leading cause of death for young and middle-aged women (National Institute of Allergy and Infectious Diseases 2012). Reasons for the greater susceptibility of women than men to autoimmune diseases are not well understood. Some researchers point to a possible protective effect conferred by androgens (hormones that are at higher levels in males than females) (Voskul 2011). New research suggests that an important contributing factor may be male–female differences in intestinal bacteria—differences which in some way affect hormone levels (Markle *et al.* 2013).Among the consequences of women's greater susceptibility to autoimmune diseases is that women are more likely to suffer from chronic pain. Ironically, women's complaints of pain are more likely than men's to be dismissed as emotional in origin and to be untreated, and clinical trials of pain medication have often omitted women (Edwards 2013).

Gender is also a factor in patterns of some infectious diseases, such as malaria, tuberculosis, and a variety of other diseases that are spread from person to person. In some cultures, girls are less likely than boys to be vaccinated against common diseases (Borooah 2004). Studies in Africa show that adolescent girls and pregnant women are particularly vulnerable to malaria; pregnant adolescents, who often face stigma and negative attitudes when they seek prenatal medical care, are especially vulnerable (World Health Organization 2007). Gender differences in sleeping arrangements, and the way labor is divided according to gender roles, may sometimes determine exposure to the mosquitoes that carry malaria. For instance, if women work outside before dawn, or if men do most of their work in the forest, their work may place them at high risk of being bitten by mosquitoes. Gender norms may also affect access to health care services when malaria is suspected. For example, a woman may need her husband's permission to visit a clinic, or a man may feel he cannot give priority to traveling to a clinic when he has economically important work to do close to home. Women often bear the heaviest burden of malaria and other tropical diseases because they have the main responsibility of caring for ill family members; however, they are often not the decision-makers with respect to treatment.

With respect to tuberculosis, the reported incidence is higher for men than for women. The reasons for this difference are poorly understood, but some analysts have suggested that, in those countries most heavily affected, the stigma of tuberculosis is seen as greater for women, discouraging them from seeking treatment (and thus from being diagnosed and counted). On the other hand, gender differences in certain behaviors may affect the progression of this disease. Smoking and alcohol abuse are linked to reduced immunity—and men are far more likely than women to smoke and abuse alcohol in the countries where tuberculosis is prevalent. Men are also less likely than women to complete treatment (World Health Organization 2002a). Clearly, gender-related norms, values and expectations can shape gendered patterns of illness in a multitude of complex ways. Some of these ways are explored in the following sections.

NUTRITION

Around the world, women are more likely than men to suffer from malnutrition. The reasons for this difference include the practice in some societies of giving priority to men and boys when food is available, and women's reduced access to the financial resources necessary to ensure food security. A large study in India showed that girls were less likely than boys to receive supplemental food and were more likely than boys to be malnourished. However, when mothers had higher individual status or lived in communities where women had higher status in general, this status apparently had a protective effect on their daughters, reducing the nutrition gap between boys and girls (Bose 2011).

Another factor contributing to women's higher levels of malnutrition is their greater need for dietary iron during reproductive years, when menstruation depletes iron, and for more protein when pregnant or breastfeeding (Food and Agriculture Organization of the United Nations n.d.). Unfortunately, when a mother is undernourished, it can set up a chain of events that causes malnutrition and its consequences to persist into future generations. An undernourished pregnant woman is more likely to die in childbirth or to give birth to an underweight baby, which may in turn lead to child mortality or serious illness, poor learning ability, and poor health and economic consequences as the child grows to adulthood (Oniang'o and Mukudi 2002).

A nutritional disadvantage for women can also be seen in older age groups. One study of homebound elders in the United States showed that, after controlling for health and demographic factors, women reported significantly lower nutrient intake than did men (Sharkey and Branch 2004). One US study showed that many elderly disabled women who report financial difficulties in acquiring food do not receive any food assistance; these women are more likely than their counterparts to experience poor quality of life, more medical conditions, and anemia (Klesges *et al.* 2001).

Where food is plentiful, women may still sometimes be more likely than men to be malnourished, perhaps because of their acceptance of the cultural notion that they must be thin. Women are more likely than men to be weight conscious and to restrict their food intake in order to lose weight (Aruguete *et al.* 2005; Yeung 2010). They are also more likely than men to emphasize the fat content of foods over nutrient levels when deciding which foods are healthy to eat (Oakes and Slotterback 2001).

STRESS

When external events or conditions are experienced as threatening or debilitating, they become stressors: sources of upset, worry, discomfort and general distress. Too much stress leads to negative health consequences; the onset of illness is often preceded by an increase in stress. Some researchers have tried to determine whether there are differences between women and men in the amount and type of stress they encounter in their environments.

Stressful life events may be unique occurrences, such as the death of a family member, loss of one's job, destruction of one's home, or being the victim of a physical attack. Stressful life conditions, on the other hand, are chronic situations that must be confronted day after day, such as food insecurity, fear of violence, overwork, or hostility from co-workers. Daily minor irritations, such as traffic, annoying telemarketing calls, or unexpected messes at home are a third cause of stress. Women tend to report higher levels of both chronic stress and minor daily stressors than men do; however, men and women report similar number of stressful life events (Matud 2004). Whereas women and men do not differ in the number of stressful life events, they may differ in the kinds of events they experience, in the magnitude and type of reaction to these events, and in their coping styles. Matud (2004) found, in a large sample of adults in Spain, that women were more likely to list family and health-related stressful events, and men were more likely to list relationship, financial, and work-related events. Women also rated their stressful life events as more negative and less controllable, and they scored higher than men on psychosomatic symptoms and psychological distress. These findings suggest that women were more affected than men by the stressors they experienced. Women were also more likely than men to use emotion-focused coping (trying to regulate their emotional responses to the situation) rather than problem-focused coping (trying to change the situation) to deal with stress.

Women are more likely than men to experience one category of stressor: sexist prejudice or discrimination. In one US sample, 99 percent of women said they had experienced a sexist event at least once in their lives; women of color reported more such incidents than Whites (Klonoff and Landrine 1995). Most common among such events were exposure to sexist or sexually degrading jokes, sexual harassment, sexist insults, and disrespectful treatment associated with being female. More than half the sample reported that being female had led to their being picked on, hit, shoved, or threatened; 40 percent said they had been denied a raise or promotion because they were women; and more than 19 percent said they had taken serious action such as filing a lawsuit or grievance because of sexist discrimination. Women's greater exposure to the stressor of sexist treatment may partially explain why they report higher rates of depressive, anxious, and somatic symptoms than men do. One survey of a sample of US students showed that women who reported experiencing frequent sexist treatment displayed significantly more such symptoms than men did, but women who reported little sexism did not differ from men on any of the symptoms measured (Klonoff and Landrine 2000).

HEALTH-RELATED BEHAVIORS ARE INFLUENCED BY GENDER STEREOTYPES

Women and men tend to differ in behaviors and attitudes linked to health outcomes. For example, women are more likely than men to engage in "preventive nutrition" by avoiding foods that are thought to be dangerous (Schüz et al. 2005). Female medical students display more positive attitudes than men toward using nutrition as a therapeutic tool (Schulman and Karney 2003). Where they have the resources, women are more likely than men to eat the recommended five servings per day of fruit and vegetables, and to be aware of the recommendations (Baker and Wardle 2003). How might these kinds of male–female differences in health behaviors be linked to gender socialization and expectations? Here are some possibilities. Part of the masculine role entails taking risks rather than being cautious. Part of the feminine role involves an orientation toward nurturing and care taking, which could encompass being knowledgeable about health issues. In many contexts it is more acceptable for women than for men to admit weakness, seek help, or take advice. And women are socialized more than men to be concerned about their bodies.

Smoking

All over the world, men are far more likely than women to use tobacco, with an average prevalence of 40 percent for men vs. nearly 9 percent for women (World Health Organization 2010b). The gender disparity is smallest in the Americas and Europe. Historically, in most countries men have been first to adopt the practice of smoking—a pattern that has been reinforced by gender roles that have traditionally deemed smoking unfeminine or unladylike. For example, the World Health Organization (2003) cites a study in Vietnam in which the most common reason given by women for avoiding tobacco was not health concerns, but that "women shouldn't smoke." For boys, on the other hand, smoking often represents masculinity and may form an important aspect of social relationships among males. Smoking advertisements tend to bolster this notion, with portrayals of men smoking while in rough terrain, undertaking adventurous or strenuous activities, and wearing rugged clothing.

Tobacco companies have targeted girls and women, particularly in developing countries, with the message that smoking is sophisticated, sexy, and associated with breaking barriers for women's roles. Furthermore, cultural emphasis on thinness for women adds to the pressure to use tobacco; many young women report that they start or continue smoking in order to avoid weight gain. In fact, women seem to gain more weight than men do after quitting smoking. Perhaps for these reasons, tobacco use appears to be increasing among girls in some countries, particularly in Asia and the Pacific region (World Health Organization 2010b).

For women more than for men, smoking appears to be associated with avoiding depression and other negative emotions (Richardson *et al.* 2012); for men, smoking is more linked to positive sensations and habit. Some studies show that it is harder for women than men to quit smoking—perhaps because they rely on it to cope with stress (Legleye *et al.* 2011; World Health Organization 2010b).

Smoking is responsible for the majority of cases of lung cancer, and is implicated in many cases of heart disease and other illnesses. As smoking rates have risen among women, the rates of lung cancer have followed, with about a 30-year lag (Weiss 1997). In the United States, the prevalence of cigarette smoking peaked for men in 1940, remained steady until 1955, and then began to

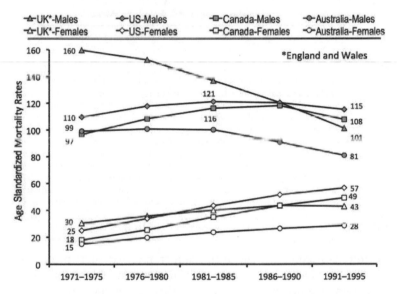

Figure 7.2: Patterns in lung cancer mortality rates by gender in four countries. Changes in lung cancer mortality rates among women and men are an example of how changes in gendered patterns of behavior can affect health. In all four countries shown here, there was a trend for lung cancer mortality rates to begin dropping among men as the delayed impact of a drop in the percentage of men who smoke took effect. For women, on the other hand, lung cancer mortality rates continued to increase steadily, reflecting a rise in women's smoking that peaked years later than the peak for men.

Source: Based on data from Table 1 in Liaw *et al.* (2005), Patterns of Lung Cancer Mortality in 23 Countries: Application of the age-period-cohort model, *BMC Public Health, 5*, online at http://www.ncbi.nlm.nih.gov/pmc/articles/PMC555565/ .

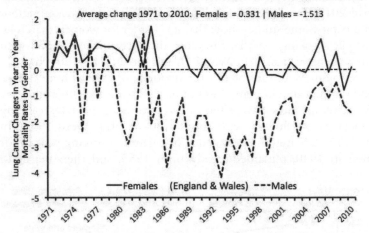

Values-lines above "0" indicate increasing mortality rates from one year to another
Values-lines below "0" indicate decreasing mortality rates from one year to another

Figure 7.3: Changes in lung cancer mortality rates in England and Wales. A detailed look at changes over time in women's and men's lung cancer mortality rates in England and Wales shows the overall tendency for women's rates to increase and men's to decrease between 1971 and 2010. The fact that most of the values for women fall above the "0" line shows that the mortality rate for women increased almost every year, although there was considerable variation in the amount of increase from year to year. Conversely, the fact that most of the values for men fall below the "0" line shows that the mortality rate for men decreased almost every year, again with considerable variation from year to year. Researchers have concluded that the increasing mortality rate for women and the decreasing mortality rate for men is a long-term consequence of changes in gendered patterns of smoking behavior.

Source: Based on data from Cancer Research UK (2010), *Lung cancer mortality statistics* (Figure 2.2), at http://www.cancerresearchuk.org/cancer-info/cancerstats/types/lung/mortality/.

decline; consequently, the lung cancer rate for men peaked in 1990 and then began to drop. For women, whose smoking increased steadily from no higher than 2 percent in 1930 to 38 percent in 1960 and then dropped more slowly than men's, lung cancer mortality began to rise about 1965. Women's mortality rate from lung cancer has increased sixfold since 1950; lung cancer overtook breast cancer as the leading cause of death for women in the United States in the 1980s and remains a more frequent cause of death for US women (National Center for Health Statistics 2012). Compared to men, women may develop lung cancer with lower levels of smoking and are more likely to contract aggressive small cell lung cancer. Tobacco use is also especially problematic for women because their bodies metabolize nicotine more quickly if they are pregnant or using oral contraceptives (World Health Organization 2010b).

Alcohol and other drugs

Multinational studies show a consistent tendency for men more than women to use alcohol and drink heavily, and for women more than men to abstain from alcohol or give up drinking (Wilsnack *et al.* 2009). The use and abuse of drugs other than alcohol show some similarities to the patterns for alcohol. Illicit drug use and dependence is higher among males (Substance Abuse and Mental Health Services Administration 2012). The reasons for women's lower levels of alcohol and illicit drug consumption may include cultural norms that are more tolerant of male than female intoxication, and that emphasize restraint as a sign of appropriate femininity. Another partial explanation, in some contexts, may be men's greater access to money to spend on alcohol and drugs and the freedom to go out and indulge. The importance of such cultural factors is made clear by the large variation among countries in women's and men's drinking behavior. For example, one 35-country study reported rates of current drinking that ranged from 97 percent of men and 94 percent of women in Denmark to 37 percent of men and 3 percent of women in the Indian state of Karnataka (Wilsnack *et al.* 2009).

Although women drink less alcohol than men, they typically achieve higher blood alcohol concentrations than men even when they consume the same amount (Mumenthaler *et al.* 1999). This means women are likely to experience alcohol-related problems at lower levels of drinking than men. For example, studies have shown that college women reported blackouts at the same rate as men, even though they drank less (White, Jamieson-Drake and Swartzwelder 2002), and that they experienced alcohol-related physical illnesses with lower levels of drinking than men (Nolen-Hoeksema 2004).

Thus women and men may be at risk of different consequences of drinking, and these consequences may be shaped both by differences in the ways their bodies respond to alcohol and by differences in gender norms and expectations. One study examined gender differences in the consequences of drinking, after controlling for the reported amount of alcohol consumed per week and the estimated average blood alcohol level of participants. They found that, even after accounting for these variables, women who drank alcohol had a higher risk than men of developing tolerance for higher levels of alcohol, blacking out, passing out, drinking after promising not to, and getting injured. Men, on the other hand, had a higher risk than women of damaging property and going to school drunk (Sugarman, DeMartini and Carey 2009). For women in some contexts, a dangerous consequence of binge drinking is an increased vulnerability to rape (McCauley, Calhoun and Gidycz 2010). Another consequence unique to women is danger to a developing fetus of maternal alcohol use (Tsai *et al.* 2007).

Risk-taking

Men tend to engage in more physically risky behaviors than women (Byrnes, Miller and Schaffer 1999)—perhaps because taking risks is part of stereotypic masculinity (Brannon 1976). Men may use risk-taking to signal their masculinity to potential mates; for example, one study showed that young men were more likely to take risks when sexually aroused and in the presence of a romantically available woman (Baker and Maner 2009). Men seem to build up masculine "capital" by engaging in activities traditionally considered masculine. Such masculinity points might be used to bolster a man's perceived masculinity and compensate for non-masculine behaviors (de Visser and McDonnell 2013). Thus, for example, a man might be able to compensate for being a non-drinker if he takes other kinds of risks, is a good athlete, or is known to be heterosexually active.

The orientation toward risk can make men, especially certain groups of men, particularly vulnerable to accidental injury and death. For example, young working class men in Australia have been found to be very attached to a risk-heavy masculine automobile culture, which emphasizes male power and tends to exclude women (Walker, Butland and Connell 2000). Attempts to fit in with these cultural norms may encourage young men to speed, avoid seat belt use, drive while intoxicated, and engage in other risky behaviors that can lead to disastrous results. Indeed, each year almost three times as many boys and men as girls and women die from road traffic accidents around the world (World Health Organization 2002b).

For women, health-related risky behaviors may often be focused around body change strategies, such as extreme dieting or cosmetic surgery. Such behaviors are not often discussed in the framework of "risk-taking," and are less public and/or social than the kinds of risks associated with masculinity. Thus they may be overlooked when researchers try to make gender comparisons in risky behaviors.

Risky sexual behaviors

Having more sexual partners exposes an individual to increased risk of sexually transmitted disease, and it may also increase the likelihood of sexual victimization, particularly for women, by raising the probability of encountering an assaultive partner. Men appear more likely than women to engage in unprotected sex with multiple partners (Nkansah-Amankra et al. 2011). In some cultural contexts, having plenty of sex with multiple women is seen as an important aspect of masculinity (Bowleg et al. 2011; Simpson 2007).

For both women and men, one of the predictors of sexual risk-taking and other forms of health risk behaviors is a history of sexual assault. Women who have been sexually assaulted report higher levels of depression and anxiety and also more dangerous drinking and risky sexual behavior than do other women (McCauley et al. 2009; Orcutt, Cooper and Garcia 2005). In one diverse sample of US college women, women in all ethnic groups appeared to use risky sexual behavior as a way of coping with the depression and anxiety caused by sexual assault (Littleton et al. 2013). Research on male college students in the United States revealed that sexual victimization was linked to higher levels of sexual risk-taking behaviors and higher levels of problem drinking (Turchik 2012).

Exercise and fitness

In every age group, men are more likely than women to engage in the levels of regular physical activity recommended to maintain health—although the majority of members of both groups do not meet minimum guidelines in developed countries (Centers for Disease Control and Prevention 2012; Zach *et al.* 2013). Men's greater levels of participation in exercise may stem partly from gender stereotypes and norms that emphasize strength and activity for men more than for women. Linked to these stereotypes are differences in encouragement and opportunities for women and men in the realm of sports and fitness. For example, for many years, the running of marathons was considered something women could not and should not do. It was 1972 before women were allowed to compete in the famous Boston Marathon (although Roberta Gibb sneaked onto the field and completed the race in 1966 and Kathrine Switzer made a famous "unofficial" run in 1967 by registering for the race as K. V. Switzer and nonchalantly lining up with the men). There was no marathon race for women included in the Summer Olympics until 1984 (Lovett 1997). And although women have been engaged in ski-jumping for many years, only in 2014 will women's ski-jumping be included as an Olympic sport for the first time (Thomas 2011).

In countries where there are strong sanctions against women's bodies being seen by unrelated men, the restrictions on women's opportunities for exercise and sports participation have been even more stringent. For example, in some Muslim majority countries, female athletes must abide by very modest dress codes and are not permitted to join in mixed-gender fitness classes. Female athletes in these countries have adjusted by wearing a variety of very modest fitness clothing, adopting forms of exercise that allow for comfortable clothing (or solitude) and flocking to single-sex gyms and women-only beaches (Moaveni 2009). When accommodations are made for dress codes, some Muslim women have made their mark in international competitive sports. For example, an Iranian skier, Marjan Kalhor, participated in the 2010 Winter Olympics wearing a uniform that covered her body completely, and female boxers from Afghanistan have worn the hijab in competitions sponsored by the International Boxing Association

(WISE 2010). Nonetheless, Muslim women face many more barriers to exercise and fitness than do their male counterparts.

HIV/AIDS AND OTHER SEXUALLY TRANSMITTED DISEASES

Women make up more than half of the 34 million people around the world who are infected with human immunodeficiency virus (HIV), and HIV/AIDS is reported to be the leading cause of death worldwide among women of reproductive age (National Institute of Allergy and Infectious Diseases 2012). Globally, among young people aged 15 to 24, women's rates of HIV infection are twice as high as men's (UNAIDS 2012). Both biology and gender-related norms and power relations contribute to the high prevalence of this disease among women. During heterosexual intercourse, women are at higher risk than men for transmission of HIV and some other sexually transmitted infections, partly because the mucous membranes of the female reproductive tract receive substantial and protracted exposure to any virus present in seminal fluid. Women's biological vulnerability is magnified, moreover, by cultural factors: their exposure to rape, to pressure by partners to have sex without the protection of condoms, and by their frequent lack of control over high-risk behaviors of their partners—who may have unprotected sex or use intravenous drugs with shared needles (Higgins, Hoffman and Dworkin 2010). For similar reasons, women are also more vulnerable than men to a variety of other sexually transmitted diseases such as human papilloma virus (HPV), trichomoniasis, genital herpes, and chlamydia.

Men's vulnerability to HIV/AIDS is increased under conditions such as homelessness and incarceration. In the United States, for example, where the overwhelming majority of prisoners are Black men, the rate of AIDS is three times higher in the prison population than in the general population (Sabol, Couture and Harrison 2007). Interestingly, however, in some contexts men's wealth and income are positively related to HIV risk—perhaps because these resources are linked to the ability to have more leisure time, spend more on alcohol and drugs, and acquire more sexual partners. In some sub-Saharan African countries, adults in the wealthiest segments of the population have been found to have the highest prevalence of HIV (Mishra *et al.* 2007).

The impact of HIV/AIDS differs by gender. For one thing, pregnant women who are HIV positive can transmit the virus to their newborns during pregnancy, childbirth or breastfeeding— something that occurs from 15 to 45 percent of the time in the absence of effective interventions (World Health Organization 2013b). Women are also impacted in particular ways because of gender inequalities in accessing health care. The World Health Organization (2013c) notes that women may face barriers to HIV prevention and treatment because of a lack of resources, childcare responsibilities, and restrictions on their mobility and decision-making power. Men, on the other hand, may avoid seeking HIV prevention or treatment services because of fear of stigma, worry about losing their jobs, or concern that they may be perceived as weak or unmanly.

REPRODUCTIVE HEALTH AND MATERNAL MORTALITY

It is in the realm of reproductive health that differences in health-related issues between women and men are most stark, since women deal with pregnancy, childbirth, and the complications associated with these processes, and are also concerned with preventing or terminating pregnancies. Maternal mortality is a major health issue in the developing world, complicated in some cases by female genital cutting procedures that, besides their inherent dangers, leave women vulnerable to terrible injuries when giving birth. In developed countries, too, reproductive health issues impact women and men quite differently, particularly in terms of access to contraception and abortion.

Contraception and abortion

The availability of reliable ways to prevent pregnancy has a significant impact on individual heterosexual relationships and on the broader picture of male–female relations. In 2010, the fiftieth anniversary of the birth-control pill, analysts opined that it was the pill that changed women's lives (e.g. Rubin 2010). The large impact came because women taking the pill could control their reproduction, even without the knowledge and/or consent of their partners—a significant shift in the balance of power within relationships. Even if women were in relationships where they had little choice about whether to have sex, they at least did not have to face a series of unwanted pregnancies. This was a dramatic change from earlier decades, when women often bore more children than they wanted, could afford, or had the health and strength to nurture. And the development of better pills and contraceptive methods over the intervening years—now including morning-after pills—has increased women's options in this regard.

Around the world, however, in 2008 about 11 percent of women aged 15 to 49, who were married or in sexual relationships and who wanted to avoid a pregnancy, either did not have access to, or were not using, any effective method of contraception. In Africa, the unmet need for contraception was 25 percent (World Health Organization 2013d). Even where contraception is theoretically available (though perhaps not very affordable or accessible), it is not always used. In the United States, about one of every ten women who are at risk from an unintended pregnancy do not use any form of contraception; this proportion rises to almost one in five among those aged 15 to 19 (Mosher and Jones 2010).

Contraceptive methods for men have emphasized the condom and sterilization through vasectomy. The approaches have not advanced significantly for years, perhaps because, since it is women who get pregnant, women have seemed to be the most appropriate target for intervening in the process. However, there are recent reports of a possible new, reversible method of male contraception (so far tested only on mice) that uses a molecular approach to reduce sperm numbers and motility without affecting hormone levels (Matzuk et al. 2012). If such a method were successfully developed, it might increase the proportion of men who take on the major responsibility for contraception.

When contraception is unavailable or fails, women faced with unintended pregnancies may turn to abortion. In the United States, where abortion is legal, there were 16 abortions reported per 1,000 women of reproductive age in 2008, with highest rates for women aged 20 to 29 (Pazol et al. 2011). It is rare for these abortions to end in death or serious injury for the women involved; however, in developing countries, grim statistics reveal that abortion is often unsafe for women when carried out under illegal or unsanitary conditions. Worldwide, approximately 13 percent of maternal deaths (about 67,000 per year) can be traced to abortion-related complications—and almost all of these deaths occur in developing countries (World Health Organization Regional Office for Africa 2010).

Pregnancy, childbirth, and maternal health

The vast majority of women experience pregnancy at some point in their lives. Pregnancy and its outcomes and complications provide the single most obvious set of reasons why women may require health care. Life-threatening complications include severe bleeding during or after childbirth, infections, and problems linked to hypertension, heart disease, diabetes, and botched abortions.

For women in the developed world, pregnancy and childbirth are relatively safe. For example, in 2010 a woman's lifetime risk of death associated with complications of pregnancy or childbirth was one in 5,200 in Canada, one in 4,600 in the United Kingdom, and one in 2,400 in the United States (the highest rate for any industrialized country). In Afghanistan, however, the risk of maternal death was 1 in 32; in Somalia, it was 1 in 16 (World Health Organization, UNICEF, UNFPA and The World Bank, 2012). Although the number of maternal deaths decreased 47 percent worldwide from 1990 to 2010, about 800 women per day were dying in 2010, mainly in low-income countries. Poverty is a key factor in maternal mortality: research across developing countries shows a consistent link between increasing poverty and an increasing proportion of women dying from pregnancy-related causes (Paruzzolo *et al.* 2010). Within the developed countries too, maternal deaths are more common among women who lack economic resources and access to good medical care. In the United States, for example, pregnancy related deaths are more than twice as high for African American women than for other women (Centers for Disease Control and Prevention 2013) and are highest in regions of the country with high poverty rates and high immigrant populations (Singh 2010).

The health risks of pregnancy and childbirth are especially high for teenaged women, who are more likely than older women to die from maternal causes. In fact, very young mothers (aged 10 to 14 years) have maternal mortality rates up to five times those of women in their early twenties (Save the Children 2004). This consideration, along with concerns about the ability of very young mothers—particularly if they are single mothers—to provide and care for children has driven efforts to reduce teen birth rates in many countries. In the United States, a 44 percent decline in teen birth rates from 1991 to 2010, to a historic low of 34.3 births per 1,000 women aged 15 to 19, was recently announced with relief and pride by health officials (Hamilton and Ventura 2012). However, in some low income countries, women are expected to marry and begin childbearing at very young ages, often without having any power to refuse such arrangements; by some estimates, about one in every ten births around the world is to a mother who is still a child (Save the Children 2004). Among teenaged mothers in developing countries, complications of pregnancy and childbirth are the leading cause of death—and babies born to such young women also have a lower risk of survival (Save the Children 2004). In contexts where gender norms prescribe that women be kept subservient to men and not given the opportunities for education and income that would allow them more options for controlling their futures and delaying marriage and motherhood, this pattern is likely to persist.

Female genital mutilation

A traditional practice in some cultures involves a rite of passage in which a girl's genital area is cut. Sometimes called female circumcision, female genital mutilation is a cultural practice that is apparently rooted in the notion that women's sexuality is dangerous and must be controlled. As one official commented to a reporter, "It is necessary to control women's sexual urges. They must be chaste to preserve their beauty" (Haworth 2012, par. 4). In some cases, the clitoris and labia are excised completely and the genital area is sewn up; in others the clitoris and labia are partially removed. Millions of girls are affected; for example, researchers in Indonesia found that in 2010 between 86 and 100 percent of households surveyed said their daughters were subjected to genital cutting (Haworth 2012). It is estimated that in Africa 101 million girls currently aged ten years and older have undergone female genital mutilation (World Health Organization 2013e).

This procedure, which is carried out both to ensure and later to demonstrate that a girl grows into a sexually virtuous woman, is dangerous and painful, and later interferes with the woman's sexual pleasure. Furthermore, this genital cutting and sewing often creates a smaller vaginal opening, leading to obstructed labor when the woman later gives birth. Obstructed labor can produce a dangerous condition called obstetric fistula: a hole torn in the birth canal. Without repair, the fistula leads to unrelenting urinary incontinence and the possibility of infection—and the sufferer is often shamed and segregated in her community (World Health Organization 2010c).

Male circumcision, which involves surgical removal of the foreskin of the penis when the boy is a few days old, also affects millions. This procedure too has its roots in cultural and religious traditions (both Jewish and Muslim), and has sometimes been thought to improve the cleanliness of the penis. Although the research is mixed, male circumcision (unlike the procedures described above for females) may confer some potential health benefits: prevention of urinary tract infections, penile cancer, and transmission of some sexually transmitted infections (American Academy of Pediatrics 2012). International clinical trials in Africa demonstrated that men who had been randomly assigned to be circumcised had significantly lower incidence of HIV infection than control groups of men randomly assigned to be circumcised at the end of the study (Byakika-Tusiime 2008). Unlike female genital mutilation, male circumcision does not typically have any deleterious effects on sexual pleasure or expose boys to the risk of serious health problems or death.

DEPRESSION AND SUICIDE

Women and men have similar overall levels of mental health, but they differ in the frequency with which they experience specific conditions: women are more likely to experience depression and anxiety disorders; men are likely to show substance abuse, antisocial behavior, and to commit suicide (Rieker and Bird 2005). Although there is little doubt that women are more likely than men to be depressed, part of the difference in diagnosis rates may be due to gender-related stereotypes and expectations. When women and men score similarly on measures of depressive symptoms, women are more likely than men to be diagnosed as depressed by their primary care physician (Bertakis *et al.* 2001).

Beginning in adolescence, women are about twice as likely as men to be diagnosed as depressed—a ratio that seems to hold all over the world (Nolen-Hoeksema 2006; Kuehner 2003). A number of explanations have been posited for this gender difference, some focusing on the amount and kinds of distress experienced by women and men, and some focusing on how that distress is handled. Women may experience different kinds of stressors than men, or may, because of biological and socialization differences, be more likely than men to react to stress in ways that lead to depression (Nolen-Hoeksema 2006). With respect to the way women and men cope with distress, a major focus has been on rumination: focusing on and thinking about problems. Women and girls are more likely than men and boys to ruminate when they are distressed—and people who tend to ruminate when they are distressed experience more depressive symptoms and are more likely to develop major depression (McLaughlin and Nolen-Hoeksema 2011).

Social support from peers and friends is thought to buffer the effects of stress and reduce the likelihood of depression. However, one group of researchers was puzzled by the pattern that, even though adolescent girls report more supportive peer relationships than boys do, they also have higher rates of depression. Upon investigation, they discovered that adolescent girls were more likely than boys to spend time co-ruminating with their close friends—focusing their conversations mainly on problems and negative emotions (Stone *et al.* 2011). They also found that higher levels of co-rumination were associated with more, longer, and more severe episodes of depression among the sample of adolescents they studied. The causes of gender differences in rumination and co-rumination may lie in the different ways girls and boys are socialized. For example, girls apparently expect that disclosing problems to friends will make them feel cared for and understood, whereas boys expect to feel like they are wasting time (Rose *et al.* 2012)—a difference that may be rooted in early parent–child interactions that emphasize conversation for girls more than boys.

Although women are more likely than men to be depressed and to think about and attempt suicide (Nock *et al.* 2008), men are more likely than women to actually commit suicide (e.g. Powell, 2013; World Health Organization 2011a). The ratio of male to female suicides varies widely among countries, with, for example, the number of male suicides for every female suicide being 3.9 in the United States, 3.3 in Australia, 1.8 in Korea, and 2.7 in Japan (Hee Ahn *et al.* 2012). Some research suggests a narrowing of the gender difference in certain places. For example, in Canada, suicide rates appear to have been increasing in female children and adolescents and decreasing in male children and adolescents over the past three decades (Skinner and McFaull 2012). For both males and females, having been a victim of sexual assault is linked to increased likelihood of suicide attempts (Tomasula *et al.* 2012).

Some different factors may push women and men toward suicide. One South African study found, for example, that men tended to take their own lives as a means of escape when their ideals of masculinity, dominance and success were thwarted, whereas women committed suicide to protest against miserable conditions in their lives—often caused by the dominance of the men around them (Niehaus 2012). Perpetrators of a particular type of suicide—murder-suicide—in the United States are overwhelmingly male, most often use guns, and most often target family members, although a smaller group targets strangers in "rampage killings" before committing suicide (Violence Policy Center 2012). These statistics appear to fit with the idea of suicide growing out of rage and frustration at being unable to succeed in controlling a situation—as a man is supposed to be able to do—and/or the desire to escape failure by going out in a blaze of "masculine" glory. However, there is very little actual research to confirm or dispute this interpretation.

The gender differences in completed suicides obviously do not parallel gender differences in depression, and researchers have struggled to comprehend the underlying factors. Some have suggested that men are more likely than women to have access to very lethal tools for suicide, that is, firearms (Hee Ahn *et al.* 2012). Others have studied personality traits as precursors of suicide. For example, one team of researchers found higher levels of stoicism and sensation-seeking among male than female US college students—and they showed that these traits are linked to the two major facets of a construct labeled acquired capability for suicide: pain insensitivity and fearlessness about death (Witte *et al.* 2012). Both stoicism, defined as the tendency to deny, suppress and control emotion, and sensation-seeking, defined as the propensity to behave in ways that court risk, including risk of death, form key aspects of traditional ideals of masculinity. These findings suggest one way in which socialization to the masculine role may make men more vulnerable than women to suicide.

ACCESS TO MEDICAL CARE

When access to medical care is readily available, women are more likely than men to consult with physicians for physical and mental health issues. When female patients seek health care, the interactions with their physicians tend to place more emphasis on preventive care and less on physical examination and discussions about the use of alcohol and tobacco (Bertakis and Azari 2007). One explanation for the differences appears to be the constraints of the masculine gender role. One US study shows that both men and women consider seeing a doctor for minor health concerns or consulting a psychologist or psychiatrist for emotional issues as not masculine behaviors (de Visser and McDonnell 2013).

Access to medical care is often not readily available, however, because of a lack of resources. Among older Americans, women have greater health care needs but fewer economic resources than men—and in this population, women have fewer physician visits and hospital stays than men with similar health profiles (Cameron *et al.* 2010). There is considerable evidence of gender disparities in access to care, screening, treatment decisions, and follow-up care. Even in Canada, a country with universally accessible, publicly funded health care, gender has been found to be a reliable predictor of having an unmet health care need (Bryant, Leaver and Dunn 2009). In the United States, one recent review points out that women are often less likely than men to have reliable health insurance coverage, are less likely than men to be screened for colon cancer, less likely to receive certain proactive treatment for arthritic disability, less likely to receive bypass surgery for heart disease, receive less thorough examinations and follow-up when they enter hospital with chest pain, and are frequently omitted from clinical trials (Travis, Howerton and Szymanski 2012). These authors suggest that gender stereotypes and benevolent sexism may account for some of the gender disparities in decisions about medical treatment. For example, women may be deemed too frail, compared to men, to undergo certain procedures—even though such procedures may be as potentially beneficial for them as for men. Health care providers may thus tend to frame treatment options more in terms of risk when dealing with female patients, leading to a bias in terms of conservative treatment. And physicians whose prototypical heart attack patient is a middle-aged man may be slow to diagnose a heart attack in a middle-aged woman, even though women who have a heart attack are actually more likely than men to die (Travis, Meltzer and Howerton 2010).

In the developing world as well, gender inequities in access to health care are often linked to gendered norms, stereotypes and the allocation of resources. For example, women often lack economic support for seeking treatment for themselves or their children, and may sometimes have to defy the opinions of male family members in order to do so. And in some settings, women may be reluctant to deal with male health care workers (World Health Organization 2007). On the other hand, men sometimes use health care services less than women do when significant commitments of time and energy, such as walking long distances to a clinic, are involved. Men may not assign high enough priority to their health to invest so much time and energy in obtaining treatment—or perhaps masculinity ideology makes it embarrassing to appear to place so much emphasis on obtaining help.

It appears clear that attempts to understand gendered patterns of health must go beyond biological differences between women and men. Gendered cultural norms, expectations, and restrictions play a significant role in shaping threats to, and supports for, individuals' wellbeing. The lifelong impact of these cultural forces culminates in the way older age is experienced by men and women, as seen in the next chapter.

FOR FURTHER EXPLORATION

Chrisler, J.C. (ed.) (2012). *Reproductive Justice: a global concern*. (Santa Barbara, CA: Praeger.) Contributions from social scientists in many different countries examine a variety of issues related to reproductive health. Included are chapters on partner selection, power in partner relationships, genital cutting, sexual assault, trafficking and sexual exploitation, contraception and abortion, pregnancy, birthing, and public policy for reproductive justice.

Bird, Chloe E. and Rieker, P. P. (2008). *Gender and Health: the effect of constrained choices and social policies*. (New York: Cambridge University Press.) These sociologist authors examine ways in which gender differences in health may be constructed by social arrangements and societal norms and laws with respect to gender. They include discussions of the impact of gendered work and family patterns, community supports, and gender-differentiated pressures toward particular individual health choices.

Jack, Dana C. and Ali, Alisha A. (eds) (2010). *Silencing the Self Across Cultures: depression and gender in the social world*. (Oxford, UK: Oxford University Press.) The editors have gathered the perspectives of 21 contributors from 13 countries to examine the social and psychological aspects of gender differences in depression. The contributions include consideration of such factors as relationships, drugs, self-censorship, immigration, violence, and illness in the development of gendered patterns of depression in different cultural contexts.

8

THE SHAPE OF OUR FUTURE: GENDER AND THE AGING POPULATION

Aging represents the future—not only for each of us as individuals, but for many facets of our collective experience within culture. As it happens, each of us is getting older, but also we are currently in a situation in which the world's population is shifting toward an older average age. Like so many other things, the experience of aging is shaped by gender roles and expectations. Some analysts have written about a "double standard of aging," by which older women in North America are judged as unattractive, less feminine and frail, whereas older men are judged distinguished, still masculine, and wise (Deutsch, Zalenski and Clark 1986; Sontag 1979). On the other hand, some researchers have identified a mellowing of gender stereotypes with older age, so that women become more comfortable with agency, power, and authority as they age (e.g. Stewart, Ostrove and Helson 2001), whereas men become more nurturing and less concerned with dominance and competition (Sinnott and Shifren 2001; Villereal and Cavazos 2005). All this is of particular interest to gender scholars because women live longer than men—so there is an increasing majority of women as we consider older age groups.

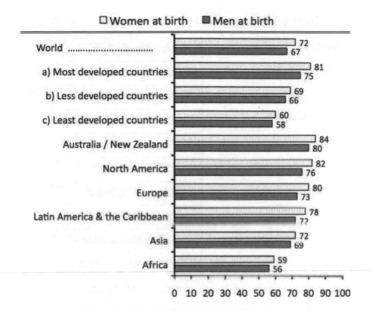

Figure 8.1: Life expectancy at birth for women and men. In all regions of the world, women's life expectancy at birth is longer than that of men. However, the difference is smaller in poorer countries.

Source: Based on data from United Nations Population Fund (2012).

CHANGING DEMOGRAPHICS: AN AGING POPULATION MEANS MORE WOMEN

In all regions and countries of the world, the proportion of people aged 60 and older is increasing. An historic threshold was crossed when, in 2000, the world's population had more people over the age of 60 than under the age of 5; by 2050 it is projected that 65 countries will have more than 30 percent of their population over the age of 60 (United Nations Population Fund 2012).

As noted in the previous chapter, women's life expectancy is longer than men's. Thus women make up the majority of persons in older age brackets, and that majority increases in size at increasing age. Worldwide, there are only 84 men for every 100 women aged 60 or over—and only 61 men for every 100 women aged 80 or over. These ratios vary somewhat by region; for example, at age 80 there are 57 men for every woman in North

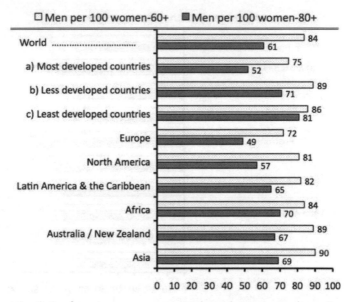

Figure 8.2: Ratio of men to women among people aged sixty years and over. Because women live longer than men, on average, there are more women than men in older segments of the population. Women outnumber men among seniors aged sixty years and over, and the proportion of women to men increases with age.

Source: Based on data from United Nations Population Fund (2012).

America, 37 men for every woman in Eastern Europe, and 64 men for every woman in Eastern Asia (United Nations Population Fund 2012). By the time they reach older age, women and men have been affected by the cumulative impact of years of differential treatment and access to resources and opportunities. Thus it is not surprising if their experiences of old age are different on many dimensions, including work, health, and relationships.

WORK AND THE GENDERED ECONOMICS OF AGING: WHO CAN AFFORD A RESTFUL RETIREMENT?

Global statistics reveal that 47 per cent of men and 23.8 per cent of women over 60 are participating in the labor force (United Nations Population Fund 2012). These proportions differ from country to country; for example, in the United States in 2009 more than 26 percent of women aged 65 to 69 and 15 percent of women aged 70 to 74 were in the civilian labor force (US Bureau of Labor Statistics 2009b). In the much poorer country of Malawi, on the other hand, the labor force participation rates for both men and women aged 65 and over are well over 90 percent (United Nations Population Fund 2012).

In recent years the proportion of women working past traditional retirement age has increased more than the proportion of men doing the same. According to the US Bureau of Labor Statistics (2008), older women are increasingly likely to be in the labor market. In the 30 years between 1977 and 2007, the labor force participation of women aged 65 and older increased by 147 percent, while that of men increased by only 75 percent. The rates of increase have continued to be different: between 2000 and 2009, a period when employment levels were relatively flat for both women and men aged 16 and older, the employment of women 65 and older rose by 161 percent, whereas the employment of similar-aged men rose by 142 percent (US Bureau of Labor Statistics 2010b). In 2012 Great Britain, 15 percent of women aged 65 to 69, and 2.8 percent of women aged 70 and older were employed full- or part-time; for men the comparable percentages were 24.3 and 6.2 (Office for National Statistics 2013).

Why might the proportion of older women in the workforce be increasing more rapidly than the proportion of men? One possibility is that, because of their disproportionate share of family responsibilities, many women joined the workforce later or had more gaps in their workforce participation than men did, leaving them not ready to retire "on schedule" because they were still building their careers. Another possibility is that, having put in fewer years of work and been paid lower salaries, women are less likely than men to have the economic resources to retire.

One thing that is clear is that a gender wage gap persists among older workers. For example, in the United States in 1979 older women's median weekly earnings were 77.6 percent of men's; 28 years later, in 2007, the women's earnings were still only 77.8 percent of men's. In 2011, the most recent year for which statistics are currently available, women aged 65 and over earned 80.1 percent of what similar-aged men earned (US Bureau of Labor Statistics 2012b). The wage gap increases with age among US women aged 15 to 64. In 2009 women in the 15-24 age range earned just over 89 percent of similar-aged men's earnings; women in the 55-64 age group earned only 60.8 percent of what similar-aged men earned; and women aged 65-74 earned only 56 percent of similar-aged men's earnings (US Census Bureau 2010).

The cumulative impact of the gender wage gap over many years of work means that women are more likely than men to have insufficient resources when they approach retirement. The situation is exacerbated by the fact that women are less likely than men to have adequate pension coverage (Renga, Molnar-Hidassy and Tisheva 2010). Traditionally, state-funded pensions were not designed to be directly available to persons who had not made contributions while in the workforce—meaning that women who spent much of their lives in homemaking roles could access pension income only through their spouses. Women are also less likely to be in jobs that provide private pensions, and because they may have put in fewer years in the workforce, have had less time to accumulate pension contributions and retirement savings. In some countries, such as the United Kingdom, the age at which women could start receiving a state pension has traditionally been lower (60) than men's (65). For all the reasons listed above, this difference makes little sense and, in some cases, may well harm women's chances of accumulating reasonable retirement savings by leading them to retire too soon. As part of a controversial overhaul of state pensions, the retirement age for women is gradually being raised to match men's in the UK, leading women to stay employed longer (BBC News 2013).

The problems with inadequate pensions and retirement income for women exist worldwide. In the United States, retired women are significantly more likely than their male counterparts to depend on Social Security payments as their only source of income (US Government Accountability Office 2012). In Britain, one study showed that, among employed women, about 45 percent of White women, more than 50 percent of Indian women, and more than 60 percent of Pakistani and Bangladeshi women had no private pensions (Department for Work and Pensions 2005). One study in Bangladesh shows that only 10 percent of retirees who receive a pension based on worker contributions are women, and many governments provide no old age security pensions to elders (United Nations Population Fund 2012). Furthermore, women's longer life expectancy means that they must stretch their already smaller retirement savings over a longer period than men must. All this adds up to considerable worry for women. The European Social Survey (2010) showed that in almost all countries surveyed women were more concerned than men that their retirement income would be inadequate to support them through their old age.

Whether or not they can afford a "restful retirement," many elders spend their early old age making large and important contributions to their families and communities through unpaid work. A decade ago, for example, the Australian government calculated that, among those in the 65 to 74 age range, women contributed 16 billion dollars per year in unpaid caregiving and voluntary work, while men contributed 10 billion dollars per year (de Vaus, Gray and Stanton 2003). For both men and women, retirement generally means a change in work, rather than its cessation.

Aging and the feminization of poverty

Women who are old and single are especially vulnerable to poverty. Because women live longer than men, they are more likely than men to lose their life partners, less likely to remarry, and spend more time at the ends of their lives living in poverty. We have already seen that women tend to have fewer retirement savings and are less likely than men to have adequate pensions. Widowhood decreases women's income (except in the rare cases where the husband leaves a large inheritance), and often pushes women over the line into poverty (Gillen and Kim 2009). In the United States, widowhood decreases a woman's household income by 37 percent, but decreases a man's by only 22 percent (US Government Accountability Office 2012).

In the United States in 2010, the poverty rate for older women was significantly higher (10.7 percent) than for men (6.7 percent). Women, minorities, and older persons living alone were more likely to be poor. Thus staggeringly high poverty rates were found for Hispanic women living alone (40.8 percent) and Black women living alone (30.7 percent) (Administration on Aging 2012). A study by the Organization for Economic Cooperation and Development (2011b) found older women to be at higher risk of poverty than older men in twenty-seven out of thirty countries. The largest gender gaps were found in Ireland, Finland, and Norway, where older women's poverty rates were more than 10 percentage points higher than older men's—but large gaps also existed in Austria, Italy, Japan, the Slovak Republic, and the United States.

GENDERED ASPECTS OF AGING AND HEALTH

Gender stereotypes and age stereotypes interact; women, already stereotyped as weaker than men, are viewed as increasingly frail as they age. Stereotypes of post-menopausal women include frailty, poverty, disengagement, and dependency (Velkoff and Kinsella 1998). The impact of such stereotypic images is evident in research showing that young people view "old age" as starting earlier for women than for men (Barrett and von Rohr 2008).

For men, masculine stereotypes of dominance and sexual agency interact with age stereotypes to shape anti-aging messages to men. Older men are targeted by advertisements urging them to forestall aging via supplemental testosterone, to continue to view women in terms of their sexual availability, and to continue in their senior years to prove masculinity through competence and competition (Calasanti and King 2007). Clearly, gender stereotypes play a role in individuals' experience of aging and health.

Media messages to older men and women

Both the popular and scientific media produce competing narratives of aging and contradictory messages aimed at older women and men (Lips and Hastings 2012). Ads in the popular media careen between portrayals of silver-haired, carefree, heterosexual couples enjoying a leisurely retirement of golf and Caribbean cruises, and depictions of older individuals wincing in pain as they try to move. The medical literature sounds dire warnings about decline in the form of arthritis, osteoporosis and erectile dysfunction, but also preaches healthy diet, exercise and fitness as ways to hold back the ravages of aging.

Along with increases in the proportion of older people in the population has come a rise in targeting of seniors by advertisers— and many of the advertisements tout products that are supposed to make people look and feel younger. Whereas older women were once ignored in the media or treated as anything but sexy, they are now bombarded by the message that they ought to do or buy whatever is necessary to maintain their sex appeal. At the same time, powerful and accomplished mature women in the public eye, such as Hillary Clinton, Helen Clark, and Angela Merkel, are sometimes deliberately portrayed as unattractive and unlikeable—with stereotypic attributions such as "ice queen," unflattering photographs emphasizing wrinkles and sags, and abrasive-sounding quotes (Vandiver 2011). The media message to older women seems to be that they should try to keep their focus on beauty rather than talent, and strive to be more like Sophia Loren than Christine Lagarde.

Older men are also targeted by media messages that exhort them to look and act younger than their age. For example, a torrent of advertisements advises men on ways to prevent or reverse hair loss or greying. Yet the media also provides many favorable images of men in their seventies and eighties—in which craggy faces are shown as interesting and full of character and grey hair is linked to distinction. We may think of Clint Eastwood, Harrison Ford, Sean Connery and many others as older men who are allowed to be seen as attractive and interesting, but it is more difficult to come up with similar-aged women who are portrayed equally favorably.

Women, men, bodies and fitness at older ages

Aging is correlated with changes in our physical bodies: changes in appearance, and in the ease with which we see, hear, think, and move. Indeed, the body is the crucial locus for the social construction of aging. Theorists in both women's studies and psychology have articulated theories of embodiment to analyze the impact of aging on individuals.

Not surprisingly, physical appearance is a central aspect of women's experience of aging (Maguire 2008). Women are judged heavily on their appearance, and a youthful appearance is prized as a *sine qua non* of women's attractiveness. Not surprisingly, then, many women express concerns about how they can hold back the tide of changes in appearance (wrinkles, grey hair, sagging breasts, weight gain) that often come with advancing age. These concerns are frequently translated into spending money on a wide variety of anti-aging treatments, ranging from expensive skins creams to cosmetic surgery. One market research firm projects annual spending on anti-aging products in the US market alone will reach $114 billion by 2015 (Crary 2011). And in 2010 there were 84,685 cosmetic surgery procedures performed on patients aged 65 and older, the majority of them women, in the United States (Ellin 2011).

Although we may decry the association of age with unattractiveness in women and exhort women to think of aging as beautiful, there are real and serious cultural reasons for women's concerns about "looking old." Research by psychologists shows clearly that, not only are negative stereotypes of the aged pervasive, but these stereotypes are often internalized. In other words, through a lifelong process of first observing and then experiencing the prejudiced evaluations directed at old persons, older persons begin to accept the stereotypes and apply them to themselves. Furthermore, the more strongly these stereotypes are internalized, the more they become self-fulfilling prophecies: older persons who accept that they are frail, incapable, vulnerable, become less healthy and less capable on a variety of dimensions.

Levy (2009) proposes a *stereotype embodiment theory* that outlines how individuals assimilate stereotypes of aging from the surrounding culture, leading to self-definitions that influence their own functioning and health. Aging, she argues, is at least in part a social construct—so while we ought to try to change negative stereotypes of aging, we should also acknowledge the real impact of the current stereotypes on older persons. When individuals resist the appearance changes associated with aging through such strategies as coloring their hair, trying to lose weight, or even seeking cosmetic surgery, they are responding to a genuine threat from their social environment. Dismissive or disparaging reactions of others to older persons can literally drag those older persons down and confirm the stereotypes.

Women are apparently judged more negatively than men for the effects of aging (Tiggemann 2004), but men too are subject to media pressures to maintain a youthful appearance. However, the research is scant and mixed as to how serious this concern is for men as they age. Whereas some research suggests older men respond neutrally or positively to the ways their appearance changes with age (Halliwell and Dittmar 2003), and that older men may experience less body dissatisfaction than younger men (Peat *et al.* 2011), other researchers have found that men were more distressed than women by age-related changes in body appearance (Kaminski and Hayslip 2006).

Stereotypes about aging bodies are not all about appearance, however; they are also about physical strength and weakness—and both women and men are targeted by competing messages in this domain. On the one hand, older individuals are warned of the many health dangers and possibilities of decline with age; on the other, they are offered strategies for staving off these dangers through drugs and lifestyle changes. However, the cultural messages targeted at women and men are somewhat different, shaped by stereotypes of femininity and masculinity.

When stereotypes of femininity and aging are combined, their emphases on weakness, delicacy and frailty are mutually reinforcing; they are unlikely to convey strength and power. Even media portrayals of older women that are meant to depict positive aging, such as television advertisements for bone-strengthening drugs, tend to focus on fluidity and flexibility rather than power and strength. Such images are countered to some extent by a relatively new media focus on outstanding older female athletes, such as the 79-year-old American "iron nun" who completes triathlons (Rickman and Wares 2010) or the South African "soccer grannies" who play the game both for its health benefits and in defiance of social norms that prescribe a dignified sedentary lifestyle for grandmothers (Dixon 2010). However, the latter images can often be taken as notable simply because they are unusual, and may be more easily discounted than the constant drumbeat of images that focus on decline. As is the case with appearance, exposure to images related to physical strength is likely to affect the ways aging is embodied—and thus experienced and lived—by women. If Levy's (2009) stereotype embodiment theory is correct, we might expect that an older woman who watches television and/or reads magazines in a Western culture is likely to have internalized the expectation that, as she ages, her bones will become increasingly fragile, her joints painful, her muscles weak, her stamina increasingly limited. The internalized expectancies turn into self-fulfilling prophecies, causing individuals to circumscribe their own activities—perhaps resulting in the very loss of physical capacity contained in the expectations.

In terms of their attitudes toward their aging bodies, women and men's concerns and sources of dissatisfaction appear to differ in emphasis, with women focusing more strongly on their appearance and men on the functionality of their bodies (Halliwell and Dittmar 2003). For men, strength and a muscular physique are an aspect of masculinity, and men generally express more desire than women for a lean, muscular body (Tiggemann, Martins and Kirkbride 2007). However, even as they become less muscular, older men may be somewhat protected from the effects of body dissatisfaction by satisfaction in other dimensions of masculinity. For example, masculinity also entails achievement, success, self-confidence, and independence—all things that may be higher in older men than in younger men.

In terms of actual behavior, it appears that individuals in older age ranges continue a gender-differentiated pattern of physical activity. For example, in the United States, women (64.7 percent) are more likely than men (52.8 percent) to report that they never exercise (Pleis, Lucas and Ward 2009). Over the age of 65, 35.9 percent of women, as opposed to 44 percent of men, engage in the recommended physical activity level of 30 minutes per day/5 days per week of moderate physical activity (Centers for Disease Control and Prevention 2010a). At older ages, the pattern of gender differences continues, with only 16.4 percent of women 75-84 years old engaging in regular physical activity, as compared to 26.2 percent of men (Centers for Disease Control and Prevention 2010b).

For those who engage in it, physical activity has important benefits: both older women and older men who are athletically active tend to be able to challenge some of the typical thinking about aging, and to focus their self-views on capability age rather than numerical age (Eman 2012). Even in the oldest age groups, men who maintain good levels of physical activity suffer less cognitive decline than men whose activity levels drop (van Gelder *et al.* 2004). Among older women too, physical activity is linked with a reduced risk of cognitive decline: among one large sample of women aged 65 and older, women with higher levels of physical activity were between 26 percent and 34 percent less likely to experience a reduction in their cognitive abilities over 6 to 8 years (Yaffe *et al.* 2001). And research on elite senior athletes participating in the Senior Olympics showed that, between ages 50 and 75, performance declined very slowly (about 3.4 percent per year) for both men and women who continued competition. For women, the decline was greater for speed than for endurance; for men, declines on both dimensions occurred at a similar rate. Among these active seniors, subjective physical and mental health was significantly higher than in the US population as a whole (Wright and Perricelli 2008).

Disability and disease

Despite the evidence that older individuals can maintain healthy active lives, a major emphasis in research on aging continues to be illness, disability, and decline. So dominant is this emphasis that some critics have complained that useful data on health, fitness, and strength in older age groups is in very short supply. For example, research on bone health provides no definition of a healthy skeletal system during the older years, and has focused almost solely on how to treat bone disease and bone injury among the elderly (Wright and Perricelli 2007).

Yet there are some important issues with respect to disability and disease in older age groups that cannot be ignored. One in particular is the rise in Alzheimer's disease and other forms of dementia among elders in developed nations, where an increasing number of individuals can expect to live to older ages. For example, a recent longitudinal population based study estimated that in 2010 there were 4.7 million people aged 65 and older suffering from Alzheimer's disease in the United States—and that as the population ages, this number will nearly triple to 13.8 million by 2050 (Hebert *et al.* 2013). Globally, the total number of people with dementia is projected to almost double every 20 years—to a total of 115.4 million in 2050 (United Nations Population Fund 2012).

Since women, on average, live longer than men, they are more likely to be diagnosed with Alzheimer's disease. There is also some evidence that, in addition to their longer life expectancy, women are at increased risk, relative to men, of Alzheimer's disease and of more rapid cognitive decline once it develops—although the reasons for this increased risk are not clear. Men, on the other hand, have a higher risk than women of vascular dementia (a much less common form of dementia), most likely linked to other heart and blood vessel problems that are relatively common in older men (Dunkin 2009). Besides their greater likelihood of experiencing Alzheimer's disease, women's longer lifespan makes it more likely that they will be engaged in caring for a spouse or other family member with the disease.

In addition to dementia, there is an increased prevalence of other disabilities with older age, and disability is more likely among women and among people in low-income countries. Visual impairment, hearing loss, and osteoarthritis are the most common forms of disability in both developed and developing countries, but they are much more prevalent in developing countries (United Nations Population Fund 2012). A number of studies show that, whereas women live longer than men, they experience more disabilities related to activities of daily living in old age. For example, a study in Singapore showed that, among people aged 65 and older, women, in comparison to men, could expect a larger proportion of their remaining years to include bone and joint problems, hypertension, vision impairments, and walking difficulties (Yong, Saito and Chan 2011). A US study found that, after controlling for resource differences, women of all racial/ethnic groups experienced more disability-related limitations in their ability to function than did White men or men of the same race/ethnicity (Warner and Brown 2011). Among the oldest old, women experience more illnesses, tend to describe themselves as less healthy, have lower scores on such functional capacity measures as gait and balance, experience more depression, and report lower levels of subjective well-being than men (Smith and Baltes 1998). Women's greater experience of disability appears to be linked both to their tendency to recover more slowly from illness or injury and the lower likelihood that they will die from these events (Hardy *et al.* 2008).

One significant source of injury, illness and unhappiness in old age is elder abuse and neglect. In one large community-based survey in the United States, 1 in 10 respondents aged 60 years or older reported emotional, physical, or sexual mistreatment or neglect in the previous year—with the most significant risk factor being a lack of social support (Acierno *et al.* 2010). Although elder abuse is often discussed in gender-neutral terms, it appears that gender is an important factor. Some studies have indicated that women are more likely than men to be victims of elder abuse (e.g. Hightower 2010; Kissal and Beşer 2011). One Canadian study of family medical practice clients produced an estimate that the prevalence of elder abuse ranged from 13.6 to 15.2 percent among women and from 9.1 to 9.7 percent among men (Yaffe *et al.* 2007). An early comprehensive population-based study in the United States revealed that some 450,000 elderly persons had been abused or neglected in 1996. In the typical case, the victim was a white woman, aged about 78, and the perpetrator was her son, aged between 41 and 54 (National Center on Elder Abuse 1998). A more recent comprehensive study, using data from the National Incident-Based Reporting System in the United States between 2000 and 2005, also found that victims were more likely to be female (about 53 percent), and that more than 70 percent of perpetrators were male (Krienert, Walsh and Turner 2009). In the latter study, male abusers were found more likely to abuse men and female abusers more likely to abuse women; however, male elders were more likely to be abused by a woman than by another man. As in other forms of violence, men were more likely than women to be abused by a stranger or acquaintance; women were more likely than men to be abused by a son or daughter, spouse, or other family member. Women were also more likely than men to be abused in their homes. Men were more likely than women to be victims of aggravated assaults and to report major injuries; women were more likely to experience simple assaults and intimidation and to report either no injury or minor injury. The latter finding suggests that some of the abuse experienced by women may be hidden and difficult to identify.

Certain economic and cultural factors may increase the risk of elder abuse. In cultures where women's social and economic status relative to men is especially low, elderly women are likely to be at higher risk than men for neglect as well as abuse, especially if they are widowed (World Health Organization 2011b). However, research also suggests that the risk for elder abuse increases where the abuser is financially dependent on the elderly person (Krienert, Walsh and Turner 2009). Abuse has also been linked to compassion fatigue and frustration—suggesting that more adequate societal supports for caregivers might reduce the incidence of abuse (Krienert, Walsh and Turner 2009).

It is likely that the relationship between gender and vulnerability to elder abuse is complicated by the availability of social support, financial dependence, and gender stereotypes. Social support has been found to be a protective factor against elder maltreatment (Melchiorre et al. 2013), and women are likely to have higher levels of social support than men during the early part of old age. However, since women live longer than men, they may spend more years in relative isolation, having outlived much of their social network. Women are also more likely than men to be poor in old age, and thus may find themselves financially dependent on family care-takers—leaving them more vulnerable to abuse by those care-takers. For men, vulnerability to abuse in old age may be increased by masculinity stereotypes that do not encompass the possibility of men as victims—making it difficult for men to report such abuse and for observers such as health professionals to see it (Kosberg 2007).

One study using mock criminal cases found that women were more likely than men to believe the testimony of alleged victims of elder abuse and to render a guilty verdict—and this difference was largest when the alleged perpetrator was the elder's daughter (Golding et al. 2005). The researchers suggest that women's greater readiness to believe that abuse occurred in such situations may be linked to their capacity to identify with both the caregiver and the recipient of care—both roles they know they are likely to inhabit at some point.

The gendering of caregiving

Women are more likely than men both to need and to provide caregiving services in their old age. In terms of need, a study by the European Commission indicates that women in the European Union are between 1.1 and 2.8 times more likely than men to receive institutional care, and between 1.5 and 2.8 times more likely than men to receive formal in-home care during their senior years (Bettio and Verashchagina 2010). Women's greater need for formal care in older age is linked in part to their longer lifespan and the related tendency to outlive a spouse. In the United States in 2010, 70 percent of men, but only 41 percent of women aged 65 and older lived with a spouse. Among women aged 75 and older, 47 percent lived alone (Administration on Aging 2012). In Great Britain, 63 percent of women and 35 percent of men aged 75 and older lived alone in 2008 (Office for National Statistics 2010). Thus most older women encounter the illnesses and disabilities of old age without a spouse, whereas most men encounter them *with* a spouse and can often expect to be cared for by that spouse.

The need to provide health care for family members disproportionately burdens women. One recent sixteen-country study showed that almost two-thirds of persons over the age of 50 who were providing unpaid informal care were women (Organization for Economic Cooperation and Development 2011a). In the United States, where there is no national childcare policy, and arrangements for pre-school and after school care for children of employed parents tend to be a patchwork, grandparents often fill in the gaps. One group of researchers calculated that women and men over the age of 65 spend an average of 1.9 hours and 1.6 hours per day on unpaid childcare (Bianchi, Folbre and Wolf 2012). Even in countries and regions where governments and/or employers provide childcare resources, older women and men still provide a significant amount of informal care for children. For example, in Denmark and the Netherlands, more than 60 percent of women and 40 percent of men aged 60 to 65 provide some care for their grandchildren (Croda and Gonzalez-Chapela 2005).

One of the factors driving the necessity for elders to provide caregiving to children is the prevalence of children who have been orphaned by AIDS, natural disasters, or wars. The impact of HIV/AIDS, in particular, has been the subject of much attention in the international community. Grandparents usually end up as the primary care-takers of AIDS orphans in Asia and Africa (Nyambedha, Wandibba and Aagaard-Hansen 2003; Subbarao and Coury 2004). In one study of communities in rural Kenya, 1 of every 3 children had lost one parent and 1 of every 9 children had lost both parents (Nyambedha, Wandibba and Aagaard-Hansen 2003). Their grandparent care-takers encountered significant hardships in providing education, food and medical care for these children. Furthermore, because their own children had died, these elderly caretakers were deprived of the higher status, respect, and entitlement to be cared for that had traditionally been accorded older persons in the community. Even grandparents with few resources tend, in such situations, to become providers rather than receivers of care. One South African study shows that AIDS orphans are more likely to be taken in by grandparents in the poorest economic groups (Ardington et al. 2009). Most of the grandparents taking responsibility for AIDS orphans are women; however, some evidence suggests that, for those who take it on, this caretaking role may be harder on men than on women. A study of AIDS caregivers in two slum districts of Nairobi revealed that men who were caregivers reported higher levels of disability and severe health problems than men who were not caregivers; no such differences between caregivers and non-caregivers were found for women (Chepngeno-Langat et al. 2011). The authors suggest that one reason for the gender differences may be that men do not expect to have to become active care-takers in this situation and have not developed appropriate coping strategies. However, in many settings, gender norms and stereotypes work against women, assigning lower value to their needs, health, and lives than to men's, and prescribing that it is their duty to provide care for others, even at the cost of their own wellbeing (Olowu 2012).

Much of the informal caregiving provided by the elderly, however, is directed at adults, most frequently parents and spouses (Organization for Economic Cooperation and Development 2011a). Although, up to at least age 65, women provide the bulk of this care, demographic changes such as increases in men's life expectancy have increased the likelihood that men will take on caregiving roles for spouses. For example, a few years ago in the UK, among those older than 65, men actually became more likely than women to be caring for a spouse (Office for National Statistics 2004). Among persons 75 and older, men are now as likely or more likely than women to be caregivers in many countries, including Germany, Greece, Belgium, and Austria; however, women still predominate as informal caregivers in other countries, such as France, Switzerland, and the Czech Republic (Organization for Economic Cooperation and Development 2011a). Although there is a shortage of research that focuses specifically on male caregivers, there is some evidence that they seek help from others less often than female caregivers, that they are less aware of available community services, and that they are concerned about appearing to be incompetent and weak if they signal that they cannot manage the caregiving situation on their own (Baker and Robertson 2008). All of these responses are congruent with traditional expectations for masculinity.

Although caregiving is often informal, there is often very little choice involved, and it can take a large physical and emotional toll on caregivers. Researchers have found, for example, that caregivers of a spouse with dementia experience stress that results in lowered immunity response to vaccines, slower wound healing, and higher inflammation—and that some measures of psychological wellbeing, such as depression and loneliness, do not rebound to normal levels even three years after the death of the cared-for spouse (Glaser et al. 2000, Gouin, Hantsoo and Kiecolt-Glaser 2008; Robinson Whelen et al. 2001). Caregivers also often neglect their own self-care, because they are too busy or too wrapped up in their caregiving tasks to pay attention to their own wellbeing; this too contributes to negative health consequences (Vitaliano, Zhang and Scanlan 2003). The prevalence of mental health problems is estimated to be 20 percent higher among caregivers than non-caregivers (Organization for Economic Cooperation and Development 2011a).

There is some evidence that even when women and men provide equivalent amounts and types of care, women experience a higher subjective burden of care (e.g. they may be more likely than men to say that they feel trapped or that providing care is an excessive burden) (del Pino-Casado *et al.* 2012; Pinquart and Sorensen 2003). One important source of stress for a caregiver is exposure to the suffering of the person receiving care; this exposure can, through empathy or mirroring of the care recipient's feelings, provoke strong emotional responses that contribute to the caregiver's psychological and physical distress. Some theorists have argued that, since it is well-established that women are more sensitive than men to others' emotions and more empathetic under many conditions, they may be more distressed than men by the suffering of a care recipient—particularly one to whom they have a close relationship (Monin and Schulz 2009).

The toll on caregivers can also be financial, since caregiving may involve taking time away from paid work—something that most women, in particular, can ill afford to do. Caregiving is associated with unemployment, temporary and part-time work, reduction in hours of paid work, lower income, early retirement, and an increased risk of poverty (Organization for Economic Cooperation and Development 2011a). The increased risk of lower income and poverty is particularly striking for female caregivers.

Of course, not all caregiving is informal; paralleling the growth of the aging population, there is a large and growing long-term care workforce in developed countries. Most of these workers (90 percent in the United States; 84 percent in England) are female and many are women of color (56 percent in the United States; 17 percent in England) (Hussein 2011; Institute for Women's Policy Research 2012). They fill jobs as nurse aids, nursing assistants, orderlies, personal care attendants, home care workers, and other paraprofessional caregivers to the elderly or disabled in hospitals, nursing homes, day care settings, and private homes. It is projected that there will be a need for 6 million such direct care workers in the United States by 2050 (Bouchard 2013).

Furthermore, a growing proportion of these women are immigrants from countries where they cannot find good jobs (Browne and Braun 2008). In 2011, 28 percent of direct care workers in the United States were foreign-born (Institute for Women's Policy Research 2012). The availability of these immigrant women workers fills an important need in countries such as the United States, but it may also fuel the devaluation of eldercare as a profession by keeping wages low. In the United States, wages for direct-care workers are significantly lower than the median wage for all US workers, and about 45 percent of these workers live in households earning below 200 percent of the federal poverty income level (Paraprofessional Healthcare Institute 2011). Another problem is that the countries from which these workers come may find their own supply of both formal eldercare workers and informal family caretakers drained. It is difficult to predict the impact of the latter development on the gendering of caregiving in these "source" countries.

IDENTITY AND RELATIONSHIPS: WIDOWHOOD, SOCIAL NETWORKS, SOCIAL SUPPORT

A growing body of research shows that both social isolation (having little social contact, living alone, without a partner or a network of social support) and feeling lonely (being dissatisfied with the frequency and/or closeness of one's social contacts) may be connected to poor health outcomes. For example, one prospective study of over 2,000 elderly people in the Netherlands found that older persons who report feeling lonely are at higher risk for dementia, even if they are not, by objective measures, socially isolated (Holwerda *et al.* 2012). A study of a nationally representative US sample of individuals aged 50 and over found that feelings of loneliness were associated with increased mortality risk over a 6-year period (Luo *et al.* 2012). Another study of 6,500 British people aged 52 and older found that both social isolation and loneliness were linked to increased mortality from all causes, but that only the effect of social isolation was independent of other predictors of mortality (Steptoe *et al.* 2013). Other research has shown that both socially isolated and lonely individuals are at higher risk for cardiovascular disease, high blood pressure, and heightened inflammatory response to stress (Steptoe *et al.* 2013).

These findings suggest big problems for older people, who are much more likely than younger people to be isolated and lonely. For example, the European Social Survey (2010) revealed that 27 percent of respondents aged 50 and older said they met friends, relatives or colleagues once a month or less. Furthermore, there is a gender dimension to this issue, as women are especially likely to be isolated in older age. In some European countries, for example, more than 40 percent of women aged 65 and older live alone, and one report from Bosnia and Herzegovina found older women to be one of the most socially excluded groups in that society (United Nations Population Fund 2012). In the large British sample studied by Steptoe and his colleagues (2013), there was no male–female difference in social isolation, but women were significantly more likely than men to be lonely.

Women's increased risk for isolation and loneliness in old age may be linked to their longer lifespan, tendency to outlive their spouses, and their greater likelihood of experiencing depression and other illnesses. However, the gender difference turns out to be somewhat complicated. Yes, women are more likely than men to find themselves widowed in their senior years (Antonucci *et al.* 2002). For example, in the United States in 2010, there were four times as many widows (8.7 million) as widowers (2.1 million) (Administration on Aging 2012). However, in developed countries, widowhood seems to be harder on men than on women (Stroebe, Stroebe and Schut 2001), and marital status seems to have a larger effect on loneliness for men than for women (Rokach *et al.* 2007). This may be because, for men, marriage is likely to be both central to their feelings of intimate attachment and emotional wellbeing *and* a key aspect in their wider social involvement (perhaps because their wives mediate social arrangements or because they are more likely to socialize as couples than as individuals). Thus when men lose their wives, they lose not only an important close relationship but also a link to a variety of other social relationships. For women, marriage offers one source of intimate attachment, but they are also likely to find both emotional and social support in other close ties with friends and family members (Dykstra and de Jong Gierveld 2004). Women, even in their 70s, have larger social networks than men, and these networks tend to be less impacted than men's by widowhood or divorce (McLaughlin *et al.* 2010). Researchers have found that in some countries the positive quality of older women's social relations can counteract and make up for the negative emotional consequences and resource deficits they face in terms of financial security and health (Antonucci *et al.* 2002). Even under the difficult conditions found in Kenyan slums, elderly women apparently maintain larger, stronger social networks than men, allowing them to be more resourceful and cooperative in dealing with needs for food, information, and health care (Mudege and Ezeh 2009).

As a spouse is often the most important provider of a wide variety of kinds of support and care, widowhood demands that the affected person seek out new sources of social and practical support to compensate for the loss of a partner. Since, as we have noted, women tend to have larger support networks than men, finding such substitute support may be easier for them than for men. Studies of how widows compensate for losing a spouse have suggested that they do seek out new sources of support—by establishing new ties, rekindling older relationships that have been dormant, or seeking new kinds of help and support from existing relationships. However, the older women in one study did not appear to gain the kinds of compensatory benefits in emotional health that might be expected. In fact, the widows who achieved the most social network substitution actually experienced more loneliness and depression. The researchers speculate that this relationship may be due to a pattern in which the most lonely and distressed women worked most diligently to create new ties (Zettel and Rook 2004).

In cultures where a woman is seen as deriving her identity and status, as well as her livelihood, from her husband, the impact of widowhood on women may be more dire than on men. In some areas of Africa, a widow risks being labeled and persecuted as a witch (Rosenblatt and Nkosi 2007). In parts of rural India, a widow may be considered a non-person; there is even a tradition (called *Sati*, now illegal, but still practiced on occasion) that a widow should throw herself on the funeral pyre of her husband, since her life is no longer worth living; there is no parallel tradition for widowers (Vijayakumar 2004). Attitudes toward widows continue to evolve in India, and middle-class widows in urban settings can now often anticipate rebuilding their lives as single women (Czerenda 2010). However, one Indian study of a nationally representative sample of persons aged 60 and over revealed that widowed persons of both genders were more vulnerable than married persons in terms of health status and access to health care services, but widows were the most disadvantaged group (Sreerupa and Rajan 2010).

PURPOSE AND MEANING: RETHINKING WHAT MATTERS

Although aging is associated with a variety of losses and declines in certain areas, older people tend to adapt by readjusting their priorities, goals, and ways of functioning. The process has been described as *selective optimization with compensation* (Baltes and Baltes 1990), referring to a narrowing of one's set of goals by picking only the most important as targets of one's resources, and using alternative methods or resources to make up for losses or deficiencies. This winnowing of goals may take somewhat different forms for women and men, especially if they have been engaged in traditional gender roles. For example, men may re-think the importance of career achievement and success and women may question the necessity of placing so much importance on the feminine ideals of pleasing others, looking attractive, and putting the needs of others before their own.

For women, moving into older age may sometimes be associated with a new sense of freedom: moving in new directions and stepping out of the constraints of feminine stereotypes and roles (Arnold 2005). Whereas, for women, aging often used to be framed mainly as the loss of reproductive roles and transition to an "empty nest," it is now apparent that midlife and older age present women with a variety of opportunities to enhance self-development, confidence, and self-acceptance (Picard 2000).

As individuals narrow their goals and focus in concert with aging, one interesting result appears to be that they focus more on emotion-related goals than on information-related goals—and they emphasize the positive emotions. Framing this process as *socioemotional selectivity* (Carstensen, Fung and Charles 2003), researchers have used it to explain why older age is linked, somewhat unexpectedly, to happiness. The theory posits that, with age, adults realize that remaining life is short, and begin to focus on reducing the amount of time they spend on negative emotions and experiences. In other words, they make choices in order to better meet their needs and protect their emotional health. In line with this theory, older adults appear to respond with less anger and to disengage more from offending interpersonal situations than younger adults do (Charles and Carstensen 2008).

In laboratory experiments they pay less attention to, and recall, fewer negative stimuli than younger people do—a phenomenon labeled the *positivity effect* (Carstensen and Mikels 2005).

Although there is still a shortage of research, there are some indications that women and men may emphasize different strategies in achieving this focus on the positive. For example, women seem more likely than men to focus on positive social exchanges (experiencing care, support and companionship) to buffer or ameliorate the damaging impact on their emotions of negative social exchanges (tension, conflict, neglect) (Fiori et al. 2013). This may be because, as we have seen, women tend to place more emphasis on social networks and interpersonal relationships than men do (Antonucci and Jackson 1987).

For both men and women, there is some evidence for a shift away from traditional gender expectations with increasing age. Transitions such as job loss or retirement, or the illness or loss of a spouse, may cause men to re-evaluate long held assumptions and beliefs about aspects of gender roles such as division of labor, or important sources of identity (Emslie, Hunt and O'Brien 2004). For women, age may sometimes be accompanied by a stronger sense of their own power and inner strength (Friedman and Pines 1992; Todd, Friedman and Kariuki 1990). Most of the vast literature on gender roles, norms, and stereotypes has focused on the young; as we move into a future that includes an increasing proportion of older women and men, many questions remain to be answered about gender and aging.

FOR FURTHER EXPLORATION

Muhlbauer, V., and Chrisler, J.C. (eds) (2007). *Women over 50: psychological perspectives.* (New York: Springer.) This collection of ten chapters examines the challenges and opportunities associated with women's entry into the "middle" time of life, commonly thought of as a bridge to old age. The issues are considered from a research perspective and range from body image, love and sex, relationships, and retirement, to empowerment.

Cruikshank, Margaret (2013). *Learning to be Old: gender, culture, and aging.* (Lanham, MD: Rowman and Littlefield, Inc.) This book, framed by a feminist perspective, takes a good look at cultural myths about aging and the fears people have about an aging population. The book focuses on the American situation, but most of the issues are relevant to many countries. Included are discussions of sickness and social roles, overmedication, ageism, the different experiences of different ethnic and economic groups and "countercultural gerontology."

Lamb, Sarah (2000). *White Saris and Sweet Mangoes: aging, gender, and body in North India.* (Berkeley, CA: University of California Press.) The author, an anthropologist, explores the expectations and practices associated with aging and gender in one part of the world—and in doing so sheds light on many broad assumptions about older women and men. Through fascinating stories of individuals in Mangaldihi, India, she entices the reader to examine issue of economics, health, separation, widowhood, death, and love.

United Nations Population Fund (2012). *Ageing in the Twenty-first Century: a celebration and a challenge.* Available at http://unfpa.org/ageingreport/. This comprehensive report analyzes the issues raised by the rapid aging of the world's population. Consideration of the many ways in which gender and ageing are linked is included in every chapter.

EPILOGUE:
THE FUTURE OF GENDER

In her incisive book, *The Dialectic of Sex*, Shulamith Firestone (1970) offered a radical feminist analysis of the oppression of women—along with even more radical solutions. Firestone argued that inequality between women and men was rooted in the biological assignment to women of the task of childbearing. As a goal of the feminist revolution, she envisioned a future in which reproduction would, through advances in technology, be separated from both sexuality and gender: conception would happen through artificial inseminations and gestation would take place, not in women's bodies, but in artificial wombs in carefully controlled environments. By divorcing the act of sex from procreation and the female body from pregnancy and childbirth, Firestone posited that the biological, genital, distinction between women and men would cease to matter. Male privilege would be undercut, and the stage would be set for cultural equality between women and men.

As a vision of the future, Firestone's scenario was startling and controversial. More than forty years later, despite advances in reproductive technology that have significantly weakened the link between sex and pregnancy, there appears to be little appetite for her imagined world of laboratory-dominated reproduction. However, many might still agree that, by focusing on childbearing, she had honed in on what may well be the key issue among barriers to gender equality. In the developing world, women's health is often held hostage to their roles as mothers. As we have seen, maternal mortality and maternity-related illnesses take an enormous toll on women in regions of the world where availability of good health care is scant, childbearing is emphasized as the key task for women, and access to control over reproduction is elusive at best. That toll is exacerbated in cultures that place a lower value on women's lives than on men's.

In developed countries, maternal mortality is less common, but the motherhood penalty appears to be a major economic issue. We have seen that motherhood is associated with lower pay and fewer advancement opportunities for employed women; that the logistics of balancing childcare with paid work remain difficult for many women; that mothers, much more often than fathers, are forced to make impossible choices between attending to family responsibilities and focusing on their jobs. Women, not men, are still deemed to be the primary care-takers of children and families; this assumption colors government and corporate policies about employment, and can disadvantage women at every stage of their working life. Furthermore, the association of women with motherhood seems to strengthen gender stereotypes that emphasize caring and "softness" as opposed to the competence and decisiveness expected of public leaders and high-achieving workers. (Even though anyone who has been a mother is well aware that competence and decisiveness are critical aspects of this role.)

It is difficult to imagine a scenario in which the health, economic, and social stereotype-related disadvantages linked to motherhood would vanish completely—without doing away with the biological necessity for women to bear the children. Perhaps that is why Firestone focused her revolutionary vision on separating reproduction from sex and pregnancy, and why science fiction writer Ursula LeGuin (1969) fantasized a world where there were not two sexes, but one—and anyone could become pregnant. Neither of these solutions is realistic, but they do help us to identify the extent to which female–male relations are shaped by childbearing—and perhaps to envision a world in which more gender equality is possible.

Predicting the future of gender relations, in a world where those relations are now in flux, cannot be done with precision. Yet there are many signs that the strict definition of gender roles with respect to family and work has eroded dramatically. In developed countries, women have moved into the paid workforce in large numbers, often becoming primary breadwinners for their families (Galinsky, Aumann and Bond 2011). To some extent, women's increasing presence in the paid workforce has driven policy changes (parental leave, child care arrangements, flexible work schedules) that support workers needing to balance family and employment responsibilities. There are still too many regions of the world where education for women is a low priority; however, in countries where women have equal access to education, women are quickly becoming more highly educated than men. Women now hold more positions of public leadership than ever before, although they still form a small minority in such roles. Thus in terms of women's movement into roles traditionally reserved for men, there is evidence of a momentum which, although not unstoppable, is unlikely to be easily reversed. Even in regions of the world where restrictions on them are most draconian, women and girls are pushing up against barriers, often risking their lives to gain opportunities for education, self-expression, health care for themselves and their families, and protection from sexual violence. It does not seem unreasonable to predict that women's roles will continue to expand and change, and that these changes will result in greater gender equality. Since a significant body of research suggests that greater societal gender equality is associated with lower levels of sexual violence, intimate partner violence, and maternal and child mortality, and with higher levels of economic prosperity, health, and happiness, the goal of increasing equality has been adopted by many world organizations.

What of changes in men's roles? In some contexts and on some dimensions, women have been encouraged to be more flexible in the ways they enact femininity. However, social definitions of masculinity have often been more rigid, and pressures on men to live up to masculine ideals have been strong. Men have been slower to change, most likely because societies have traditionally assigned lower status to feminine-stereotyped behaviors, but they too have moved into roles previously restricted to the other gender. There are more men in such traditionally female "caring" professions as nursing and social work, and even a small but significant minority of men who are fulltime homemakers. Furthermore, both men and women are now less likely than in earlier years to insist on a traditional division of family roles in which the man earns more money and the woman is the primary caretaker of the home and children—and men's attitudes have changed more than women's toward acceptance of the notion that employed women can be good mothers. However, for men, the biggest change may be more subtle than a change in jobs or primary roles. Once sharing or ceding the role of main breadwinner in the family, a man may have to shift his sources of identity and self-esteem away from a traditional (and higher-status) masculine emphasis on successful competition and external accomplishments. Instead, his contributions to child-rearing, keeping the home running smoothly, and maintaining a good relationship with his spouse become more important. If men have difficulty adapting to this change, they may struggle with lowered self-esteem, psychological distress, and even depression (Dunlop and Mletzko 2011). Yet some men have found these changes liberating and exhilarating (Round 2006).

Social change is bound to be an uneven and sometimes frustrating process—and its results are rarely unequivocally positive. Some women and men worry that values traditionally associated with femininity, such as care for others, may lose prominence as more women move into more competitive and individualistic lifestyles. Some worry that societies will lose their competitive edge if they restructure their institutions to accommodate the demands of family responsibilities for all their workers and encourage men to share those responsibilities. It can hardly be denied that both caring and achievement, both the capacity for empathy and the capacity for toughness, both openness to compromise and unwavering determination, are qualities much needed for the smooth functioning of societies, institutions, families, and interpersonal relationships. Yet if all such qualities are useful, why insist on dividing them up between women and men? And why, in particular, assign lower status to those "soft" qualities linked to femininity?

Debates may persist, but in a context of rapidly changing technology and global media reach, the tide of change in women's roles is unlikely to be turned back. And because we are connected, because we live and work together, changes in women's roles are inevitably linked to changes in the behaviors, attitudes, and feelings that are expected of men. As women and men journey together into a future that appears dynamic and uncertain, there will be a continuing necessity to question long-held assumptions and experiment with new roles. Perhaps the greatest allure of the journey is in not knowing exactly where it will lead.

FOR FURTHER EXPLORATION

World Bank (2012). *World Development Report 2012: Gender Equality and Development.* Available at http://econ.worldbank.org/ WBSITE/EXTERNAL/EXTDEC/EXTRESEARCH /EXTWDRS/EXTWDR2012/0,,menuPK:7778074 ~pagePK:7778278~piPK:7778320~theSitePK:7778063 ~contentMDK:22851055,00.html. Through charts and graphs, text, maps, and videos, this report details recent progress on gender equality around the world and shows where change has been fast and slow. It illustrates the connections between gender equality and a variety of positive outcomes. Finally, it explores the factors that tend to promote and retard change in the direction of greater equality between women and men and makes policy recommendations.

GLOSSARY

Affirmative action—a constellation of proactive intervention strategies aimed at increasing the proportion of women and other underrepresented groups who have access to educational and employment opportunities.

Ambivalent sexism—a constellation of attitudes made up of both negative and positive feelings and beliefs about women or men.

Androgyny—the combination of both feminine and masculine qualities.

Bases of power—resources (such as reward, punishment, legitimacy, expertise) that can be used to back up attempts to exert power.

Benevolent sexism—warm but condescending stereotypic attitudes toward women or men. Includes attitudes that each gender is naturally better at certain things, and that women and men need each other to be complete.

Cognitive theories of gender development—theories that emphasize the child's role as an active seeker of the correct ways to be and behave as a boy or a girl.

Descriptive gender stereotypes—beliefs about what typical men and women are like.

Double bind—for women in leadership roles, refers to the dilemma that, if they behave in too feminine a way, they will not be seen as effective leaders, but if they behave in too masculine a way, they will be disliked and disparaged.

Double standard—the use of different standards of acceptable sexual behavior for women and men.

Evolutionary psychology—theoretical approach that locates the origin of male–female behavioral differences in the pressures for reproductive success. This approach says men and women are different because different qualities and strategies have led to reproductive success for the two groups across many generations.

Fatherhood premium—tendency for male workers who are fathers to be paid more than non-fathers.

Feminism—a set of diverse ideologies that center on the idea that inequalities between women and men should be challenged.

Gender—socially constructed category involving a constellation of stereotypes, norms, and roles for various forms of masculinity, femininity, and androgyny.

Gender identity—the private sense of oneself as male or female or as a member of a third gender category.

Gender role—set of behaviors culturally prescribed for women or men.

Gender token—the only woman or man (one of very few) in a particular occupational or educational setting numerically dominated by members of the other gender.

Glass ceiling—metaphor used to describe the situation in which women appear to encounter an invisible barrier as they try to advance to higher levels of leadership.

Glass escalator—metaphor used to describe a constellation of subtle mechanisms and pressures that enhance men's advancement in female-dominated professions.

Honor killing—sanctioned killing of a wife or daughter who has behaved "inappropriately," in order to protect the honor of her family.

Hook-up—sexual activity with no expectation of commitment.

Hostile sexism—derogatory beliefs about women or men based on their gender.

Human capital model—an economic model that describes differences in employment earnings as explainable by differences in the employment-related investments (e.g., education, time at work) workers make.

Implicit stereotypes—stereotypes that operate automatically, below the level of awareness.

Influence styles—approaches to making requests or demands of others (direct or indirect).

Interactionist theories—theories based on the idea that biology and environment interact to influence developmental outcomes.

Intersexed—having both male and female biological markers.

Intimate justice—a theory that focuses on the way social and political inequalities can affect women's and men's experience of intimate relationships.

Lack of fit—refers to the notion that, because of a mismatch between her/his qualities and the requirements of the job, a certain type of individual is not a good match for a certain type of job. Used in the literature on gender and work to describe the assumed mismatch between women and managerial jobs.

Misogyny—hatred of, or disdain for, women.

Modern sexism—a subtle form of sexism that entails a lack of support for policies designed to promote equality-oriented changes in gender relations, antagonism toward women's demands for access and inclusion, and denial that gender discrimination still exists (also called **neosexism**).

Motherhood penalty—tendency for women workers who are mothers to experience a loss of cumulative employment earnings.

Nature vs. nurture—debate about the relative contributions of biology and environment to human (and other animal) development.

Neosexism—a subtle form of sexism that entails a lack of support for policies designed to promote equality-oriented changes in gender relations, antagonism toward women's demands for access and inclusion, and denial that gender discrimination still exists (also called **modern sexism**).

Old-fashioned sexism—the open endorsement of stereotypic judgments about, and differential treatment of, women and men.

Positivity effect—the tendency found among older people to devote more of their attention and memory to positive rather than negative stimuli (see also **socioemotional selectivity theory**).

Possible selves—individuals' specific images and fantasies of what they could be or become in the future.

Prescriptive gender stereotypes—beliefs about what men and women should be like in order to conform to society's expectations.

Psychoanalytic theory—theoretical approach that locates differences between women and men in early childhood relationships with parents.

Relational aggression—aggression that hurts or threatens another person by damaging her or his relationships and/or social status.

Role incongruity—refers to the situation where two roles that an individual is trying to fulfill have conflicting requirements. This concept is sometimes invoked to describe the difficulty of fulfilling contradictory requirements of the female role and those of a leadership role.

Selective optimization with compensation—process by which older individuals are theorized to adapt to losses in functioning: by targeting their resources to a narrower set of goals and priorities and compensating for any deficiencies by using alternative approaches.

Sex—biological category of male or female.

Sexism—evaluative judgments of individuals based on gender.

Sex chromosomes—the 23rd pair of chromosomes in humans: XX for females, XY for males.

Sexual economics theory—theory that in cultures where women have fewer sources of power than men, they work to enhance their power by restricting sexual activity.

Sexual orientation—tendency to be attracted sexually to members of one's own or the other sex, or to both.

Sexual self-schema—the way a person conceptualizes her/himself as a sexual being.

Social dominance theory—theoretical approach that posits that, in hierarchically-oriented societies, women are socialized toward values that are hierarchy-attenuating and men toward values that are hierarchy-enhancing.

Social roles theory—argues that women and men occupy different roles because each gender is expected to have the qualities necessary for those roles, and that performing those roles reinforces and develops these qualities, thus supporting gender stereotypes.

Socialization—processes used to teach and encourage individuals to conform to societal norms and expectations.

Social-cultural theories—theories that emphasize the role of social structures and power relations in the production of behavioral differences between groups (in this case, women and men).

Socioemotional selectivity theory—theory that, as they grow older, adults realize their remaining life is short, and so tend to reduce the amount of time they devote to negative emotions and experiences.

Stereotype embodiment theory—theory that suggests people incorporate cultural stereotypes (for example, of frailty associated with aging) into self-definitions that, in turn, affect their own physical functioning and health.

Stereotype threat—awareness of being judged according to negative stereotypes about one's group.

Transactional leadership—a style that focuses on reaching set goals, completing tasks, assigning rewards and punishments based on performance, and detecting errors.

Transformational leadership—a style of leadership that focuses on motivating followers to perform at a high level and in the process to develop their own leadership potential. The style includes four aspects: stimulating followers to think innovatively, motivating followers to contribute to a shared vision, showing consideration and support for followers' concerns and development, and modeling one's own ideals, values and beliefs.

Transgendered—an individual who is not comfortable with the gender category to which she or he has been assigned.

BIBLIOGRAPHY

50 Most Powerful Women in Business (2012). *CNN Money*. Retrieved February 1, 2013 from http://money.cnn.com/magazines/fortune/most-powerful-women/

Abella, R.S. (1984). *Report of the Commission on Equality in Employment* (Vol. 1). Ottawa, Canada: Minister of Supply and Services.

Acierno, R., Hernandez, M.A., Amstadter, A.B., Resnick, H.S., Stever, K., Muzzy, W. and Kilpatrick, D.G. (2010). Prevalence and correlates of emotional, physical, sexual, and financial abuse and potential neglect in the United States: The National Elder Mistreatment Study. *American Journal of Public Health* **100**, 292–97. doi: 10.2105/AJPH.2009.163089

Adams, T.M. and Fuller, D.B. (2006). The words have changed but the ideology remains the same: Misogynistic lyrics in rap music. *Journal of Black Studies* **36**, 938–57. doi: 10.1177/0021934704274072

Administration on Aging (2012). Profile of older Americans. Department of Health and Human Services. Retrieved from http://www.aoa.gov/Aging_Statistics/Profile/2011/Index.aspx

Adreoni, J. and Petrie, R. (2008). Beauty, gender and stereotypes: evidence from laboratory experiments. *Journal of Economic Psychology* **29**, 73–93.

Aida, Y. and Falbo, T. (1991). Relationships between marital satisfaction, resources, and power strategies. *Sex Roles* **24**, 43–56. doi: 10.1007/BF00288702

Ali, A.H. (2007). *Infidel*. New York: Free Press.

Ali, S., Sophie, R., Imam, A.M., Khan, F.I., Ali, S.F., Shaikh, A. and Farid-ul-Hasnain, S. (2011). Knowledge, perceptions and myths regarding infertility among selected adult population in Pakistan: a cross-sectional study. *BMC*

Public Health **11**, 760. doi: 10.1186/1471-2458-11-760. Retrieved from http://www.biomedcentral.com/1471-2458/11/760

All Things Considered (2011, November 13). A look at media, gender in "Miss Representation." National Public Radio. Accessed at http://www.npr.org/2011/11/13/142288599/a-look-at-media-gender-in-miss-representation

American Academy of Pediatrics (2012). Circumcision policy statement. *Pediatrics* **130**, 585–86. doi: 10.1542/peds.2012-1989

Andersen, B.L. and Cyranowski, J.M. (1994). Women's sexual self-schema. *Journal of Personality and Social Psychology* **67**, 1079–1100. doi: 10.1037/0022-3514.67.6.1079

Andersen, B.L., Cyranowski, J.M. and Espindle, D. (1999). Men's sexual self-schema. *Journal of Personality and Social Psychology* **76**, 645–61. doi: 10.1037/0022-3514.76.4.645

Antonucci, T.C. and Jackson, J. (1987). Social support, interpersonal efficacy, and health: a life course perspective. In L.L. Carstensen and B.A. Edelstein (eds), *Handbook of Clinical Gerontology*, pp 291–311. New York: Pergamon.

Antonucci, T.C., Lansford, J.E., Akiyama, H., Smith, J., Baltes, M.M., Takahashi, K., Fuhrer, R. and Dartigues, J-F. (2002). Differences between men and women in social relations, resource deficits, and depressive symptomatology during later life in four nations. *Journal of Social Issues* **58**, 767–83. doi: 10.1111/1540-4560.00289

Apfelbaum, E. (1993). Norwegian and French women in high leadership positions: the importance of cultural contexts upon gendered relations. *Psychology of Women Quarterly* **17**, 409–29. doi: 10.1111/j.1471-6402.1993.tb00653.x

Archer, J. (2000). Sex differences in aggression between heterosexual partners: a meta-analytic review. *Psychological Bulletin* **126**, 651–80.

Archer, J. (2004). Sex difference in aggression in real-world settings: a meta-analytic review. *Review of General Psychology* **8**, 291–322. doi: 10.1037/1089-2680.8.4.291

Ardington, C., Case, A., Islam, M., Lam, D., Leibbrandt, M., Menendez, A. and Olgiati, A. (2009, February). *The impact of AIDS on intergenerational support in South Africa: evidence from the Cape Area Panel Study*. Paper prepared for the conference on "The Impact of AIDS on Older Persons in Africa and Asia." University of Michigan. Retrieved from http://www.princeton.edu/~accase/downloads/AIDS_and_intergenerational_support_in_Cape_Town.pdf

Arias, I. and Pape, K.T. (1999). Psychological abuse: Implications for adjustment and commitment to leave violent partners. *Violence and Victims* **14**, 55–67.

Arnold, E. (2005). A voice of their own: women moving into their fifties. *Health Care for Women International* **26**, 630–51. doi: 10.1080/07399330500177014

Aruguete, M.S., DeBord, K.A., Yates, A. and Edman, J. (2005). Ethnic and gender differences in eating attitudes among black and white college students. *Eating Behaviors* **6**, 328–36. doi: 10.1016/j.eatbeh.2004.01.014

Asgari, S., Dasgupta, N., and Stout, J.G. (2012). When do counterstereotypic ingroup members inspire versus deflate? The effect of successful professional women on young women's leadership self-concept. *Personality and Social Psychology Bulletin* **38**, 370–83. doi: 10.1177/0146167211431968

Associated Press (2011, April 26). In a first, women surpass men in college degrees. Retrieved from http://www.cbsnews.com/2100-201_162-20057608.html

Australian Institute of Criminology (2001). *Australian crime – facts and figures 2002*. Retrieved from http://www.aic.gov.au/publications/facts/2001/

Auyeung, B., Baron-Cohen, S., Ashwin, E., Knickmeyer, R., Taylor, K., Hackett, G. and Hines, M. (2009). Fetal testosterone predicts sexually differentiated childhood behavior in girls and boys. *Psychological Science* **20**, 144–48. doi: 10.1111/j.1467-9280.2009.02279.x

AWARE (2008). Research study on workplace sexual harassment, 2008. Retrieved from http://www.aware.org.sg/wp-content/uploads/AWARE_Research_Study_on_Workplace_Sexual_Harassment.pdf

Baker, A.H. and Wardle, J. (2003). Sex differences in fruit and vegetable intake in older adults. *Appetite* **40**, 269–75. doi: 10.1016/S0195-6663(03)00014-X

Baker, K.L. and Robertson, N. (2008). Coping with caring for someone with dementia: reviewing the literature about men. *Aging and Mental Health* **12**, 413–22.

Baker Jr., M.D. and Maner, J.K. (2009). Male risk-taking as a context-sensitive signaling device. *Journal of Experimental Social Psychology* **45**, 1136–39. doi: 10.1016/j.jesp.2009.06.006

Balsam, K.F. and Szymanski, D.M. (2005). Relationship quality and domestic violence in women's same-sex relationships: the role of minority stress. *Psychology of Women Quarterly* **29**, 258–69. doi: 10.1111/j.1471-6402.2005.00220.x

Baltes, P.B. and Baltes, M.M. (1990). Psychological perspectives on successful aging: The model of selective optimization with compensation. In P. B. Baltes and M. M. Baltes (eds), *Successful aging: perspectives from the behavioral sciences*, pp. 1–34. New York: Cambridge University Press.

Barnes, J.E. and Nissenbaum, D. (2013, January 24). Combat ban for women to end. *The Wall Street Journal*. Retrieved from http://online.wsj.com/article/SB10001424127887323539804578260123802564276.html

Barrett, A.E., and von Rohr, C. (2008). Gendered perceptions of aging: an examination of college students. *International Journal of Ageing and Human Development* **67**, 359–86.

Bass, B.M. and Avolio, B.J. (1994). *Improving organizational effectiveness through transformational leadership.* Thousand Oaks, CA: Sage.

Baumeister, R.F. and Mendoza, J.P. (2011). Cultural variations in the sexual marketplace: gender equality correlates with more sexual activity. *The Journal of Social Psychology* **151**, 350–60. doi: 10.1080/00224545.2010.481686

Baumeister, R.F., Catanese, K.R. and Vohs, K.D. (2001). Is there a gender difference in strength of sex drive? Theoretical views, conceptual distinctions, and a review of relevant evidence. *Personality and Social Psychology Review* **5**, 242–73.

BBC News (2012, November 14). EU defends women-on-boards plans. Retrieved from http://www.bbc.co.uk/news/business-20322317

BBC News (2013, January 14). "Simple" flat-rate state pension unveiled. Retrieved from http://www.bbc.co.uk/news/business-21017013

Bennett, J. (2010, July 19). The beauty advantage. *Newsweek.* Retrieved from http://www.thedailybeast.com/newsweek/2010/07/19/the-beauty-advantage.html

Berenbaum, S.A., Blakemore, J.E.O. and Beltz, A. M. (2011). A role for biology in gender-related behavior. *Sex Roles* **64**, 804–25. doi: 10.1007/s11199-011-9990-8

Bernard, M. (2013, January 24). With women in combat, will military finally address epidemic of sexual assault? *The Washington Post.* Blog post. Retrieved from http://www.washingtonpost.com/blogs/she-the-people/wp/2013/01/24/with-woman-in-combat-will-military-finally-address-epidemic-of-sexual-assault/

Bertakis, K.D. and Azari, R. (2007). Patient gender and physician practice style. *Journal of Women's Health* **16**, 859–68.

Bertakis, K.D., Helms, L.J., Callahan, E.J., Azari, R., Leigh, P. and Robbins, J.A. (2001). Patient gender differences in the diagnosis of depression in primary care. *Journal of Women's Health and Gender Based Medicine* **10**, 689–98.

Besler, P. (2005) *Forced Labour and Human Trafficking: estimating the profits.* Working paper. Geneva: International Labour Office. Retrieved from http://papers.ssrn.com/sol3/papers.cfm?abstract_id=1838403

Bettio, F. and Verashchagina, A. (2010). *Long-Term Care for the Elderly. Provisions and providers in 33 European countries.* Luxembourg: Publications Office of the European Union. Retrieved from http://ec.europa.eu/justice/gender-equality/files/elderly_care_en.pdf

Bianchi, S., Folbre, N. and Wolf, D. (2012), Unpaid care work. In N. Folbre (ed.), *For Love and Money: care provision in the United States*, pp. 40–64. New York: Russell Sage Foundation.

Bikorimana, D. (2012, May 15). Rwanda: the land of gender equality? *Think Africa Press.* Retrieved from http://thinkafricapress.com/rwanda/women-gender-equality

Black, M.C. (2011). Intimate partner violence and adverse health consequences: implications for clinicians. *American Journal of Lifestyle Medicine* **5**, 428–39.

Black, M.C., Basile, K.C., Breiding, M.J., Smith, S.G., Walters, M.L., Merrick, M.T., Chen, J. and Stevens, M.R. (2011). *The National Intimate Partner and Sexual Violence Survey (NISVS): 2010 Summary Report.* Atlanta, GA: National Center for Injury Prevention and Control, Centers for Disease Control and Prevention. Retrieved from http://www.cdc.gov/ViolencePrevention/pdf/ NISVS_Executive_Summary-a.pdf

Borooah, V.K. (2004). Gender bias among children in India in their diet and immunisation against disease. *Social Science and Medicine* **58**, 1719–31. doi: 10.1016/S0277-9536(03)00342-3

Bose, S. (2011). The effect of women's status and community on the gender differential in children's nutrition in India. *Journal of Biosocial Science* **43**, 513–33. doi: 10.1017/S002193201100006X

Bosson, J.K., Vandello, J.A., Burnaford, R.M., Weaver, J.R. and Wasti, S.A. (2009). Precarious manhood and displays of physical aggression. *Personality and Social Psychology Bulletin* **35**, 623–34. doi: 10.1177/0146167208331161

Bostwick, T.D. and DeLucia, J.L. (1992). Effects of gender and specific dating behaviors on percpetions of sex willingness and date rape. *Journal of Social and Clinical Psychology* **11**, 14–25.

Bouchard, S. (2013, March 12). Immigration reform may solve long-term care worker shortage. *Health Care Finance News*. Retrieved from http://www. healthcarefinancenews.com/news/immigration-reform-may-solve-long-term-care-worker-shortage

Bowleg, L., Teti, M., Massie, J.S., Patel, A., Malebranche, D.J. and Tschann, J.M. (2011). 'What does it take to be a man? What is a real man?': Ideologies of masculinity and HIV sexual risk among black heterosexual men. *Culture, Health and Sexuality* **13**, 545–59. doi: 10.1080/13691058.2011.556201

Boyle, K. (2011). Producing abuse: selling the harms of pornography. *Women's Studies International Forum* **34**, 593–602. doi: 10.1016/j.wsif.2011.09.002

Boyle, M., Georgiades, K., Cullen, J. and Racine, Y. (2009). Community influences on intimate partner violence in India: women's education, attitudes towards mistreatment and standards of living. *Social Science and Medicine* **69**, 691–97. doi: 10.1016/j.socscimed.2009.06.039

Bradley, S.J., Oliver, G.D., Chernick, A.B. and Zucker, K.J. (1998). Experiment of nurture: ablatio penis at 2 months, sex reassignment at 7 months, and a psychosexual follow-up in young adulthood. *Pediatrics* **102**(1), e9.

Bradshaw, C., Kahn, A.S. and Saville, B.K. (2010). To hook up or date: which gender benefits? *Sex Roles* **62**, 661–69. doi: 10.1007/s11199-010-9765-7

Brannon, R. (1976). The male sex role: our culture's blueprint for manhood and what it's done for us lately. In D. David and R. Brannon (eds), *The Forty-nine Percent Majority*. Reading, MA: Addison-Wesley.

Braun, S., Peus, C. and Frey, D. (2012). Is beauty beastly? Gender-specific effects of leader attractiveness and leadership style on followers' trust and loyalty. *Zeitschrift für Psychologie* **220**, 98–108. doi: 10.1027/2151-2604/a000101

Brescoll, V.L. (2011). Who takes the floor and why: gender, power, and volubility in organizations. *Administrative Science Quarterly* **56**, 622–41. doi: 10.1177/0001839212439994

Brescoll, V.L., and Uhlmann, E.L. (2008). Can an angry woman get ahead? Status conferral, gender, and expression of emotion in the workplace. *Psychological Science* **19**, 268–75. doi: 10.1111/j.1467-9280.2008.02079.x

Brescoll, V.L., Uhlmann, E.L., Moss-Racusin, C. and Sarnell, L. (2012). Masculinity, status, and subordination: why working for a gender stereotype violator causes men to lose status. *Journal of Experimental Social Psychology* **48**, 354–57. doi: 10.1016/j.jesp.2011.06.005

Bridges, A.J., Wosnitzer, R., Scharrer, E., Sun, C. and Liberman, R. (2010). Aggression and sexual behavior in best-selling pornography videos: a content analysis update. *Violence Against Women* **16**, 1065–85. doi: 10.1177/1077801210382866

Brinkman, B.G., Garcia, K. and Rickard, K.M. (2011). "What I wanted to do was...". Discrepancies between college women's desired and reported responses to gender prejudice. *Sex Roles* **65**, 344–55. doi: 10.1007/s11199-011-0020-7

Brown, M. and Rounsley, D. (1996). *True selves: understanding transsexualism for families, friends, coworkers, and helping professionals*. San Francisco, CA: Jossey-Bass.

Browne, C.V. and Braun, K.L. (2008). Globalization, women's migration, and the long-term-care workforce. *The Gerontologist* **48**, 16–24. doi: 10.1093/geront/48.1.16

Brownmiller, S. (1999). *In Our Time: memoir of a revolution*. New York: Dell Publishing.

Bryant, T., Leaver, C. and Dunn, J. (2009). Unmet healthcare need, gender, and health inequalities in Canada. *Health Policy* **91**, 24–32. doi: 10.1016/j.healthpol.2008.11.002

Budig, M. and England, P. (2001). The wage penalty for motherhood. *American Sociological Review* **66**, 204–25.

Byakika-Tusiime, J. (2008). Circumcision and HIV infection: assessment of causality. *AIDS and Behavior* **12**, 835–41.

Byrnes, J., Miller, D. and Schaffer, W. (1999). Gender differences in risk-taking: a meta-analysis. *Psychological Bulletin* **125**, 367–83.

Calasanti, T. and King, N. (2007). "Beware of the estrogen assault": Ideals of old manhood in anti-aging advertisements. *Journal of Aging Studies* **21**, 357–68. doi: 10.1016/j.jaging.2007.05.003

Cameron, K.A., Song, J., Manheim, L.M. and Dunlop, D.D. (2010). Gender disparities in health and healthcare use among older adults. *Journal of Women's Health* **19**, 1643–50. doi: 10.1089/jwh.2009.1701

Cancer Research UK (2012). *Worldwide cancer statistics.* Retrieved from http://www.cancerresearchuk.org/cancer-info/cancerstats/world/cancer-worldwide-the-global-picture

Card, N.A., Stucky, B.D., Sawalani, G.M. and Little, T.D. (2008). Direct and indirect aggression during childhood and adolescence: a meta-analytic review of gender differences, intercorrelations, and relations to maladjustment. *Child Development* **79**, 1185–1229. doi: 10.1111/j.1467-8624.2008.01184.x

Carstensen, L.L., and Mikels, J. (2005). At the intersection of emotion and cognition: aging and the positivity effect. *Current Directions in Psychological Science* **14**, 117–21.

Carstensen, L.L., Fung, H.H. and Charles, S.T. (2003). Socioemotional selectivity theory and the regulation of emotion in the second half of life. *Motivation and Emotion* **27**, 103–23.

Catalano, S.M. (2012, November 27). *Intimate partner violence, 1993-2010.* US Bureau of Justice Statistics. Retrieved from http://bjs.ojp.usdoj.gov/index.cfm?ty=pbdetail&iid=4536

Catalyst (2006). *Different Cultures, Similar Perceptions: stereotyping of Western European business leaders.* New York: Catalyst. Retrieved from http://www.catalyst.org/knowledge/different-cultures-similar-perceptions-stereotyping-western-european-business-leaders

Catalyst (2007). *The Double-bind Dilemma for Women in Leadership: damned if you do, doomed if you don't.* New York: Catalyst. Retrieved from http://www.catalyst.org/knowledge/double-bind-dilemma-women-leadership-damned-if-you-do-doomed-if-you-dont-0

Catalyst (2012a). *2012 Catalyst census: Fortune 500.* New York: Catalyst. Retrieved from http://www.catalyst.org/knowledge/2012-catalyst-census-fortune-500-appendix-5%E2%80%94companies-25-or-more-women-executive-officers

Catalyst (2012b). Knowledge Center. Women on Boards. Retrieved from http://www.catalyst.org/knowledge/women-boards

Catalyst (2013, January 3). *Women CEOs of the Fortune 500.* New York: Catalyst. Retrieved from http://www.catalyst.org/knowledge/women-ceos-fortune-500

Centers for Disease Control and Prevention (2010a). US Physical Activity Statistics. Accessed at http://apps.nccd.cdc.gov/PASurveillance/DemoCompareResultV.asp?ErrorMsg=3andYears=andState=andCT=andCat=

Centers for Disease Control and Prevention (2010b). National Center for Health Statistics. Health Data Interactive. Accessed at www.cdc.gov/nchs/hdi.htm

Centers for Disease Control and Prevention (2012). *Physical Activity. Data and Statistics*. Retrieved from http://www.cdc.gov/physicalactivity/data/facts.html

Centers for Disease Control and Prevention (2013). *Pregnancy mortality surveillance system*. Retrieved from http://www.cdc.gov/reproductivehealth/Maternal InfantHealth/PMSS.html

Chan, D.K.-S., Lam, C.B., Chow, S.Y. and Cheung, S.F. (2008). Examining the job-related, psychological and physical outcomes of workplace sexual harassment: a meta-analytic review. *Psychology of Women Quarterly* **32**, 362–76.

Chang, A., Sandhofer, C.M., and Brown, C.S. (2011). Gender biases in early number exposure to preschool-aged children. *Journal of Language and Social Psychology*, **30**, 440–450. doi: 10.1177/0261927X11416207

Charles, M. (2011). A world of difference: International trends in women's economic status. *Annual Review of Sociology* **37**, 355–71. doi: 10.1146/annurev.soc.012809.102548

Charles, M. and Grusky, D.B. (2004). *Occupational Ghettos: the worldwide segregation of women and men*. Stanford, CA: Stanford University Press.

Charles, S.T. and Carstensen, L.L. (2008). Unpleasant situations elicit different emotional responses in younger and older adults. *Psychology and Aging* **23**, 495–504. doi: 10.1037/a0013284

Chemers, M.M. (1997). *An Integrative Theory of Leadership*. Mahwah, NJ: Erlbaum.

Chesler, P. (2010). Worldwide trends in honor killings. *The Middle East Quarterly* **17**(2), 3–11. Retrieved from http://www.meforum.org/2646/worldwide-trends-in-honor-killings

Chepngeno-Langat, G., Madise, N., Evandrou, M. and Falkingham, J. (2011). Gender differentials on the health consequences of care-giving to people with AIDS-related illness among older informal carers in two slums in Nairobi, Kenya. *AIDS Care* **23**, 1586–1594. doi: 10.1080/09540121.2011.569698

Chia, S.C. and Gunther, A.C. (2006). How media contribute to misperceptions of social norms about sex. *Mass Communication and Society* **9**, 301–20. doi: 10.1207/s15327825mcs0903_3

Chivers, M.L., Seto, M.C., Lalumière, M.L., Laan, E. and Grimbos, T. (2010). Agreement of self-reported and genital measures of sexual arousal in men and women: a meta-analysis. *Archives of Sexual Behavior* **39**, 5–56. doi: 10.1007/s10508-009-9556-9

Cialdini, R.B. and Griskevicius, V. (2010). Social influence. In R.F. Baumeister and E.J. Finkel (eds), *Advanced Social Psychology: the state of the science*, pp. 385–417. New York: Oxford University Press.

Clark, K.A., Biddle, A.K., and Martin, S.L. (2002). A cost-benefit analysis of the violence against women act of 1994. *Violence Against Women*, **8**, 417–428. doi: 10.1177/10778010222183143

Clark, K.A., Biddle, A.K. and Martin, S.L. (2003). A cost-benefit analysis of the violence against women act of 1994: Erratum. *Violence Against Women* **9**, 136. doi: 10.1177/107780103762562609

Clement, S. (2011, November 15). Workplace harassment drawing wide concern. *The Washington Post*. Retrieved from http://www.washingtonpost.com/politics/2011/11/15/gIQACBryPN_story.html

Cognard-Black, A.J. (2004). Will they stay, or will they go? Sex-atypical work among token men who teach. *The Sociological Quarterly* **45**, 113–39. doi: 10.1111/j.1533-8525.2004.tb02400.x

Cohen, P.N. (2012, September 29). Debunking the end of men, "Myth of male decline" edition. Web log post. Retrieved from http://familyinequality.wordpress.com/2012/09/29/debunking-end-of-men-myth-of-male-decline-edition/

Collins, R.L. (2011). Content analysis of gender roles in media: where are we now and where should we go? *Sex Roles* **64**, 290–98. doi: 10.1007/s11199-010-9929-5

Collins, V.E. and Carmody, D.C. (2011). Deadly love: images of dating violence in the "Twilight Saga". *Affilia: Journal of Women and Social Work* **26**, 382–94.

Constitution of the Republic of Rwanda (2003). Retrieved from http://www.rwandahope.com/constitution.pdf

Corbett, C. and Hill, C. (2012). *Graduating to a pay gap: the earnings of women and men one year after college graduation*. Washington, DC: American Association of University Women.

Correll, S. J. (2004). Constraints into preferences: gender, status, and emerging career aspirations. *American Sociological Review* **69**, 93–113. doi: 10.1177/000312240406900106

Coughlin, P. and Wade, J.C. (2012). Masculinity ideology, income disparity, and romantic relationship quality among men with higher earning female partners. *Sex Roles* **67**, 311–22. doi: 10.1007/s11199-012-0187-6

Crary, D. (2011, August 20). Boomers will be pumping billions into anti-aging industry. *The Huffington Post*. Retrieved from http://www.huffingtonpost.com/2011/08/20/boomers-anti-aging-industry_n_932109.html

Crawford, M. (2010). *Sex Trafficking in South Asia: telling Maya's Story*. Abingdon, UK: Routledge.

Crick, N.R., Ostrov, J.M. and Kawabata, Y. (2007). Relational aggression and gender: an overview. In D.J. Flannery, A.T. Vazsonyi and I.D. Waldman (eds), *The Cambridge Handbook of Violent Behavior and Aggression*, pp. 245–59. New York: Cambridge University Press. doi: 10.1017/CBO9780511816840.012

Croda, E. and Gonzalez-Chapela, J. (2005). How do European older adults use their time? In A. Börsch-Supan, A. Brugiavini, H. Jürges, J. Mackenbach, J. Siegrist and G. Weber (eds), *Health, Ageing and Retirement in Europe – First Results from the Survey of Health, Ageing and Retirement in Europe*, pp. 265–71.

Mannheim, MEA. Retrieved from www.share-project.org/uploads/tx_sharepublications/CH_5.6.pdf

Crosby, F.J., Iyer, A. and Sincharoen, S. (2006). Understanding affirmative action. *Annual Review of Psychology*, **57**, 585–611. doi: 10.1146/annurev.psych.57.102904.190029

Crown Prosecution Service (UK) (2011, December 4). Domestic violence: the facts, the issues, the future. Speech by the Director of Public Prosecutions, Kerei Starmer QC. Retrieved from http://www.cps.gov.uk/news/articles/domestic_violence_-_the_facts_the_issues_the_future/

Cvencek, D., Meltzoff, A.N. and Greenwald, A.G. (2011). Math-gender stereotypes in elementary school children. *Child Development* **82**, 766–79. doi: 10.1111/j.1467-8624.2010.01529.x

Czerenda, A.J. (2010). The meaning of widowhood and health to older middle-class Hindu widows living in a south Indian community. *Journal of Transcultural Nursing* **21**, 351–60. doi: 10.1177/1043659609360715

Dabbous, Y. and Ladley, A. (2010). A spine of steel and a heart of gold: newspaper coverage of the first female Speaker of the House. *Journal of Gender Studies* **19**, 181–94. doi: 10.1080/09589231003695971

Daly, M. (2011). What adult worker model? A critical look at recent social policy reform in Europe from a gender and family perspective. *Social Politics: International Studies in Gender, State and Society* **18**, 1–23. doi: 10.1093/sp/jxr002

D'Aprano, Z. (2001). *Kath Williams: the unions and the fight for equal pay.* Melbourne, Australia: Spinifex Press.

Davis, K., Norris, J., George, W.H., Martell, J. and Heiman, J.R. (2006). Rape-myth congruent beliefs in women resulting from exposure to violent pornography: effects of alcohol and sexual arousal. *Journal of Interpersonal Violence* **21**, 1208–1223. doi: 10.1177/0886260506290428

de Vaus, D., Gray, M. and Stanton, D. (2003). *Measuring the value of unpaid household, caring and voluntary work of older Australians.* Research Paper No. 34. Melbourne, Australia: Australian Institute of Family Studies. Available from www.pc.gov.au/__data/assets/pdf_file/0011/14033/sub010.pdf

de Visser, R.O. and McDonnell, E.J. (2013). "Man points": masculine capital and young men's health. *Health Psychology* **32**, 5–14. doi: 10.1037/a0029045

del Pino-Casado, R., Frías-Osuna, A., Palomino-Moral, P.A. and Martínez-Riera, J.R. (2012). Gender differences regarding informal caregivers of older people. *Journal of Nursing Scholarship* **44**, 349–57. doi: 10.1111/j.1547-5069.2012.01477.x

Den Dulk, L. (2005). Workplace work-family arrangements: a study and explanatory framework of differences between organizational provisions in different welfare states. In S.A.Y. Poelmans (ed.). *Work and Family: an international research perspective*, pp. 211–38. Mahwah, NJ: Lawrence Erlbaum.

Department for Work and Pensions (2005). Women and pensions: the evidence. Retrieved from http://www.dwp.gov.uk/docs/women-pensions.pdf

Deutsch, F.M., Zalenski, C.M. and Clark, M.E. (1986). Is there a double standard of aging? *Journal of Applied Social Psychology* **16**, 771–85.

Diamond, M. and Sigmundson, H.K. (1997). Sex reassignment at birth: long-term review and clinical implications. *Archives of Pediatric Medicine* **151**, 298– 304.

Diekman, A.B. and Eagly, A.H. (2000). Stereotypes as dynamic constructs: women and men of the past, present, and future. *Personality and Social Psychology Bulletin* **26**, 1171–1188. doi: 10.1177/0146167200262001

Diekman, A.B., Eagly, A.H., Mladinic, A. and Ferreira, M.C. (2005). Dynamic stereotypes about women and men in Latin America and the United States. *Journal of Cross-Cultural Psychology* **36**, 209–26. doi: 10.1177/00220 22104272902

Dill, K.E., and Thill, K.P. (2007). Video game characters and the socialization of gender roles: young people's perceptions mirror sexist media depictions. *Sex Roles* **57**, 851–64. doi: 10.1007/s11199-007-9278-1

Dixon, R. (2010, June 21). They kick like grannies, proudly. *Los Angeles Times*. Accessed at http://www.globalaging.org/elderrights/world/2010/soccer. htm

Donohoe, M. T. (2005, December 13). War, rape and genocide: from ancient times to the Sudan. Abstract #108859. Presentation at the annual meeting of the American Public Health Association, Philadelphia, PA, USA. https://apha. confex.com/apha/133am/techprogram/paper_108859.htm

Downing, N.E. and Roush, K.L. (1985). From passive acceptance to active commitment: a model of feminist identity development for women. *The Counseling Psychologist* **13**, 695–709. doi: 10.1177/0011000085134013

Dunkin, J.J. (2009). Aging and gender. In E. Fletcher-Janzen (ed.), *The Neuropsychology of Women. Issues of diversity in clinical neuropsychology*, pp. 209– 23. New York: Springer Science + Business Media. doi: 10.1007/978-0-387-76908-0_10

Dunlop, B.W. and Mletzko, T. (2011). Will current socioeconomic trends produce a depressing future for men? *The British Journal of Psychiatry* **198**, 167–68. doi: 10.1192/bjp.bp.110.084210

Dykstra, P.A. and de Jong Gierveld, J. (2004). Gender and marital-history differences in emotional and social loneliness among Dutch older adults. *Canadian Journal on Aging* **23**, 141–55. doi: 10.1353/cja.2004.0018

Eagly, A.H. (1987). *Sex differences in social behavior: A social role interpretation*. Hillsdale, NJ: Erlbaum.

Eagly, A.H. and Carli, L.L. (2003). Finding gender advantage and disadvantage: systematic research integration is the solution. *Leadership Quarterly* **14**, 851–59. doi: 10.1016/j.leaqua.2003.09.003

Eagly, A.H. and Carli, L.L. (2007). *Through the Labyrinth: the truth about how women become leaders*. Boston, MA: Harvard Business School Publishing.

Eagly, A.H. and Karau, S.J. (2002). Role congruity theory of prejudice toward female leaders. *Psychological Review* **109**, 573–98. doi: 10.1037/0033-295X.109.3.573

Eagly, A.H. and Steffen, V.J. (1986). Gender and aggressive behavior: a meta-analytic review of the social psychological literature. *Psychological Bulletin* **100**, 309–30. doi: 10.1037/0033-2909.100.3.309

Eagly, A.H., Johannesen-Schmidt, M.C. and van Engen, M.L. (2003). Transformational, transactional, and laissez-faire leadership styles: a meta-analysis comparing women and men. *Psychological Bulletin* **129**, 569–91. doi: 10.1037/0033-2909.129.4.569

Eagly, A.H., Mladinic, A. and Otto, S. (1991). Are women evaluated more favorably than men? An analysis of attitudes, beliefs, and emotions. *Psychology of Women Quarterly* **15**, 203–216. doi: 10.1111/j.1471-6402.1991.tb00792.x

Eagly, A.H., Karau, S.J., Miner, J.B. and Johnson, B.T. (1994). Gender and motivation to manage in hierarchic organizations: a meta-analysis. *The Leadership Quarterly* **5**(2), 135–59. doi: 10.1016/1048-9843(94)90025-6

Edwards, L. (2013, March 16). The gender gap in pain. *The New York Times*. Retrieved from http://www.nytimes.com/2013/03/17/opinion/sunday/women-and-the-treatment-of-pain.html?ref=painand_r=1and

Eichstedt, J.A., Serbin, L.A., Poulin-Dubois, D. and Sen, M.G. (2002). Of bears and men: infants' knowledge of conventional and metaphorical gender stereotypes. *Infant Behavior and Development* **25**, 296–310. doi: 10.1016/S0163-6383(02)00081-4

Elder, W.B., Brooks, G.R. and Morrow, S.L. (2012). Sexual self-schemas of heterosexual men. *Psychology of Men and Masculinity* **13**, 166–79. doi: 10.1037/a0024835

Ellin, A. (2011, August 8). The golden years, polished with surgery. *The New York Times*. Retrieved from http://www.nytimes.com/2011/08/09/health/09plastic.html?pagewanted=alland_r=0

Elmer, V. (2012, April 8). Workplace pregnancy discrimination cases on the rise. *The Washington Post*. Retrieved from http://articles.washingtonpost.com/2012-04-08/business/35450871_1_pregnancy-discrimination-eeoc-pregnant-women

Ely, R.J., Insead, H.I. and Kolb, D.M. (2011). Taking gender into account: theory and design for women's leadership development programs. *Academy of Management Learning and Education* **10**, 474–93.

Eman, J. (2012). The role of sports in making sense of the process of growing old. *Journal of Aging Studies* **26**, 467–475. doi: 10.1016/j.jaging.2012.06.006

Emmers-Sommer, T.M. and Allen, M. (1999). Variables related to sexual coercion: a path model. *Journal of Social and Personal Relationships* **16**, 659–78.

Emslie, C., Hunt, K. and O'Brien, R. (2004). Masculinities in older men: a qualitative study in the west of Scotland. *The Journal of Men's Studies* **12**, 207–26. doi: 10.3149/jms.1203.207

Epstein, M., Calzo, J.P., Smiler, A.P. and Ward, L.(2009). "Anything from making out to having sex": Men's negotiations of hooking up and friends with benefits scripts. *Journal of Sex Research* **46**, 414–24. doi: 10.1080/00224490902775801

Equality Law (2012, May 30). Half of female workforce fear sexual harassment at work. Retrieved from http://www.equalitylaw.co.uk/news/2378/66/Half-of-female-workforce-fear-sexual-harassment-at-work/

Erchull, M.J., Liss, M., Wilson, K.A., Bateman, L., Peterson, A. and Sanchez, C.E. (2009). The feminist identity development model: relevant for young women today? *Sex Roles* **60**, 832–42. doi: 10.1007/s11199-009-9588-6

Evans, O. and Steptoe, A. (2002). The contribution of gender-role orientation, work factors and home stressors to psychological well-being and sickness absence in male- and female-dominated occupational groups. *Social Science and Medicine* **54**, 481–92. doi: 10.1016/S0277-9536(01)00044-2

European Commission (2012). *Women in economic decision-making in the EU: Progress Report.* Luxembourg: Publications office of the European Union Retrieved from http://csdle.lex.unict.it/docs/labourweb/Women-in-economic-decision-making-in-the-EU-Progress-report-/2828.aspx

European Social Survey (2010). Retrieved from http://www.europeansocial survey.org/index

Fallon, A. (2011, June 2). VS Naipaul finds no woman writer his literary match—not even Jane Austen. *The Guardian.* Accessed at http://www.guardian.co.uk/books/2011/jun/02/vs-naipaul-jane-austen-women-writers

Federal Bureau of Investigation (2011). *Crime in the United States, 2011.* Expanded offense data. Retrieved from http://www.fbi.gov/about-us/cjis/ucr/crime-in-the-u.s/2011/crime-in-the-US-2011/offenses-known-to-law-enforcement/expanded-offense-data

Federal Bureau of Investigation (2012). *Hate Crime Statistics, 2011.* Retrieved from http://www.fbi.gov/about-us/cjis/ucr/hate-crime/2011/narratives/victims

Female power (2009, December 30). *The Economist.* Retrieved from http://www.economist.com/node/15174418?story_id=15174418

Ferraro, K. J. (2003). The words change, but the melody lingers. The persistence of the Battered Woman Syndrome in criminal cases involving battered women. *Violence Against Women* **9**, 110–29, doi: 10.1177/1077801202238432

Fiori, K.L., Windsor, T.D., Pearson, E.D. and Crisp, D.A. (2013). Can positive social exchanges buffer the detrimental effects of negative social exchanges? Age and gender differences. *Gerontology* **59**, 40–52. doi: 10.1159/000339747

Firestone, S. (1970). *The Dialectic of Sex*. New York: William Morrow and Company.

Fishman, P.M. (1978). Interaction: the work women do. *Social Problems* **25**, 397–406. doi: 10.1525/sp.1978.25.4.03a00050

Fiske, S.T., Bersoff, D.N., Borgida, E., Deaux, K. and Heilman, M.E. (1991). Social science on trial: use of sex stereotyping research in *Price Waterhouse v. Hopkins*. *American Psychologist* **46**, 1049–1060. doi: 10.1037/0003-066X.46.10.1049

Floge, L. and Merrill, D.M. (1986). Tokenism reconsidered: male nurses and female physicians in a hospital setting. *Social Forces* **64**, 925–47. doi: 10.2307/2578787

Food and Agriculture Organization of the United Nations (no date). Retrieved February 25, 2013 from http://www.fao.org/docrep/012/al184e/al184e00.pdf

Forbes, C.E. and Schmader, T. (2010). Retraining attitudes and stereotypes to affect motivation and cognitive capacity under stereotype threat. *Journal of Personality and Social Psychology* **99**, 740–54. doi: 10.1037/a0020971

Foster, B.L. (1976). Friendship in rural Thailand. *Ethnology* **15**, 251–67.

Frank, M., Farnsworth, J., Esposito, S. and Hopper, J. (2012, September 27). Rock Center, NBC News. Retrieved from http://rockcenter.nbcnews.com/_news/2012/09/27/14123062-victims-of-sexual-assault-in-military-say-brass-often-ignore-pleas-for-justice?lite

French, J.R. and Raven, B. (1959). The bases of social power. In D. Cartwright (ed.), *Studies in social power*, pp. 150-67. Oxford, UK: University of Michigan Press.

Freud, S. (1960). *A General Introduction to Psychoanalysis* (trans. J. Riviere). New York: Washington Square Press. (Original work published 1924.)

Friedman, A. and Pines, A.M. (1992). Increase in Arab women's perceived power in the second half of life. *Sex Roles* **26**, 1–9. doi: 10.1007/BF00290121

Frieze, I.H. (2005). *Hurting the One You Love: violence in intimate relationships*. Belmont, CA: Wadworth/Thompson Learning.

Frieze, I.H. (2008). Social policy, feminism, and research on violence in close relationships. *Journal of Social Issues* **64**, 665–84.

Frisby, C.M. (2010, Summer-Fall). Sticks 'n stones may break my bones, but words they hurt like hell: derogatory words in popular songs. *Media Report to Women*, pp. 12–18.

Funk, L.C. and Werhun, C.D. (2011). "You're such a girl!" The psychological drain of the gender-role harassment of men. *Sex Roles* **65**, 13–22. doi 10.1007/s11199-011-9948-x

Galinsky, E., Aumann, K. and Bond, J.T. (2011). *Times are changing. Gender and generation at work and at home*. Families and Work Institute. Retrieved from http://familiesandwork.org/site/research/reports/Times_Are_Changing.pdf

Garcia, J.R. and Reiber, C. (2008). Hook-up behavior: a biopsychosocial perspective. *The Journal of Social, Evolutionary, and Cultural Psychology* **2**, 192–208.

Garcia, J.R., Reiber, C., Massey, S.G. and Merriwether, A.M. (2012). Sexual hookup culture: a review. *Review of General Psychology* **16**, 161–76. doi: 10.1037/a0027911

Gavey, N. (2005). *Just Sex? The cultural scaffolding of rape.* Hove, UK: Routledge.

Giancola, P.R., Helton, E.L., Osborne, A.B., Terry, M.K., Fuss, A.M. and Westerfield, J.A. (2002). The effects of alcohol and provocation on aggressive behavior in men and women. *Journal of Studies on Alcohol* **63**, 64–73.

Gillen, M. and Kim, H. (2009). Older women and poverty transition: consequences of income source changes from widowhood. *Journal of Applied Gerontology* **28**, 320–41. doi: 10.1177/0733464808326953

Giunta, T.K. (ed.) (2011). *Breaking the Glass Ceiling: women in the boardroom.* Washington DC: Paul Hastings. Retrieved from http://www.paulhastings.com/assets/pdfs/Gender_Parity_on_Corporate_Boards.pdf

Glaser, R., Sheridan, J., Malarkey, W.B., MacCallum, R.C. and Kiecolt-Glaser, J.K. (2000). Chronic stress modulates the immune response to a pneumococcal pneumonia vaccine. *Psychosomatic Medicine* **62**, 804–807.

Glass, C.M., Haas, S.A. and Reither, E.N. (2010). The skinny on success: body mass, gender and occupational standing across the life course. *Social Forces* **88**, 1777–1806. doi: 10.1353/sof.2010.0012

Glauber, R. (2007). Marriage and the motherhood wage penalty among African Americans, Hispanics, and Whites. *Journal of Marriage and Family* **69**, 951–61.

Glauber, R. (2008). Race and gender in families and at work: the fatherhood wage premium. *Gender and Society* **22**, 8–30.

Glick, P. and Fiske, S.T. (1996). The Ambivalent Sexism Inventory: differentiating hostile and benevolent sexism. *Journal of Personality and Social Psychology* **70**, 491–512. doi: 10.1037/0022-3514.70.3.491

Glick, P., Diebold, J., Bailey-Werner, B. and Zhu, L. (1997). The two faces of Adam: ambivalent sexism and polarized attitudes toward women. *Personality and Social Psychology Bulletin* **23**, 1323–1334. doi:10.1177/01461672972312009

Glick, P., Larsen, S., Johnson, C. and Branstiter, H. (2005). Evaluations of sexy women in low- and high-status jobs. *Psychology of Women Quarterly* **29**, 389–95. doi: 10.1111/j.1471-6402.2005.00238.x

Glick, P., Lameiras, M., Fiske, S.T., Eckes, T., Masser, B., Volpato, C., Manganelli, A.M., Pek, J.C.X., Huang, L., Sakalli-Uğurlu, N., Castro, Y.R., D'Avila Pereira, M.L., Willemsen, T.M., Brunner, A., Six-Materna, I. and Wells, R. (2004). Bad but bold: ambivalent attitudes toward men predict gender inequality in 16 nations. *Journal of Personality and Social Psychology* **86**, 713–28. doi: 10.1037/0022-3514.86.5.713

Goitein, S.D. (1971). Formal friendship in the medieval near east. *Proceedings of the American Philosophical Society* **115**, 484–89.

Goldberg, P.A. (1968). Are women prejudiced against women? *Trans-action* **5**, 28–30.

Goldin, C. and Rouse, C. (2000). Orchestrating impartiality: the impact of "blind" auditions on female musicians. *American Economic Review* **90**, 715–41.

Golding, J.M., Yozwiak, J.A., Kinstle, T.L. and Marsil, D.F. (2005). The effect of gender in the perception of elder physical abuse in court. *Law and Human Behavior* **29**, 605–14. doi: 10.1007/s10979-005-6831-8

Good, C., Aronson, J. and Harder, J.A. (2008). Problems in the pipeline: stereotype threat and women's achievement in high-level math courses. *Journal of Applied Developmental Psychology* **29**, 17–28. doi: 10.1016/j.appdev.2007.10.004

Gossett, J.L. and Byrne, S. (2002). "CLICK HERE": a content analysis of Internet rape sites. *Gender and Society* **16**, 689–709. doi: 10.1177/089124302236992

Gotta, G., Green, R., Rothblum, E., Solomon, S., Balsam, K. and Schwartz, P. (2011). Heterosexual, lesbian, and gay male relationships: a comparison of couples in 1975 and 2000. *Family Process* **50**, 353–76. doi: 10.1111/j.1545-5300.2011.01365.x

Gouin, J.P., Hantsoo, L. and Kiecolt-Glaser, J.K. (2008). Immune dysregulation and chronic stress among older adults: a review. *Neuroimmunomodulation* **15**, 251–59. doi:000156468[pii]10.1159/000156468

Halila, S. (2008). The new female Muslim thinkers or DWEMS (Daring Women as Enlightened Muslim Scholars). *The International Journal of the Humanities* **6**. Retrieved from http://thehumanities.com/publications/journal/

Hall, D.T., Lee, M.D., Kossek, E.E. and Las Heras, M. (2012). Pursuing career success while sustaining personal and family well being: a study of reduced-load professionals over time. *Journal of Social Issues* **68**, 742–66.

Halliwell, E. and Dittmar, H. (2003). A qualitative investigation of women's and men's body image concerns and their attitudes toward aging. *Sex Roles* **49**, 675–84.

Halpern, D.F. (2012). *Sex Differences in Cognitive Abilities* (4th edn). New York: Psychology Press.

Hamilton, B.E. and Ventura, S.J. (2012, April). *Birth Rates for US Teenagers Reach Historic Lows for All Age and Ethnic Groups*. NCHS Data Brief, Number 89. Hyattsville, MD: National Center for Health Statistics. Retrieved from http://www.cdc.gov/nchs/data/databriefs/db89.htm

Hardy, S.E., Allore, H.G., Guo, Z. and Gill, T.M. (2008). Explaining the effect of gender on functional transitions in older persons. *Gerontology* **54**, 79–86. doi: 10.1159/000115004

Hausmann, R., Tyson, L.D. and Zahidi, S. (2012). *The Global Gender Gap Report 2012*. World Economic Forum. Retrieved from http://www.weforum.org/issues/global-gender-gap

Haworth, A. (2012, November 17). The day I saw 248 girls suffering genital mutilation. *The Observer*. Retrieved from http://www.guardian.co.uk/society/2012/nov/18/female-genital-mutilation-circumcision-indonesia

Health Canada (2002). *Violence against women. Impact of violence on women's health*. Retrieved from http://www.hc-sc.gc.ca/

Hebert, L.E., Weuve, J., Scherr, P.A. and Evans, D.A. (2013). Alzheimer disease in the United States (2010–2050) estimated using the 2010 census. *Neurology*; Published online before print February 6, 2013. doi: 10.1212/WNL.0b013e31828726f5. Retrieved from http://www.neurology.org/content/early/2013/02/06/WNL.0b013e31828726f5

Hee Ahn, M., Park, S., Ha, K., Choi, S.H. and Hong, J.P. (2012). Gender ratio comparisons of the suicide rates and methods in Korea, Japan, Australia, and the United States. *Journal of Affective Disorders*, **142**, 161–165. doi: 10.1016/j.jad.2012.05.008

Heilman, M.E. (1983). Sex bias in work settings: the lack of fit model. *Research in Organizational Behavior* **5**, 269–98.

Heilman, M.E. and Alcott, V.B. (2001). What I think you think of me: women's reactions to being viewed as beneficiaries of preferential selection. *Journal of Applied Psychology* **86**, 574–82.

Heilman, M.E. and Stopeck, M.H. (1985). Being attractive, advantage or disadvantage? Performance-based evaluations and recommended personnel actions as a function of appearance, sex, and job type. *Organizational Behavior and Human Decision Processes* **35**, 202–15.

Henry, N. (2010). The impossibility of bearing witness: Wartime rape and the promise of justice. *Violence Against Women* **16**, 1098–1119. doi: 10.1177/1077801210382860

Higgins, J.A., Hoffman, S. and Dworkin, S.L. (2010). Rethinking gender, heterosexual men, and women's vulnerability to HIV/AIDS. *American Journal of Public Health* **100**, 435–45. doi: 10.2105/AJPH.2009.159723

Hightower, J. (2010). Abuse in later life: when and how does gender matter? In G. Gutman and C. Spencer (eds), *Aging, Ageism and Abuse: moving from awareness to action*. Elsevier Insights, pp. 17–29. San Diego, CA: Elsevier Academic Press.

"Hillary Clinton on life after being Secretary of State: 'I hope to get to sleep in.'" (2013, January 30). *The Huffington Post*. Retrieved from http://www.huffingtonpost.com/2013/01/30/hillary-clinton-sleep-deprivation_n_2581005.html?ir=Healthy+Living

Hodge, D.R. and Lietz, C.A. (2007) The international sexual trafficking of women and children: a review of the literature. *Journal of Women and Social Work* **22**, 163–74. doi:10.1177/0886109907299055

Hodges, M.J. and Budig, M.J. (2010). Who gets the daddy bonus? Organizational hegemonic masculinity and the impact of fatherhood on earnings. *Gender and Society* **24**, 717–45. doi: 10.1177/0891243210386729

Holwerda, T.J., Deeg, D.J.H., Beekman, A.T.F., van Tilburg, T.G., Stek, M.L., Jonker, C. and Schoevers, R.A. (2012). Feelings of loneliness, but not social isolation, predict dementia onset: results from the Amsterdam Study of the Elderly (AMSTEL). *Journal of Neurology, Neurosurgery and Psychiatry.* doi:10.1136/jnnp-2012-302755 (Retrieved from http://jnnp.bmj.com/content/early/2012/11/06/jnnp-2012-302755)

Horne, S., Matthews, S. and Detrie, P. (2001). Look it up under 'F': dialogues of emerging and experienced feminists. *Women and Therapy* **23**, 5–18.

Howard, J.A., Blumstein, P. and Schwartz, P. (1986). Sex, power, and influence tactics in intimate relationships. *Journal of Personality and Social Psychology* **51**, 102–09. doi: 10.1037/0022-3514.51.1.102

Hoyt, C.L. and Simon, S. (2011). Female leaders: injurious or inspiring role models for women? *Psychology of Women Quarterly* **35**, 143–57. doi: 10.1177/0361684310385216

Hussein, S. (2011, May 11). *Migrants and the state of long term care in England: opportunities and challenges.* Social Care Workforce Research Unit, King's College, London, UK. Retrieved from http://www.academia.edu/2424356/Migrants_and_the_state_of_long_term_care_in_England_opportunities_and_challenges_Filling_the_Gaps_on_the_Impacts_of_Immigration

Hyde, J.S. (1984). How large are gender differences in aggression? A developmental meta-analysis. *Developmental Psychology* **20**, 722–36.

Imperato-McGinley, J., Peterson, R.E., Gautier, T. and Sturla, E. (1979). Androgens and the evolution of male gender identity among male pseudohermaphrodites with a 5-alph-reductase deficiency. *New England Journal of Medicine* **310**, 839–40.

Institute for Women's Leadership (2011). *Women's Leadership Fact Sheet.* Retrieved from http://iwl.rutgers.edu/documents/njwomencount/womenHeadsofStates.pdf

Institute for Women's Policy Research (2012). Calculations of data from the Current Population Survey Outgoing Rotation Groups for 2010 and 2011 based on Center for Economic and Policy Research CPS ORG Uniform Extracts, Version 1.7. Washington, DC.

International Labour Organization (2012a). *Domestic workers.* Retrieved from http://www.ilo.org/global/topics/domestic-workers/lang—en/index.htm

International Labour Organization (2012b). Time for women to get on board. Retrieved from http://www.ilo.org/global/about-the-ilo/newsroom/features/WCMS_192102/lang—en/index.htm

Inter-Parliamentary Union (2012). *Women in national parliaments* (as of October 31, 2012). Retrieved from http://www.ipu.org/wmn-e/classif.htm

Iron Ladies of Liberia (2008). Independent Lens: Public Broadcasting System. http://www.pbs.org/independentlens/ironladies/

Jansma, L.L., Linz, D.G., Mulac, A. and Imrich, D.J. (1997). Men's interactions with women after viewing sexually explicit films: does degradation make a difference? *Communication Monographs* **64**, 1–24. doi: 10.1080/03637759709376402

Jarman, J., Blackburn, R.M. and Racko, G. (2012). The dimensions of occupational gender segregation in industrial countries. *Sociology* **46**, 1003–1019. doi:10.1177/0038038511435063

Jewkes, R. (2012) *Rape Perpetration: a review.* Pretoria, SA, Sexual Violence Research Initiative. Retrieved from http://www.svri.org/RapePerpetration.pdf

Johnson, K., Scott, J., Rughita, B., Kisielewski, M., Asher, J., Ong, R. and Lawry, L. (2010). Association of sexual violence and human rights violations with physical and mental health in territories of the Eastern Democratic Republic of Congo. *JAMA* **304**, 553–62. doi:10.1001/jama.2010.1086

Johnson, M.P. and Ferraro, K.J. (2000). Research on domestic violence in the 1990s: making distinctions. *Journal of Marriage and the Family* **62**, 948–63.

Johnson, S.K., Podratz, D.E., Dipboye, R.L. and Gibbons, E. (2010). Physical attractiveness biases in ratings of employment suitability: tracking down the "beauty is beastly" effect. *The Journal of Social Psychology* **150**, 301–18. doi: 10.1080/00224540903365414

Johnson, T.D. (2008). *Maternity leave and employment patterns: 2001-2003* (Report No. P70–113). Retrieved from http://www.census.gov/prod/2008pubs/p70-113.pdf

Jones, A.S., Dienemann, J., Schollenberger, J., Kub, J., O'Campo, P., Gielen, A.C. and Campbell, J.C. (2006). Long-term costs of intimate partner violence in a sample of female HMO enrollees. *Women's Health Issues* **16**, 252–61.

Kahn, A.S., Jackson, J., Kully, C., Badger, K. and Halvorsen, J. (2003). Calling it rape: differences in experiences of women who do or do not label their sexual assault as rape. *Psychology of Women Quarterly* **27**, 233–42. doi: 10.1111/1471-6402.00103

Kaminski, P.L. and Hayslip, B. (2006). Gender differences in body esteem among older adults. *Journal of Women and Aging* **18**, 19–35.

Kanter, R.M. (1977). *Men and Women of the Corporation.* New York: Basic Books.

Kaukinen, C. (2004). Status compatibility, physical violence, and emotional abuse in intimate relationships. *Journal of Marriage and the Family* **66**, 452–71.

Khalid, R. (1997). Perceived threat of violence and coping strategies: a case of Pakistan women. *Journal of Behavioral Sciences* **8**, 43–54.

Killeen, L.A., Lopez-Zafra, E. and Eagly, A.H. (2006). Envisioning oneself as a leader: comparisons of women and men in Spain and the United States. *Psychology of Women Quarterly* **30**, 312–22.

Kilmartin, C. (2009). *The Masculine Self* (4th edn). Cornwall-on-Hudson, NY: Sloan Publishing.

Kimball, M. (1995). *Feminist Visions of Gender Similarities and Differences.* Binghamton, NY: Haworth.

Kissal, A. and Beşer, A. (2011). Elder abuse and neglect in a population offering care by a primary health care center in Izmir, Turkey. *Social Work in Health Care* **50**, 158–75. doi: 10.1080/00981389.2010.527570

Klesges, L.M., Pahor, M., Shorr, R.I., Wan, J.Y., Williamson, J.D. and Guralnik, J.M. (2001). Financial difficulty in acquiring food among elderly disabled women: results from the Women's Health and Aging Study. *American Journal of Public Health* **91**, 68–75.

Klonoff, E.A., and Landrine, H. (1995). The Schedule of Sexist Events: a measure of lifetime and recent sexist discrimination in women's lives. *Psychology of Women Quarterly* **19**, 439–72. doi: 10.1111/j.1471-6402.1995.tb00086.x

Klonoff, E.A. and Landrine, H. (2000). Sexist discrimination may account for well-known gender differences in psychiatric symptoms. *Psychology of Women Quarterly* **24**, 93–99. doi: 10.1111/j.1471-6402.2000.tb01025.x

Koenig, A.M., Eagly, A.H., Mitchell, A.A. and Ristikari, T. (2011). Are leader stereotypes masculine? A meta-analysis of three research paradigms. *Psychological Bulletin* **137**, 616–42. doi: 10.1037/a0023557

Koivunen, J.M., Rothaupt, J.W. and Wolfgram, S.M. (2009) Gender dynamics and role adjustment during the transition to parenthood: current perspectives. *The Family Journal* 17, 323–28. doi: 10.1177/1066480709347360

Kosberg, J.I. (ed.) (2007). *Abuse of Older Men.* New York: Routledge.

Koss, M.P. (1988). Hidden rape: incidence, prevalence, and descriptive characteristic of sexual aggression and victimization in a national sample of college students. In A.W. Burgess (ed.), *Sexual Assault* (Vol. 2), pp. 3–25. New York: Garland.

Krienert, J.L., Walsh, J.A. and Turner, M. (2009). Elderly in America: a descriptive study of elder abuse examining National Incident-Based Reporting System (NIBRS) data, 2000–2005. *Journal of Elder Abuse and Neglect* **21**, 325–45. doi: 10.1080/08946560903005042

Kristof, N.D. (2005, June 14). Raped, kidnapped and silenced. *The New York Times.* Retrieved January 15, 2009 from http://www.nytimes.com/2005/06/14/opinion/14kristof.html

Kruijver, F., Zhou, J.-N., Pool, C., Hofman, M., Gooren, L. and Swaab, D. (2000). Male-to-female transsexuals have female neuron numbers in a limbic nucleus. *Journal of Clinical Endocrinology and Metabolism* **85**, 2034–2041.

Kruse, M., Sørensen, J., Brønnum-Hansen, H. and Helweg-Larsen, K. (2011). The health care costs of violence against women. *Journal of Interpersonal Violence* **26**, 3494–3508. doi: 10.1177/0886260511403754

Kudo, T. (2013, January 25). I killed people in Afghanistan. Was I right or wrong? *The Washington Post*. Retrieved from http://articles.washingtonpost.com/2013-01-25/opinions/36539894_1_bomb-strikes-afghanistan-enemy-fire

Kuehner, C. (2003). Gender differences in unipolar depression: an update of epidemiological findings and possible explanations. *Acta Psychiatrica Scandinavica* **108**, 163–74. doi: 10.1034/j.1600-0447.2003.00204.x

Kunkel, D., Eyal, K., Finnerty, K.L., Biely, E. and Donnerstein, E. (2005). *Sex on TV 4*. Menlo Park, CA: Henry J. Kaiser Family Foundation.

Lambert, N.M., Negash, S., Stillman, T.F., Olmstead, S.B. and Fincham, F.D. (2012). A love that doesn't last: pornography consumption and weakened commitment to one's romantic partner. *Journal of Social and Clinical Psychology* **31**, 410–38. doi: 10.1521/jscp.2012.31.4.410

Lansford, J.E., Skinner, A.T., Sorbring, E., Giunta, L.D., Deater-Deckard, K., Dodge, K.A., Malone, P.S., Oburu, P., Pastorelli, C., Tapanya, S., Tirado, L.M.U., Zelli, A., Al-Hassan, S.M., Alampay, L.P., Bacchini, D., Bombi, A.S., Bornstein, M.H. and Chang, L. (2012). Boys' and girls' relational and physical aggression in nine countries. *Aggressive Behavior* **38**, 298–308. doi: 10.1002/ab.21433

Latu, I.M., Mast, M.S., Lammers, J. and Bombari, D. (2013). Successful female leaders empower women's behavior in leadership tasks. *Journal of Experimental Social Psychology* (Published online before print), doi: 10.1016/j.jesp.2013.01.003

Latu, I.M., Stewart, T.L., Myers, A.C., Lisco, C.G., Estes, S.B. and Donahue, D.K. (2011). What we "say" and what we "think" about female managers: explicit versus implicit associations of women with success. *Psychology of Women Quarterly* **35**, 252–66. doi: 10.1177/0361684310383811

Laughlin, L. (2011). Maternity leave and employment patterns: 2006–2008. *Current Population Report*, pp. 70–128, Washington, DC: US Census Bureau. Retrieved from http://www.census.gov/prod/2011pubs/p70-128.pdf

Lawson, K.M. and Lips, H.L. (in press). The role of self-perceived agency and job attainability in women's impressions of successful women. *Journal of Applied Psychology*.

Leaper, C. and Smith, T.E. (2004). A meta-analytic review of gender variations in children's language use: talkativeness, affiliative speech, and assertive speech. *Developmental Psychology* **40**, 993–1027. doi: 10.1037/0012-1649.40.6.993

Legal Information Institute, Cornell University Law School (2012). 89–1215. International Union, United Automobile, Aerospace and Agricultural Implement Workers of America, UAW *et al.* v. Johnson Controls, Inc. Retrieved from http://www.law.cornell.edu/supct/html/89-1215.ZS.html

Legleye, S., Khlat, M., Beck, F. and Peretti-Watel, P. (2011). Widening inequalities in smoking initiation and cessation patterns: a cohort and gender analysis in

France. *Drug and Alcohol Dependence* **117**, 233–41. doi: 10.1016/j. drugalcdep.2011.02.004

Legon, J. (2003). Mom, soldier and Hopi Indian: 'She fought and died valiantly.' CNN.com. Retrieved from http://edition.cnn.com/SPECIALS/2003/iraq/ heroes/piestewa.html

LeGuin, U.K. (1969). *The Left Hand of Darkness*. New York: Ace Books.

Lenton, R.L. (1995). Power versus feminist theories of wife abuse. *Canadian Journal of Criminology* **37**, 305–30.

Levy, B. (2009). Stereotype embodiment: a psychosocial approach to aging. *Current Directions in Psychological Science* **18**, 332–36. doi: 10.1111/j. 1467-8721.2009.01662.x

Linos, N., Khawaja, M. and Kaplan, R.L. (2012). Women's acceptance of spousal abuse in Iraq: prevalence rates and the role of female empowerment characteristics. *Journal of Family Violence* **27**, 625–33. doi: 10.1007/s10896-012-9462-0

Lips, H.M. (2000). College students' visions of power and possibility as moderated by gender. *Psychology of Women Quarterly* **24**, 39–43. doi: 10.1111/j.1471-6402.2000.tb01020.x

Lips, H.M. (2001). Envisioning positions of leadership: the expectations of university students in Virginia and Puerto Rico. *Journal of Social Issues* **57**, 799–813. doi: 10.1111/0022-4537.00242

Lips, H.M. (2013). The gender pay gap: challenging the rationalizations: perceived equity, discrimination, and the limits of human capital models. *Sex Roles* **68**, 169–85. doi:10.007/s11199-012-0165-z

Lips, H.M. and Hastings, S.L. (2012). Competing discourses for older women: agency/leadership vs. disengagement/retirement. *Women and Therapy* **35**, 1–20.

Lisak, D.M., and Miller, P.M. (2002). Repeat rape and multiple offending among undetected rapists. *Violence and Victims* **17**, 73–84. doi: 10.1891/vivi.17.1.73.33638

Little, A. (2012, October 10). Australian Prime Minister schools misogynist in awesome rant. *Ms.blog*. Retrieved from http://msmagazine.com/blog/2012/10/10/australian-prime-minister-schools-misogynist-in-awesome-rant/

Littleton, H.L., Grills-Taquechel, A.E., Buck, K.S., Rosman, L. and Dodd, J.C. (2013). Health risk behavior and sexual assault among ethnically diverse women. *Psychology of Women Quarterly* **37**, 7–21. doi: 10.1177/0361684312451842

Llanos, B. (2011). *Unseeing Eyes: media coverage and gender in Latin American elections*. International Institute for Democracy and Electoral Assistance. Retrieved from http://www.idea.int/publications/unseeing-eyes/index.cfm

Lockwood, P. (2006). "Someone like me can be successful": Do college students need same gender role models? *Psychology of Women Quarterly* **30**, 36–46. doi: 10.1111/j.1471-6402.2006.00260.x

Lord, C.G. and Saenz, D.S. (1985). Memory deficits and memory surfeits: differential cognitive consequences of tokenism for tokens and observers. *Journal of Personality and Social Psychology* **49**, 918–26. doi: 10.1037/0022-3514.49.4.918

Lovett, C. (1997). *Olympic Marathon*. Westport, CT: Greenwood Publishing Group.

Luo, Y., Hawkley, L.C., Waite, L.J. and Cacioppo, J.T. (2012). Loneliness, health, and mortality in old age: a national longitudinal study. *Social Science and Medicine* **74**, 907–14. doi: 10.1016/j.socscimed.2011.11.028

Lyn, C. and Mullan, K. (2011). How mothers and fathers share childcare: a cross-national time-use comparisons. *American Sociological Review* **76**, 834–61. doi: 10.1177/0003122411427673

Lyndon, A.E., Sinclair, H.C., MacArthur, J., Fay, B., Ratajack, E. and Collier, K.E. (2012). An introduction to issues of gender in stalking research. *Sex Roles* **66**, 299–310. doi: 10.1007/s11199-011-0106-2

Maass, A., Cadinu, M., Guarnieri, G. and Grasselli, A. (2003). Sexual harassment under social identity threat: the computer harassment paradigm. *Journal of Personality and Social Psychology* **85**, 853–70.

Magnusson, E. and Marecek, J. (2012). *Gender and Culture in Psychology: theories and practices*. New York: Cambridge University Press.

Maguire, M. (2008). "Fade to Grey": older women, embodied claims and attributions in English university departments of education. *Women's Studies International Forum* **31**, 474–82. doi: 10.1016/j.wsif.2008.09.001

Mahabeer, P. (2011). Sexual harassment still pervasive in the workplace. *AOL. com*. Retrieved from http://jobs.aol.com/articles/2011/01/28/sexual-harassment-in-the-workplace/

Malamuth, N.M., Hald, G.M. and Koss, M. (2012). Pornography, individual differences in risk and men's acceptance of violence against women in a representative sample. *Sex Roles* **66**, 427–39. doi: 10.1007/s11199-011-0082-6

Manohar, S.V. and Kirpal, B.N. (1997, August). "Vishaka and Ors vs State Of Rajasthan and Ors on 13 August 1997". Supreme Court of India **241**, http://www.webcitation.org/6891WS3sS.

Marino, K. (2011, October 3). Rethinking the causes of wartime rape. The Clayman Institute for Gender Research, Stanford University. Retrieved from http://gender.stanford.edu/news/2011/rethinking-causes-wartime-rape

Markle, J.G.M., Frank, D.N., Mortin-Toth, S., Robertson, C.E., Feazel, L.M., Rolle-Kampczyk, U., von Bergen, M., McCoy, K.D., Macpherson, A.J. and Danska, J.S. (2013). Sex differences in the gut microbiome drive hormone-dependent regulation of autoimmunity. *Science*, published online January 17. doi: 10.1126/science.1233521. Retrieved from http://www.sciencemag.org/content/early/2013/01/16/science.1233521

Markus, H. and Nurius, P. (1986). Possible selves. *American Psychologist* **41**, 954–69.

Martin, C.L. and Ruble, D. (2004). Children's search for gender clues. *Current Directions in Psychological Science* **13**, 67–70. doi: 10.1111/j.0963-7214.2004.00276.x

Martinot, D., Bagès, C. and Désert, M. (2012). French children's awareness of gender stereotypes about mathematics and reading: when girls improve their reputation in math. *Sex Roles* **66**, 210–19. doi: 10.1007/s11199-011-0032-3

Matud, M.P. (2004). Gender differences in stress and coping styles. *Personality and Individual Differences* **37**, 1401–1415. doi: 10.1016/j.paid.2004.01.010

Matzuk, M.M., McKeown, M.R., Filippakopoulos, P., Li, Q., Ma, L., Agno, J.E., Lemieux, M.E., Picaud, S., Yu, R.N., Qi, J., Knapp, S. and Bradner, J.E. (2012). Small-molecule inhibition of BRDT for male contraception. *Cell* **150**, 673–84. doi: 10.1016/j.cell.2012.06.045

McCauley, J.L., Calhoun, K.S., and Gidycz, C.A. (2010). Binge drinking and rape: a prospective examination of college women with a history of previous sexual victimization. *Journal of Interpersonal Violence* **25**, 1655–1668. doi: 10.1177/0886260509354580

McCauley, J., Ruggiero, K.J., Resnick, H.S., Conoscenti, L.M. and Kilpatrick, D.G. (2009). Forcible, drug–facilitated, and incapacitated rape in relation to substance use problems: results from a national sample of college women. *Addictive Behaviors* **34**, 458–62. doi: 10.1016/j.addbeh.2008.12.004

McClelland, S.I. (2009). *Intimate Justice: sexual satisfaction in young adults* (Doctoral dissertation). Available from ProQuest Dissertations and Theses database.

McClelland, S.I. (2010). Intimate justice: A critical analysis of sexual satisfaction. *Social and Personality Compass* **4**(9), 663–80. doi: 10.1111/j.1751-9004.2010.00293.x

McHugh, M.C., Livingston, N.A. and Ford, A. (2005). A postmodern approach to women's use of violence: developing multiple and complex conceptualizations. *Psychology of Women Quarterly* **29**, 323–36. doi: 10.1111/j.1471-6402.2005.00226.x

McLaughlin, D., Vagenas, D., Pachana, N.A., Begum, N. and Dobson, A. (2010). Gender differences in social network size and satisfaction in adults in their 70s. *Journal of Health Psychology* **15**, 671–79. doi: 10.1177/1359105310368177

McLaughlin, K. and Nolen-Hoeksema, S. (2011). The role of rumination in promoting and preventing depression in adolescent girls. In T.J. Strauman, P.R. Costanzo and J. Garber (eds), *Depression in Adolescent Girls: science and prevention*. Duke Series in Child Development and Public Policy, pp. 112–29. New York: Guilford Press.

McNamara, C.L. and Marsil, D.F. (2012). The prevalence of stalking among college students: the disparity between researcher- and self-identified victimization. *Journal of American College Health* **60**, 168–74. doi: 10.1080/07448481.2011.584335

Melchiorre, M.G., Chiatti, C., Lamura, G., Torres-Gonzales, F., Stankunas, M., Lindert, J., Ioannidi-Kapolou, E., Barros, H., Macassa, G. and Soares, J.F.J. (2013). Social support, socio-economic status, health and abuse among older people in seven European countries. *PLoS One* **8**: e54856. Published online January 30. doi: 10.1371/journal.pone.0054856

Michael, R.T., Gagnon, J.H., Laumann, E.O. and Kolata, G. (1994). *Sex in America.* Boston: Little, Brown.

Minturn, L., Boyd, D. and Kapoor, S. (1978). Increased maternal power status changes in socialization in a restudy of Rajput mothers of Khalapur, India. *Journal of Cross-Cultural Psychology* **9**, 483–98. doi: 10.1177/002202217894007

Mishra V., Assche, S.B., Greener, R., Vaessen, M., Hong, R., Ghys, P.D., Boerma, J.Y., Van Assche, A., Khan, S. and Rutstein, S. (2007). HIV infection does not disproportionately affect the poorer in sub-Saharan Africa. *AIDS* **21**(Suppl 7), S17–S28.

Mitchell, J. (2012, December 4). Women notch progress. Females now constitute one-third of nation's rank of doctors and lawyers. *The Wall Street Journal.* Retrieved from http://online.wsj.com/article/SB10001424127887323717004578159433220839020.html?mod=WSJ_WSJ_US_News_5

Moaveni, A. (2009, August 16). How to work out while Muslim—and female. *Time.com.* Retrieved from http://www.time.com/time/magazine/article/0,9171,1924488,00.html

Monin, J.K. and Schulz, R. (2009). Interpersonal effects of suffering in older adult caregiving relationships. *Psychology and Aging* **24**, 681–95. doi: 10.1037/a0016355

Mosher, W.D. and Jones, J. (2010). Use of contraception in the United States: 1982–2008. *Vital and Health Statistics* 2010, Series 23, No. 29, Retrieved from http://www.cdc.gov/nchs/data/series/sr_23/sr23_029.pdf

Moss-Racusin, C.A., Dovidio, J.F., Brescoll, V.L., Graham, M.J. and Handelsman, J. (2012). Science faculty's subtle gender biases favor male students. *PNAS* **109**, 16474–16479. doi:10.1073/pnas.1211286109

Mudege, N.N. and Ezeh, A.C. (2009). Gender, aging, poverty and health: survival strategies of older men and women in Nairobi slums. *Journal of Aging Studies* **23**, 245–57.

Mumenthaler, M.S., Taylor, J.L., O'Hara, R. and Yesavage, J.A. (1999). Gender differences in moderate drinking effects. *Alcohol Research and Health* **23**, 55–64.

Muzzatti, B. and Agnoli, F. (2007). Gender and mathematics: attitudes and stereotype threat susceptibility in Italian children. *Developmental Psychology* **43**, 747–59. doi: 10.1037/0012-1649.43.3.747

National Center for Health Statistics (2012). *Health, United States 2011.* Hyattsville MD. Retrieved from http://www.cdc.gov/nchs/data/hus/hus11.pdf

National Center on Elder Abuse. (1998). Retrieved from http://www.aoa.gov/AoARoot/AoA_Programs/Elder_Rights/Elder_Abuse/docs/ABuseReport_Full.pdf

National Heart, Lung, and Blood Institute, US Department of Health and Human Services (2011). *How does heart disease affect women?* Retrieved from http://www.nhlbi.nih.gov/health/health-topics/topics/hdw/

National Institute of Allergy and Infectious Diseases (2012). *Gender-specific health challenges facing women.* Retrieved from http://www.niaid.nih.gov/topics/womenshealth/pages/diseases.aspx

Neft, N. and Levine, A.D. (1997). *Where women stand: an international report on the status of women in 140 countries.* New York: Random House.

Nelson, D. (2012, December 19). Gang rape of Indian woman sparks mass protests. *The Telegraph.* Retrieved from http://www.telegraph.co.uk/news/worldnews/asia/india/9755913/Gang-rape-of-Indian-woman-sparks-mass-protests.html

Niehaus, I. (2012). Gendered endings: narratives of male and female suicides in the South African lowveld. *Culture, Medicine and Psychiatry* **36**, 327–47. doi: 10.1007/s11013-012-9258-y

Nkansah-Amankra, S., Diedhiou, A., Agbanu, H.L.K., Harrod, C. and Dhawan, A. (2011). Correlates of sexual risk behaviors among high school students in Colorado: analysis and implications for school-based HIV/AIDS programs. *Maternal and Child Health Journal* **15**, 730–41. doi: 10.1007/s10995-010-0634-3

Nock, M.K., Borges, G., Bromet, E.J., Alonso, J., Angermeyer, M., Beautrais, A., Bruffaerts, R., Chiu, W.T., de Girolamo, G., Gluzman, S., de Graaf, R., Gureje, O., Haro, J.M., Huang, Y., Karam, E., Kessler, R.C., Lepine, J. P., Levinson, D., Medina-Mora, M.E., Ono, Y., Posada-Villa, J. and Williams, D. (2008). Cross-national prevalence and risk factors for suicidal ideation, plans and attempts. *The British Journal of Psychiatry* **192**, 98–105. doi: 10.1192/bjp.bp.107.040113

Nolen, S. (2005, Spring). "Not women anymore …"The Congo's rape survivors face pain, shame and AIDS. *Ms. Magazine.* Retrieved from http://www.msmagazine.com/spring2005/congo.asp

Nolen-Hoeksema, S. (2004). Gender differences in risk factors and consequences for alcohol use and problems. *Clinical Psychology Review* **24**, 981–1010.

Nolen-Hoeksema, S. (2006). The etiology of gender differences in depression. In C.M. Mazure, and G.P. Keita (eds), *Understanding Depression in Women: applying empirical research to practice and policy*, pp. 9–43. Washington, DC: American Psychological Association **xvii**, 163 pp. doi: 10.1037/11434-001

Nowak, P. (2012, January 5). US leads the way in porn production, but falls behind in profits. *Canadian Business*. Retrieved from http://www.canadianbusiness.com/blogs-and-comment/u-s-leads-the-way-in-porn-production-but-falls-behind-in-profits/

Nowinski, S.N. and Bowen, E. (2012). Partner violence against heterosexual and gay men: prevalence and correlates. *Aggression and Violent Behavior* **17**, 36–52. doi: 10.1016/j.avb.2011.09.005

Nyambedha, E., Wandibba, S. and Aagaard-Hansen, J. (2003). Retirement lost— the new role of the elderly as caretakers for orphans in western Kenya. *Journal of Cross-Cultural Gerontology* **18**, 33–52.

Oakes, M.E. and Slotterback, C.S. (2001). Gender differences in perceptions of the healthiness of foods. *Psychology and Health* **16**, 57–65. doi: 10.1080/08870440108405489

Obermeyer, C.M. (1992). Islam, women, and politics: the demography of Arab countries. *Population and Development Review* **18**, 33–60.

Office for National Statistics (2004). *Focus on older people: health and caring*. Retrieved from http://www.statistics.gov.uk/cci/nugget.asp?id=882

Office for National Statistics (2010, September 30). Statistical Bulletin: *Older people's day 2010*. Retrieved from http://www.ons.gov.uk/ons/search/index.html?pageSize=50andsortBy=noneandsortDirection=noneand newquery=Focus+On+Older+People

Office for National Statistics (2011). *UK mothers in the labour market*. Retrieved from http://www.ons.gov.uk/ons/rel/lmac/mothers-in-the-labour-market/2011/mothers-in-the-labour-market—-2011.html#tab-More-mothers-working-now-than-ever-before

Office for National Statistics (2013). Pension trends—Chapter 4: *The labour market and retirement, 2013 edition*. Retrieved from http://www.ons.gov.uk/ons/dcp171766_297899.pdf

Okimoto, T.G. and Brescoll, V.L. (2010). The price of power: power seeking and backlash against female politicians. *Personality and Social Psychology Bulletin* **36**, 923–36. doi: 10.1177/0146167210371949

Olowu, D. (2012). Gendered imbalances in AIDS-related burden of care: lessons from Lesotho. *Gender and Behaviour* **10**, 4344–4357.

O'Neill, O.A. and O'Reilly, C. (2011). Overcoming the backlash effect: self-monitoring and women's promotions. *Journal of Occupational and Organizational Psychology* **84**, 825–32. doi: 10.1111/j.2044-8325.2010.02008.x

Oniang'o, R. and Mukudi, E. (2002). Nutrition and gender. In *Nutrition: a foundation for development*. Geneva, Switzerland: United Nations Standing Committee on Nutrition. Retrieved from http://www.unscn.org/files/Publications/Briefs_on_Nutrition/Brief7_EN.pdf

Opolade, D. (2012, July 10). The fairer leaders. *The New York Times*. Retrieved from http://latitude.blogs.nytimes.com/2012/07/10/african-states-ahead-of-the-west-in-female-political-representation/

Orcutt, H.K., Cooper, M.L. and Garcia, M. (2005). Use of sexual intercourse to reduce negative affect as a prospective mediator of sexual revictimization. *Journal of Traumatic Stress* **18**, 729–39. doi: 10.1002/jts.20081

Organization for Economic Cooperation and Development (2011a). *Help wanted? Providing and paying for long-term care*. OECD Publishing. Retrieved from http://www.oecd.org/els/health-systems/helpwantedprovidingand payingforlong-termcare.htm

Organization for Economic Cooperation and Development (2011b). Old-age income poverty. In *Pensions at a Glance 2011: Retirement-income Systems in OECD and G20 Countries*. OECD Publishing. Retrieved from http://dx.doi.org/10.1787/pension_glance-2011-28-en

Overall, N.C., Sibley, C.G. and Tan, R. (2011). The costs and benefits of sexism: resistance to influence during relationship conflict. *Journal of Personality and Social Psychology* **101**, 271–90. doi: 10.1037/a0022727

Oxfam (2012). *Fifty years later: women and social change in Cuba*. Retrieved from http://www.oxfam.ca/sites/default/files/imce/women-social-change-cuba.pdf

Paek, H., Nelson, M.R. and Vilela, A.M. (2011). Examination of gender-role portrayals in television advertising across seven countries. *Sex Roles* **64**, 192–207. doi:10.1007/s11199-010-9850-y.

Pagelow, M.D. (1993). Justice for victims of spouse abuse in divorce and child custody cases. *Violence and Victims* **8**, 69–83.

Paludi, M.A. and Strayer, L.A. (1985). What's in an author's name? Differential evaluations of performance as a function of author's name. *Sex Roles* **12**, 353–61. doi: 10.1007/BF00287601

Paraprofessional Healthcare Institute (2011, February). Who are direct-care workers? *PHI Facts 3*. Retrieved from http://phinational.org/sites/phinational.org/files/clearinghouse/PHI%20Facts%203.pdf

Parks-Stamm, E.J., Heilman, M.E. and Hearns, K.A. (2008). Motivated to penalize: women's strategic rejection of successful women. *Personality and Social Psychology Bulletin* **34**, 237–47. doi: 10.1177/0146167207310027

Parrot, A. and Cummings, N. (2006). *Forsaken Females: the global brutalization of women*. Lanham, MD: Rowan and Littlefield.

Parsons, T. and Bales, R.F. (1955). *Family Socialization and Interaction Process*. Glencoe, IL: Free Press.

Paruzzolo, S., Mehra, R., Kes, A. and Ashbaugh, C. (2010). Targeting poverty and gender inequality to improve maternal health. New York: Women Deliver. Retrieved from http://www.womendeliver.org/assets/Targeting_poverty.pdf

Pazol, K., Zane, S.B., Parker, W.Y., Hall, L.R., Berg, C. and Cook, D.A. (2011, November 25). Abortion surveillance—United States, 2008. Atlanta, GA: CDC National Center for Chronic Disease Prevention and Health Promotion, Division of Reproductive Health. Retrieved from http://www.cdc.gov/mmwr/preview/mmwrhtml/ss6015a1.htm?s_cid=ss6015a1_w

Peat, C.M., Peyerl, N.L., Ferraro, F.R. and Butler, M. (2011). Age and body image in caucasian men. *Psychology of Men and Masculinity* **12**, 195–200. doi: 10.1037/a0021478

Phillips, L.M. (2000). *Flirting with Danger*. New York: New York University Press.

Picard, C. (2000). Pattern of expanding consciousness in midlife women: creative movement and the narrative as modes of expression. *Nursing Science Quarterly* **13**, 150–57.

Pinquart, M. and Sorensen, S. (2003). Differences between caregivers and non-caregivers in psychological health and physical health: a meta-analysis. *Psychology and Aging* **18**, 250–67.

Pleis, J.R., Lucas, J.W. and Ward, B.W. (2009). *Summary health statistics for US adults: National Health Interview Survey, 2008*. National Center for Health Statistics, Vital Health Stat 10 (242). Retrieved from http://www.cdc.gov/nchs/data/series/sr_10/sr10_242.pdf

Population Council (2004). *Forced sexual relations among married young women in developing countries*. Retrieved from http://www.popcouncil.org/pdfs/popsyn/PopulationSynthesis1.pdf

Powell, J. (2013, January 23). Suicide is a gender issue that can no longer be ignored. *The Guardian*. Retrieved from http://www.guardian.co.uk/commentisfree/2013/jan/23/suicide-rates-men-gender-issue

Pratto, F. and Walker, A. (2004). The bases of gendered power. In A.H. Eagly, A.E. Beall and R.J. Sternberg (eds), *The Psychology of Gender* (2nd edn), pp. 242–68. New York: Guilford Press.

Prentice, D.A. and Carranza, E. (2002). What women should be, shouldn't be, are allowed to be, and don't have to be: the contents of prescriptive gender stereotypes. *Psychology of Women Quarterly* **26**, 269–81. doi: 10.1111/1471-6402.t01-1-00066

Puhl, R. and Brownell, K.D. (2001). Bias, discrimination and obesity. *Obesity Research* **9**, 788–805.

QuotaProject (2013). Global database of quotas for women. http://www.quotaproject.org/

Ragonese, M. (2002). Riot Grrrls castrate "cock rock" in New York. *Off Our Backs* **32**, 5/6, 27–31.

Raven, B.H. (1992). A power/interaction model of interpersonal influence: French and Raven thirty years later. *Journal of Social Behavior and Personality* **7**, 217–44.

Reggio, I. (2010). The influence of the mother's power on her child's labor in Mexico. *IDEAS*. Retrieved from http://ideas.repec.org/p/cte/werepe/we101305.html

Reid, P. and Finchilescu, G. (1995). The disempowering effects of media violence against women on college women. *Psychology of Women Quarterly* **19**, 397–411. doi: 10.1111/j.1471-6402.1995.tb00082.x

Renga, S., Molnar-Hidassy, D. and Tisheva, G., European Network of Experts in the Field of Gender Equality (2010). *Direct and indirect gender discrimination in old-age pensions in 33 European Countries*. European Commission, Directorate-General for Justice. Retrieved from http://ec.europa.eu/justice/gender-equality/files/conference_sept_2011/dgjustice_oldagepensions publication3march2011_en.pdf

Reyns, B.W., Henson, B. and Fisher, B.S. (2012). Stalking in the twilight zone: extent of cyberstalking victimization and offending among college students. *Deviant Behavior* **33**, 1–25. doi: 10.1080/01639625.2010.538364

RFI (2011, July 31). Indian women protest sexual violence in Delhi's first SlutWalk. Accessed at http://www.english.rfi.fr/node/102830

Richardson, A., He, J-P., Curry, L. and Merikangas, K. (2012). Cigarette smoking and mood disorders in US adolescents: sex-specific associations with symptoms, diagnoses, impairment and health services use. *Journal of Psychosomatic Research* **72**, 269–75. doi: 10.1016/j.jpsychores.2012.01.013

Richardson, D.S. (2005). The myth of female passivity: thirty years of revelations about female aggression. *Psychology of Women Quarterly* **29**, 238–47.

Rickman, R. and Wares, C. (2010, June 9). Catholic nun raises the bar for older athletes. SecondAct.com. Accessed at http://www.secondact.com/2010/06/sister-madonna/

Rieker, P.P. and Bird, C.E. (2005). Rethinking gender differences in health: why we need to integrate social and biological perspectives. *Journal of Gerontology Series B*, **60B**, 40–47.

Roberts, R. and Argetsinger, A. (2012, June 7). Jeremy Bernard speaks! First male White House social secretary on the night his job was on the line. *The Reliable Source*. Retrieved from http://www.washingtonpost.com/blogs/reliable-source/post/jeremy-bernard-speaks-first-male-white-house-social-secretary-on-the-night-his-job-was-on-the-line/2012/06/06/gJQA o6fWJV_blog.html

Robinson-Whelen, S., Tada, Y., MacCallum, R.C., McGuire, L. and Kiecolt-Glaser, J.K. (2001). Long-term caregiving: what happens when it ends? *Journal of Abnormal Psychology* **110**, 573–84. doi: 10.1037/0021-843X.110.4.573

Rogers, A.A. (2003). Power in marriage: a multidisciplinary and cross-cultural investigation. Unpublished doctoral dissertation, Southern Illinois University. *Dissertation Abstracts International*: Section B: The Sciences and Engineering, **63** (7-B).

Rokach, A., Matalon, R., Rokach, B. and Safarov, A. (2007). The effects of gender and marital status on loneliness of the aged. *Social Behavior and Personality* **35**, 243–54. doi: 10.2224/sbp.2007.35.2.243

Rose, A.J., Schwartz-Mette, R.A., Smith, R.L., Asher, S.R., Swenson, L.P., Carlson, W. and Waller, E.M. (2012). How girls and boys expect disclosure about problems will make them feel: implications for friendships. *Child Development* **83**, 844–63.

Rose, S.M. and Zand, D. (2002). Lesbian dating and courtship from young adulthood to midlife. *Journal of Lesbian Studies* **6**, 85–109. doi: 10.1300/J155v06n01_09

Rosenberg, R. (1982). *Beyond separate spheres: intellectual origins of modern feminism.* New Haven, CT:Yale University Press.

Rosenblatt, P.C. and Nkosi, B.C. (2007). South African Zulu widows in a time of poverty and social change. *Death Studies* **31**, 67–85. doi: 10.1080/07481180600995214

Roth, L.M. (2006). *Selling Women Short: gender and money on Wall Street.* Princeton, NJ: Princeton University Press.

Rothman, E.F., Exner, D. and Baughman, A.L. (2011). The prevalence of sexual assault against people who identify as gay, lesbian, or bisexual in the United States: a systematic review. *Trauma, Violence, and Abuse* **12**, 55–66. doi: 10.1177/1524838010390707

Round, A. (2006, May 17). The happy house-husbands of Brussels. *The Telegraph.* Retrieved from http://www.telegraph.co.uk/expat/4200102/The-happy-house-husbands-of-Brussels.html

Rubin, R. (2010, May 8). The pill: 50 years of birth control changed women's lives. *USA Today.* Retrieved from http://usatoday30.usatoday.com/news/health/2010-05-07-1Apill07_CV_N.htm

Rudman, L.A. and Fairchild, K. (2004). Reactions to counterstereotypic behavior: the role of backlash in cultural stereotype maintenance. *Journal of Personality and Social Psychology* **87**, 157–76.

Rudman, L.A. and Glick, P. (1999). Feminized management and backlash toward agentic women: the hidden costs to women of a kinder, gentler image of middle managers. *Journal of Personality and Social Psychology* **77**, 1004–1010. doi: 10.1037/0022-3514.77.5.1004

Rudman, L.A. and Glick, P. (2008). *The Social Psychology of Gender: How Power and Intimacy Shape Gender Relations.* New York: Guilford Press.

Rudman, L.A. and Kilianski, S. E. (2000). Implicit and explicit attitudes toward female authority. *Personality and Social Psychology Bulletin* **26**, 1315–1328. doi: 10.1177/0146167200263001

Rudman, L.A. and Phelan, J.E. (2010). The effect of priming gender roles on women's implicit gender beliefs and career aspirations. *Social Psychology* **41**, 192–202. doi: 10.1027/1864-9335/a000027

Ruffini, C. (2010, May 5). David Obey, "Bone tired," to retire from Congress. *CBS News*. Retrieved from http://www.cbsnews.com/8301-503544_162-20004248-503544.html

Ryan, C. (2012). Field of degree and earning by selected employment characteristics: 2011. Retrieved from http://www.census.gov/prod/2012pubs/acsbr11-10.pdf

Sabol, W.J., Couture H. and Harrison, P.M. (2007). Prisoners in 2006. US Department of Justice. *Bureau of Justice Statistics Bulletin*. Retrieved from http://www.ojp.usdoj.gov/bjs/pub/pdf/p06.pdf.

Saine, C. (2012, June 11). Africa's female presidents say they offer different kind of leadership. *Voice of America*. Retrieved from http://www.voanews.com/content/africas-female-presidents-say-they-offer-different-kind-leadership/1206098.html

Santaya, P.O.T. and Walters, A.S. (2011). Intimate partner violence within gay male couples: dimensionalizing partner violence among Cuban gay men. *Sexuality and Culture: an Interdisciplinary Quarterly* **15**, 153–78. doi: 10.1007/s12119-011-9087-0

Save the Children (2004). *Children having children: state of the world's mothers 2004*. Retrieved from http://www.savethechildren.org/atf/cf/%7B9def2ebe-10ae-432c-9bd0-df91d2eba74a%7D/SOWM_2004_final.pdf

Schein, V.E. (1973). The relationship between sex role stereotypes and requisite management characteristics. *Journal of Applied Psychology* **57**, 95–100. doi: 10.1037/h0037128

Schein, V.E., Mueller, R., Lituchy, T. and Liu, J. (1996). Think manager—think male: a global phenomenon? *Journal of Organizational Behavior* **17**, 33–41. doi: 10.1002/(SICI)1099-1379(199601)17:1<33::AID-JOB778>3.0.CO;2-F

Schlehofer, M.M., Casad, B.J., Bligh, M.C. and Grotto, A.R. (2011). Navigating public prejudices: the impact of media and attitudes on high-profile female political leaders. *Sex Roles* **65**, 69–82. doi: 10.1007/s11199-011-9965-9

Schmid Mast, M. (2004). Men are hierarchical, women are egalitarian: an implicit gender stereotype. *Swiss Journal of Psychology* **63**, 107–11. doi: 10.1024/1421-0185.63.2.107

Schulman, J.A. and Karney, B.R. (2003). Gender and attitudes toward nutrition in prospective physicians. *American Journal of Health Behavior* **27**, 623–32. doi: 10.5993/AJHB.27.6.5

Schüz, B., Sniehotta, F.F., Scholz, U. and Mallach, N. (2005). Gender differences in preventive nutrition: an exploratory study addressing meat consumption after livestock epidemics. *The Irish Journal of Psychology* **26**, 101–13.

Sharkey, J.R. and Branch, L.G. (2004). Gender differences in physical performance, body composition, and dietary intake in homebound elders. *Journal of Women and Aging* **16**, 71–89. doi: 10.1300/J074v16n03_06

Sheridan, L. and Lyndon, A.E. (2012). The influence of prior relationship, gender, and fear on the consequences of stalking victimization. *Sex Roles* **66**, 340–50. doi: 10.1007/s11199-010-9889-9

Shotland, R.L. and Goodstein, L. (1992). Sexual precedence reduces the perceived legitimacy of sexual refusal: an examination of attributions concerning date rape and consensual sex. *Personality and Social Psychology Bulletin* **18**, 756–64.

Shriver, M. (2009). A woman's nation. In *The Shriver Report*. Center for American Progress. Retrieved from http://www.shriverreport.com/awn/awn.php

Sigle-Rushton, W. and Waldfogel, J. (2007). Motherhood and women's earnings in anglo-American, continental European, and Nordic countries. *Feminist Economics* **13**, 55–91.

Simon, W. and Gagnon, J. (1987). A sexual scripts approach. In J. Greer and W. O'Donohue (eds), *Theories of Human Sexuality*, pp. 363–83. New York: Plenum.

Simpson, A. (2007). Learning sex and gender in Zambia: masculinities and HIV/AIDS risk. *Sexualities* **10**, 173–88. doi: 10.1177/1363460707075799

Singh, G.K. (2010). *Maternal Mortality in the United States, 1935–2007: substantial racial/ethnic, socioeconomic, and geographic disparities persist*. US Department of Health and Human Services, Health Resources and Services Administration, Maternal and Child Health Bureau. Retrieved from http://www.hrsa.gov/ourstories/mchb75th/mchb75maternalmortality.pdf.

Sinnott, J.D. and Shifren, K. (2001). Gender and aging: gender differences and gender roles. In J.E. Birren, and K.W. Schaie (eds), *Handbook of the Psychology of Aging* (5th edn), pp. 454–76. San Diego, CA: Academic Press.

Sivakumaran, S. (2007). Sexual violence against men in armed conflict. *European Journal of International Law* **18**, 253–76. doi: 10.1093/ejil/chm013

Skinner, R. and McFaull, S. (2012). Suicide among children and adolescents in Canada: trends and sex differences, 1980–2008. *Canadian Medical Association Journal* **184**, 1029–1034. doi: 10.1503/cmaj.111867

Slaughter, A. (2012, July/August). Why women still can't have it all. *The Atlantic*. Retrieved from http://www.theatlantic.com/magazine/archive/2012/07/why-women-still-cant-have-it-all/309020/

Smeding, A. (2012). Women in Science, Technology, Engineering, and Mathematics (STEM): an investigation of their implicit gender stereotypes and stereotypes' connectedness to math performance. *Sex Roles* **67**, 617–29. doi: 10.1007/s11199-012-0209-4

Smith, J. and Baltes, M.M. (1998). The role of gender in very old age: profiles of functioning and everyday life patterns. *Psychology and Aging* **13**, 676–95. doi:10.1037/0882-7974.13.4.676

Smith, J.L., Paul, D. and Paul, R. (2007). No place for a woman: evidence for gender bias in evaluations of presidential candidates. *Basic and Applied Social Psychology* **29**, 225–33. doi: 10.1080/01973530701503069

Smith, L.C., Ramakrishnan, U., Ndiaye, A., Haddad, L. and Martorell, R. (2003). *The Importance of Women's Status for Child Nutrition in Developing Countries.* Washington, DC: International Food Policy Research Institute. Retrieved from http://www.theaahm.org/fileadmin/user_upload/aahm/docs/rr131.pdf

Smith, S.L., Pieper, K.M., Granados, A. and Choueiti, M. (2010). Assessing gender-related portrayals in top-grossing G-rated films. *Sex Roles* **62**, 774–86. doi:10.1007/s11199-009-9736-z

Smith-Spark, L. (2004, December 8). How did rape become a weapon of war? *BBC News.* Retrieved from http://news.bbc.co.uk/2/hi/in_depth/4078677.stm

Sobiraj, S., Korek, S., Weseler, D. and Mohr, G. (2011). When male norms don't fit: do traditional attitudes of female colleagues challenge men in non-traditional occupations? *Sex Roles* **65**, 798–812. doi: 10.1007/s11199-011-0057-7

Sontag, S. (1979). The double standard of aging. In J. Williams (ed.), *Psychology of Women*, pp. 462–78. New York: Academic Press.

Sotomayor, S. (2013). *My Beloved World: a memoir.* New York: Random House.

Sparkes, M. (2012, September 26). Christine Lagarde: 'Women can't have it all.' *Business Insider.* Retrieved from http://www.businessinsider.com/christine-lagarde-women-cant-have-it-all-2012-9

Spencer, S.J., Steele, C.M. and Quinn, D.M. (1999). Stereotype threat and women's math performance. *Journal of Experimental Social Psychology* **35**, 4–28.

Spender, D. (1989). *The Writing or the Sex?* New York: Pergamon.

Sreerupa and Rajan, S.I. (2010). Gender and widowhood: disparity in health status and health care utilization among the aged in India. *Journal of Ethnic and Cultural Diversity in Social Work: Innovation in Theory, Research and Practice* **19**, 287–304. doi: 10.1080/15313204.2010.523650

Steele, C.M. (1997). A threat in the air. *American Psychologist* **52**, 613–29.

Steptoe, A., Shankar, A., Demakakos, P. and Wardle, J. (2013, March 25). Social isolation, loneliness, and all-cause mortality in older men and women. Proceeding of the National Academy of Sciences of the United States of America. doi: 10.1073/pnas.1219686110. Retrieved from http://www.pnas.org/content/early/2013/03/19/1219686110.abstract

Stewart, A.J., Ostrove, J.M. and Helson, R. (2001). Middle aging in women: patterns of personality change from the 30s to the 50s. *Journal of Adult Development* **8**, 23–37. doi: 10.1023/A:1026445704288

Stone, L.B., Hankin, B.L., Gibb, B.E. and Abela, J.R.Z. (2011). Co-rumination predicts the onset of depressive disorders during adolescence. *Journal of Abnormal Psychology* **120**, 752–57. doi: 10.1037/a0023384

Storr, W. (2011, July 16). The rape of men. *The Observer*. Retrieved from http://www.guardian.co.uk/society/2011/jul/17/the-rape-of-men

Stripling, J. (2012, March 12). Survey finds a drop in minority presidents leading colleges. *The Chronicle of Higher Education*. Retrieved from http://chronicle.com/article/Who-Are-College-Presidents-/131138/

Stroebe, M., Stroebe, W. and Schut, H. (2001). Gender differences in adjustment to bereavement: an empirical and theoretical review. *Review of General Psychology* **5**, 62–83.

Subbarao, K. and Coury, D. (2004). *Reaching Out to Africa's Orphans: a framework for public action*. Washington, DC: World Bank.

Substance Abuse and Mental Health Services Administration (2012). *Results from the 2011 National Survey on Drug Use and Health: Summary of National Findings*. NSDUH Series H-44, HHS Publication No. (SMA) 12-4713. Rockville, MD: Substance Abuse and Mental Health Services Administration. Retrieved from http://www.samhsa.gov/data/NSDUH/2k11Results/NSDUHresults2011.pdf

Sugarman, D.E., DeMartini, K.S. and Carey, K.B. (2009). Are women at greater risk? An examination of alcohol-related consequences and gender. *The American Journal on Addictions* **18**: 194–97. doi: 10.1080/10550490902786991

Sugihara, Y. and Katsurada, E. (1999). Masculinity and femininity in Japanese culture: a pilot study. *Sex Roles* **40**, 635–46. doi: 10.1023/A:1018896215625

Swim, J.K. (1994). Perceived versus meta-analytic effect sizes: an assessment of the accuracy of gender stereotypes. *Journal of Personality and Social Psychology* **66**, 21–36. doi: 10.1037/0022-3514.66.1.21

Swim, J.K., and Hyers, L.L. (1999). Excuse me—what did you just say?!: women's public and private responses to sexist remarks. *Journal of Experimental Social Psychology* **35**, 68–88. doi: 10.1006/jesp.1998.1370

Swim, J.K., Aikin, K.J., Hall, W.S. and Hunter, B.A. (1995). Sexism and racism: old-fashioned and modern prejudices. *Journal of Personality and Social Psychology* **68**, 199–214. doi: 10.1037/0022-3514.68.2.199

Swim, J., Borgida, E., Maruyama, G. and Myers, D.G. (1989). Joan McKay versus John McKay: do gender stereotypes bias evaluations? *Psychological Bulletin* **105**, 409–29. doi: 10.1037/0033-2909.105.3.409

Tabar, P. (2007). "Habiibs" in Australia: language, identity and masculinity. *Journal of Intercultural Studies* **28**, 157–72.

Taylor, C.J. (2010). Occupational sex composition and the gendered availability of workplace support. *Gender and Society* **24**, 189–212. doi: 10.1177/0891243209359912

Thomas, K. (2011, April 6). After long fight for inclusion, women's ski jumping gains Olympic status. *The New York Times*. Retrieved from http://www.nytimes.com/2011/04/07/sports/skiing/07skijumping.html?_r=0

Tichenor, V. (2005). Maintaining men's dominance: negotiating identity and power when she earns more. *Sex Roles* **53**, 191–205. doi: 10.1007/s11199-005-5678-2

Tiggemann, M. (2004). Body image across the adult life span: stability and change. *Body Image* **1**, 29–41.

Tiggemann, M., Martins, Y. and Kirkbride, A. (2007). Oh to be lean and muscular: body image ideals in gay and heterosexual men. *Psychology of Men and Masculinity* **8**, 15–24.

Tijdens, K.G. and Klaveren, M. (2012). *Frozen in time: gender pay gap unchanged for 10 years*. Brussels, Belgium: International Trade Union Confederation. Retrieved from http://www.ituc-csi.org/IMG/pdf/pay_gap_en_final.pdf

Todd, J., Friedman, A. and Kariuki, P.W., (1990). Women growing stronger with age: the effect of status in the United States and Kenya. *Psychology of Women Quarterly* **14**, 567–77. doi: 10.1111/j.1471-6402.1990.tb00231.x

Tomasula, J.L., Anderson, L.M., Littleton, H.L. and Riley-Tillman, T.C. (2012). The association between sexual assault and suicidal activity in a national sample. *School Psychology Quarterly* **27**, 109–19. doi: 10.1037/a0029162

Top, T.J. (1991). Sex bias in the evaluation of performance in the scientific, artistic, and literary professions: a review. *Sex Roles* **24**, 73–106. doi: 10.1007/BF00288704

Torregrosa, L.L. (2012, May 1). Cuba may be the most feminist country in Latin America. *International Herald Tribune*. Retrieved from http://rendezvous.blogs.nytimes.com/2012/05/01/cuba-may-be-the-most-feminist-country-in-latin-america/

Tougas, F., Brown, R., Beaton, A.M. and Joly, S. (1995). Neosexism: plus ça change, plus c'est pareil. *Personality and Social Psychology Bulletin* **21**, 842–49. doi: 10.1177/0146167295218007

Travis, C.B., Howerton, D.M. and Szymanski, D.M. (2012). Risk, uncertainty, and gender stereotypes in healthcare decisions. *Women and Therapy* **35**, 207–20. doi: 10.1080/02703149.2012.684589

Travis, C.B., Meltzer, A.I. and Howerton, D.M. (2010). Gender issues in health care utilization. In J. Chrisler and D.R. McCreary (eds), *Handbook of Gender Research in Psychology* (Vol. 2), pp. 517–40. New York: Springer.

Tsai, J., Floyd, R.L., Green, P.P. and Boyle, C.A. (2007). Patterns and average volume of alcohol use among women of childbearing age. *Maternal and Child Health Journal* **11**, 437–45. doi: 10.1007/s10995-007-0185-4

Turchik, J.A. (2012). Sexual victimization among male college students: assault severity, sexual functioning, and health risk behaviors. *Psychology of Men and Masculinity* **13**, 243–55. doi: 10.1037/a0024605. Special Section: Recent Research on Sexual Harassment and Victimization of Men.

Twenge, J.M. (1997). Changes in masculine and feminine traits over time: a meta-analysis. *Sex Roles* **36**, 305–25. doi: 10.1007/BF02766650

Tyler, M. (2010). 'Now that's pornography!': violence and domination in Adult Video News. In K. Boyle (ed.), *Everyday Pornography*, pp. 50–62. London and New York: Routledge.

UNAIDS (2012). *Fact sheet: Adolescents, young people and HIV*. Retrieved from http://www.unaids.org/en/media/unaids/contentassets/documents/factsheet/2012/20120417_FS_adolescentsyoungpeoplehiv_en.pdf

UNESCO (2010). *EFA Global Monitoring Report*. Retrieved from http://gmr.uis.unesco.org/selectIndicators.aspx

Unger, R. (1979). Toward a redefinition of sex and gender. *American Psychologist* **34**, 1085–1094.

United Nations (1993, December 20). Resolution adopted by the General Assembly. *48/104. Declaration on the Elimination of Violence Against Women*. UN Documents. Retrieved from http://www.un-documents.net/a48r104.htm

United Nations (2006, July 6). *Report of the Secretary-General. In-depth study of all forms of violence against women*. United Nations Document A/61/122/Add. 1. Retrieved from http://www.un.org/womenwatch/daw/vaw/SGstudyvaw.htm

United Nations Population Fund (2000). *State of the world population 2000*. Retrieved from http://www.unfpa.org/public/cache/offonce/home/publications/pid/3453;jsessionid=4C3A8C52B424B99A07B517B2A2BDA089

United Nations Population Fund (2012). *Ageing in the twenty-first century: A celebration and a challenge*. New York: United Nations Population Fund and HelpAge International. Retrieved from http://unfpa.org/ageingreport/

US Bureau of Labor Statistics (2006). *Employed persons by detailed occupation and sex, 2005 annual averages*. Retrieved from http://www.bls.gov/cps/wlf-table11-2006.pdf

US Bureau of Labor Statistics (2009a, August 7). *Women and men in management, professional, and related occupations, 2008. TED: The Editor's Desk*. Retrieved from http://www.bls.gov/opub/ted/2009/ted_20090807.htm

US Bureau of Labor Statistics (2009b). *Household data annual averages: Table 3: employment status of the civilian noninstitutional population by age, sex, and race*. Accessed at http://www.bls.gov/cps/cpsaat3.pdf

US Bureau of Labor Statistics (2010a). *American time use survey–2009 results*. Retrieved from http://www.bls.gov/news.release/atus.toc.htm

US Bureau of Labor Statistics (2010b). Data from the Current Population survey. Employment and earnings. Household data annual averages. Accessed at http://www.bls.gov/cps/cpsa2009.pdf

US Bureau of Labor Statistics (2010c). Labor force participation rates among mothers. Retrieved from http://www.bls.gov/opub/ted/2010/ted_20100507_data.htm

US Bureau of Labor Statistics (2011). American Time Use Survey–2010. Retrieved from http://www.bls.gov/news.release/atus.toc.htm

US Bureau of Labor Statistics (2012a). *Women in the Labor Force: a databook* (yearly series). Retrieved from http://www.bls.gov/cps/demographics. htm#women

US Bureau of Labor Statistics (2012b, October). *Highlights of women's earnings in 2011*. Retrieved from http://www.bls.gov/cps/cpswom2011.pdf

US Census Bureau (2010). Current Population Survey, Annual Social and Economic supplements. Historical income tables. Accessed at http://www. census.gov/hhes/www/income/data/historical/people/index.html

US Census Bureau (2012). *Table 616. Employed civilians by occupation, sex, race, and Hispanic origian: 2010*. Retrieved from http://www.census.gov/compendia/ statab/2012/tables/12s0616.pdf

US Department of Justice (1994). *The costs of crime to victims: crime data brief.* Bureau of Justice Statistics. Retrieved from http://www.ojp.usdoj.gov.bjs/ pub/

US Department of Labor (2008). Older women workers, ages 55 and over, 2007. Accessed at http://www.dol.gov/wb/factsheets/Qf-olderworkers55-07.htm#

US Department of Labor (2010). 20 leading occupations of employed women: 2010 annual averages. Retrieved from http://www.dol.gov/wb/ factsheets/20lead2010.htm

US Equal Employment Opportunity Commission (2013, January 9). Press release: *Carrols Corp. to pay $2.5 million to settle EEOC sexual harassment and retaliation lawsuit*. Retrieved from http://www.eeoc.gov/eeoc/newsroom/ release/1-9-13.cfm

US Government Accountability Office (2012, July 19). *Retirement security:Women still face challenges*. Retrieved from http://www.gao.gov/products/GAO-12- 699

Vandiver, L. (2011). Portrayal of women in the media. Politics. Media Representation Group. Retrieved from http://mediarepresentation. wordpress.com/womenmediapolitics/

van Gelder, B.M., Tijhuis, M.A.R., Kalmijn, S., Giampaoli, S., Nissinen, A. and Kromhout, D. (2004). Physical activity in relation to cognitive decline in elderly men: the FINE Study. *Neurology* **63**, 2316–2321.

Vega, V. and Malamuth, N.M. (2007). Predicting sexual aggression: the role of pornography in the context of general and specific risk factors. *Aggressive Behavior* **33**, 104–107. doi:10.1002/ab.20172

Velkoff, V. A. and Kinsella, K. (1998). Gender stereotypes: data needs for ageing research. *Ageing International* Spring, 18–38.

Vijayakumar, L. (2004). Altruistic suicide in India. *Archives of Suicide Research* **8**, 73–80. doi: 10.1080/13811110490243804

Villereal, G.L. and Cavazos Jr, A. (2005). Shifting Identity: process and change in identity of aging Mexican-American males. *Journal of Sociology and Social Welfare* **32**, 33–41.

Vinkenburg, C.J., van Engen, M.L., Eagly, A.H. and Johannesen-Schmidt, M.C. (2011). An exploration of stereotypical beliefs about leadership styles: is transformational leadership a route to women's promotion? *The Leadership Quarterly* **22**, 10–21. http://dx.doi.org/10.1016/j.leaqua.2010.12.003

Violence Policy Center (2012). *American Roulette: Murder-Suicide in the United States* (4th edn). Washington, DC: Author. Retrieved from http://www.vpc.org/studies/amroul2012.pdf

Vitaliano, P.P., Zhang, J., and Scanlan, J. M. (2003). Is Caregiving Hazardous to One's Physical Health? A Meta-Analysis. *Psychological Bulletin*, **129**, 946–972. doi: 10.1037/0033-2909.129.6.946

von Hippel, C., Issa, M., Ma, R. and Stokes, A. (2011). Stereotype threat: antecedents and consequences for working women. *European Journal of Social Psychology* **41**, 151–61. doi: 10.1002/ejsp.749

von Hippel, C., Wiryakusuma, C., Bowden, J. and Shochet, M. (2011). Stereotype threat and female communication styles. *Personality and Social Psychology Bulletin* **37**, 1312–1324. doi: 10.1177/0146167211410439

Voskul, R. (2011). Sex differences in autoimmune diseases. *Biology of Sex Differences* 2. Retrieved from http://www.bsd-journal.com/content/2/1/1

Waldo, C.R., Berdahl, J.L. and Fitzgerald, L.F. (1998). Are men sexually harassed? If so, by whom? *Law and Human Behavior* **22**, 59–79.

Walker, L., Butland, D. and Connell, R.W. (2000). Boys on the road: masculinities, car culture, and road safety education. *The Journal of Men's Studies* **8**, 153–69. doi: 10.3149/jms.0802.153

Walters, M.L. (2011). Straighten up and act like a lady: a qualitative study of lesbian survivors of intimate partner violence. *Journal of Gay and Lesbian Social Services: The Quarterly Journal of Community and Clinical Practice* **23**, 250–70. doi: 10.1080/10538720.2011.559148

Walters, M.L., Chen J. and Breiding, M.J. (2013). *The National Intimate Partner and Sexual Violence Survey (NISVS): 2010 Findings on Victimization by Sexual Orientation.* Atlanta, GA: National Center for Injury Prevention and Control, Centers for Disease Control and Prevention. Retrieved from http://www.cdc.gov/ViolencePrevention/pdf/NISVS_SOfindings.pdf

Wang, M. and Kelan, E. (2012). The gender quota and female leadership: effects of the Norwegian gender quota on board chairs and ceos. *Journal of Business Ethics*, Dec. 14, no pagination specified. doi: 10.1007/s10551-012-1546-5

Warner, D.F. and Brown, T.H. (2011). Understanding how race/ethnicity and gender define age-trajectories of disability: an intersectionality approach. *Social Science and Medicine* **72**, 1236–1248. doi:10.1016/j.socscimed.2011.02.034

Waters, H., Hyder, A., Rajkotia, Y., Basu, S., Rehwinkel, J.A. and Butchart, A. (2004). *The Economic Dimensions of Interpersonal Violence*. Geneva: Department of Injuries and Violence Prevention, World Health Organization. Retrieved from http://whqlibdoc.who.int/publications/2004/9241591609.pdf

Watts, C. and Zimmerman, C. (2002). Violence against women: global scope and magnitude. *The Lancet*, **359** (9313), 1232–1237. doi: 10.1016/S0140-6736 (02)08221-1

Weiss, W. (1997). Cigarette smoking and lung cancer trends. A light at the end of the tunnel? *Chest* **111**, 1414–1416.

White, A.M., Jamieson-Drake, D.W. and Swartzwelder, H.S. (2002) Prevalence and correlates of alcohol-induced blackouts among college students: results of an e-mail survey. *Journal of American College Health* **51**, 117–31.

White, J.W. and Kowalski, R.M. (1994). Deconstructing the myth of the nonaggressive woman: a feminist analysis. *Psychology of Women Quarterly* **18**, 487–508. doi: 10.1111/j.1471-6402.1994.tb01045.x

White, M.J. and White, G.B. (2006). Implicit and explicit occupational gender stereotypes. *Sex Roles* **55**, 259–66. doi: 10.1007/s11199-006-9078-z

Wilkerson, J.M., Brooks, A.K. and Ross, M.W. (2010). Sociosexual identity development and sexual risk taking of acculturating collegiate gay and bisexual men. *Journal of College Student Development* **51**, 279–96. doi: 10.1353/csd.0.0131

Williams, C. (1992). The glass escalator: hidden advantages for men in the "female" professions. *Social Problems* **39**, 253–67.

Williams, J.E. and Best, D.E. (1990). *Sex and Psyche: gender and self viewed cross-culturally*. Newbury Park: Sage.

Williams, S.L. and Frieze, I.H. (2005). Patterns of violent relationships, psychological distress, and marital satisfaction in a national sample of men and women. *Sex Roles* **52**, 771–84. doi: 10.1007/s11199-005-4198-4

Wilsnack, R.W., Wilsnack, S.C., Kristjanson, A.F., Vogeltanz-Holm, N.D. and Gmel, G. (2009). Gender and alcohol consumption: patterns from the multinational GENACIS project. *Addiction* **104**, 1487–1500. doi: 10.1111/j.1360-0443.2009.02696.x

Wingfield, A.H. (2009). Racializing the glass escalator. Reconsidering men's experiences with women's work. *Gender and Society* **23**, 5–26. doi: 10.1177/0891243208323305

Winter, D.G. (1988). The power motive in women—and men. *Journal of Personality and Social Psychology* **54**, 510–19.

WISE (2010). Women's Islamic Initiative in Spirituality and Equality. Current Issues: Sports. Retrieved from http://www.wisemuslimwomen.org/currentissues/sports/

Witkowska, E. and Gådin, K.G. (2005). Have you been sexually harassed in school? What female high school students regard as harassment. *International*

Journal of Adolescent Medicine and Health **17**, 391–406. doi: 10.1515/
IJAMH.2005.17.4.391

Witte, T.K., Gordon, K.H., Smith, P.N. and Van Orden, K.A. (2012). Stoicism
and sensation seeking: male vulnerabilities for the acquired capability for
suicide. *Journal of Research in Personality* **46**, 384–92. doi: 10.1016/j.
jrp.2012.03.004

Wood, J.L., Heitmiller, D., Andreasen, N.C. and Nopoulos, P. (2008). Morphology
of the ventral frontal cortex: relationship to femininity and social cognition.
Cerebral Cortex **18**, 534–40.

Wood, J.L., Murko, V. and Nopoulos, P. (2009). Ventral frontal cortex in children:
morphology, social cognition and femininity/masculinity. *Social Cognitive and
Affective Neuroscience* **3**, 168–76.

World Health Organization (2002a). *Fact sheet: Gender and tuberculosis.* Retrieved
from http://www.who.int/gender/documents/en/TB.factsheet.pdf

World Health Organization (2002b). Gender and road traffic injuries. Retrieved
from http://www.who.int/gender/other_health/en/gendertraffic.pdf

World Health Organization (2003). Gender, health and tobacco. Retrieved from
http://www.who.int/gender/documents/Gender_Tobacco_2.pdf

World Health Organization (2005). *WHO multi-country study on women's health
and domestic violence.* Retrieved from http://www.who.int/gender/violence/
who_multicountry_study/en/

World Health Organization (2007, June). Gender, health, and malaria. Retrieved
from http://www.who.int/gender/documents/gender_health_malaria.pdf

World Health Organization (2009, November). *Fact sheet: Women's health.*
Retrieved from http://www.who.int/mediacentre/factsheets/fs334/en/
index.html

World Health Organization (2010a). *Gender and blindness—eye surgery in Egypt.*
Retrieved from http://www.who.int/gender/egypt_20101108_en.pdf

World Health Organization (2010b). *Gender, women, and the tobacco epidemic.*
Retrieved from http://www.who.int/tobacco/publications/gender/women
_tob_epidemic/en/index.html

World Health Organization (2010c). 10 facts on obstetric fistula. Retrieved from
http://www.who.int/features/factfiles/obstetric_fistula/en/index.html

World Health Organization (2011a). Suicide rates per 100,000 by country, year
and sex (Table). Retrieved from http://www.who.int/mental_health/
prevention/suicide_rates/en/

World Health Organization (2011b, August). *Elder maltreatment.* Retrieved from
http://www.who.int/mediacentre/factsheets/fs357/en/index.html

World Health Organization (2012). *World Health Statistics 2012.* Retrieved from
http://www.who.int/gho/publications/world_health_statistics/2012/en/
index.html

World Health Organization (2013a). *Global Health Observatory. NCD mortality and morbidity*. Retrieved from http://www.who.int/gho/ncd/mortality_morbidity/en/index.html

World Health Organization (2013b). HIV/AIDS. *Mother-to-child transmission of HIV*. Retrieved from http://www.who.int/hiv/topics/mtct/en/index.html

World Health Organization (2013c). Gender Women and health: Gender inequalities and HIV. Retrieved from http://www.who.int/gender/hiv_aids/en/index.html

World Health Organization (2013d). Global Health Observatory. Unmet need for family planning. Retrieved from http://www.who.int/gho/maternal_health/reproductive_health/family_planning/en/index.html

World Health Organization (2013e). *Female genital mutilation*. Retrieved from http://www.who.int/mediacentre/factsheets/fs241/en/

World Health Organization Regional Office for Africa (2010). Prevention of unsafe abortion. Retrieved from http://www.afro.who.int/en/clusters-a-programmes/frh/sexual-and-reproductive-health/programme-components/prevention-of-unsafe-abortion.html

World Health Organization, UNICEF, UNFPA and The World Bank (2012). *Trends in maternal mortality: 1990 to 2010*. Retrieved from http://www.who.int/reproductivehealth/publications/monitoring/9789241503631/en/index.html

Wright, V.J. and Perricelli, B.C. (2008). Age-related rates of decline in performance among elite senior athletes. *American Journal of Sports Medicine* **36**, 443–50.

Yaffe, K., Barnes, D., Nevitt, M., Lui, L-Y. and Covinsky, K. (2001). A prospective study of physical activity and cognitive decline in elderly women. *Archives of Internal Medicine* **161**, 1703–1708.

Yaffe, M.J., Weiss, D., Wolfson, C. and Lithwick, M. (2007). Detection and prevalence of abuse of older males: perspectives from family practice. *Journal of Elder Abuse and Neglect* **19**, 47–60. doi: 10.1300/J084v19n01_04

Yeung, W.T.L. (2010). Gender perspectives on adolescent eating behaviors: a study on the eating attitudes and behaviors of junior secondary students in Hong Kong. *Journal of Nutrition Education and Behavior* **42**, 250–58. doi: 10.1016/j.jneb.2009.05.008

Yoder, J.D. and Sinnett, L.M. (1985). Is it all in the numbers? A case study of tokenism. *Psychology of Women Quarterly* **9**, 413–18. doi: 10.1111/j.1471-6402.1985.tb00890.x

Yong, V., Saito, Y. and Chan, A. (2011). Gender differences in health and health expectancies of older adults in Singapore: an examination of diseases, impairments, and functional disabilities. *Journal of Cross-Cultural Gerontology* **26**, 189–203. doi: 10.1007/s10823-011-9143-0

Yoon, E., Funk, R. and Kropf, N. (2010). Sexual harassment experiences and their psychological correlates among a diverse sample of college women. *Affilia: Journal of Women and Social Work* **25**(1), 8–18.

Young, J.L. and James, E.H. (2001). Token majority: the work attitudes of male flight attendants. *Sex Roles* **45**, 299–319. doi: 10.1023/A:1014305530335

Zach, S., Zeev, A., Dunsky, A., Goldbourt, U., Shimony, T., Goldsmith, R. and Netz, Y. (2013). Adolescents' physical activity habits—results from a national health survey. *Child: Care, Health and Development* **39**, 103–108. doi: 10.1111/j.1365-2214.2012.01392.x

Zettel, L.A. and Rook, K.S. (2004). Substitution and compensation in the social networks of older widowed women. *Psychology and Aging* **19**, 433–43. doi:10.1037/0882-7974.19.3.433

Zillmann, D. and Bryant, J. (1982). Pornography, sexual callousness, and the trivialization of rape. *Journal of Communication* **32**, 10–21. doi: 10.1111/j.1460-2466.1982.tb02514.x

Zillmann, D. and Weaver, J.B. (1989). Pornography and men's sexual callousness toward women. In D. Zillmann and J. Bryant (eds), *Pornography: research advances and policy considerations. Communication,* pp. 95–125. Hillsdale, NJ: Lawrence Erlbaum Associates.

Zimmerman, C., Hossain, M., Yun, K., Roche, B., Morison, L. and Watts, C. (2006). *Stolen Smiles: a summary report on the physical and psychological health consequences of women and adolescents trafficked in Europe.* London: The London School of Hygiene and Tropical Medicine. Retrieved from http://genderviolence.lshtm.ac.uk/files/Stolen-Smiles-Summary.pdf

INDEX